PRACTICAL LANGUAGE TEACHING
Editors: Marion Geddes and Gill Sturtridge

Teaching Reading Skills in a Foreign Language

PRACTICAL LANGUAGE TEACHING
Editors: Marion Geddes and Gill Sturtridge

Teaching Reading Skills in a Foreign Language

Christine Nuttall

HEINEMANN

Heinemann English Language Teaching
A division of Heinemann Publishers (Oxford) Ltd
Halley Court, Jordan Hill, Oxford OX2 8EJ

OXFORD MADRID ATHENS PARIS FLORENCE
PRAGUE SÃO PAULO CHICAGO MELBOURNE
AUCKLAND SINGAPORE TOKYO GABORONE
JOHANNESBURG PORTSMOUTH (NH) IBADAN

ISBN 0 435 28973 X

Æ 11759686

🕮 British Library Cataloguing in Publication Data

Nuttall, Christine
  Teaching reading skills in a foreign language.
  —(Practical language teaching: no. 9)
  1. Reading—Study and teaching—Foreign students
  I. Title   II. Series
  428.4   LB1050

  ISBN 0-435-28973-X

Phototypesetting by Parkway Group, London and Abingdon
Printed and bound in Great Britain by
Athenæum Press Ltd, Gateshead, Tyne & Wear.

95 96 97 98 99 15 14 13

Contents

Preface

No book of this kind owes its existence to a single writer, and my debt to many others will be immediately obvious. First and foremost is the influence of the students and teachers with whom I have worked. To them, especially those at the Advanced Teacher Training College in Winneba, Ghana, I should like to dedicate the book, as a small return for all they have given to me.

It is impossible to mention here all those who deserve acknowledgement: the books I have read, the universities that have guided me, the colleagues who have shared their experience so generously. Their contribution has been so great that it seems impertinent that my own name should appear on the title page. I hope they will collectively accept this recognition that I am deeply aware of all I owe them and profoundly grateful.

I must however specifically mention certain materials produced as a result of the current renewal of interest in foreign language reading. For many insights and ideas for types of reading task, I have drawn freely on *English in Focus* (OUP), *Foundation Reading* (Chulalongkorn University Language Institute), *Reading and Thinking in English* (OUP) and *Skills for Learning* (University of Malaya/Nelson). Without the stimulus of these materials, this book would have been very different and much the poorer.

For help specifically with the text of this book, I should like to thank Alan Moore and John Moore for their time and trouble and their excellent suggestions; the publishers for their unfailing helpfulness; and finally, Gill Sturtridge and Marion Geddes for their support, without which the book would not have been written.

CEN
1981

A note to the reader

If this book seems somewhat long, I suggest that you first read Chapter 1 and then move straight to Chapters 11 and 12, which attempt to summarize the classroom application of the issues discussed in Chapters 2 to 10. You can then turn back to the earlier chapters for further details.

Abbreviations used in the text

EFL/ESL	English as a foreign/second language
FL	Foreign language (includes second language unless otherwise indicated)
he *etc.*	he *or* she *etc.*
L1	first language (mother tongue, native language)
MC	multiple choice (question)
NVM	non-verbal material (Chapter 5)
OHP	overhead projector
SPQ	signpost question (p. 158)
SQ3R	study, question, read, recite, review (p. 169)
TAS	text attack skill (Chapters 7, 8)
T/F	true/false (question)
w.p.m.	words per minute

Acknowledgements

The author and publishers wish to thank the following for permission to reproduce their materials and for providing illustrations:

Werner Soderstrom Osakeyhtio for the extract from *Ne Tulevat Takaisin* by Y. Kokko (1954); The Language Centre, University of Malaya Press/Thomas Nelson & Sons Ltd for the extracts from *Reading Projects: Science* (1979) and *Skills for Learning: Reading for Academic Study* (1979); Thomas Nelson & Sons Ltd for the extract from *Principles of Human Knowledge* by George Berkeley (1949); Andre Deutsch for the extract from *The Suffrage of Elvira* by V. S. Naipaul (1969); Collins Publishers for the extracts from *Life on Earth* by David Attenborough (Collins/BBC 1979) and *The African Child* by Camara Laye (1980); Edward Fry for allowing us to use his readability estimate (1964); Penguin Books Ltd for the extracts from Chapter 2 of *Buddhism* by Christmas Humphreys (Pelican Books, Third Edition, 1962) © Christmas Humphreys 1951 and *China: The Quality of Life* by Wilfred Burchett and Rewi Alley (Pelican Books 1976) © Wilfred Burchett 1976; McGraw-Hill Book Company for the extract from *Learning System Design* by Davis, Alexander and Yelon (1974); Oxford University Press for the extracts from *Reading and Thinking in English: Discovering Discourse* and *Reading and Thinking in English: Exploring Functions* © The British Council 1979, *English in Social Studies* by J. P. B. Allen and H. G. Widdowson © OUP 1978, *English in Physical Science* by J. P. B. Allen and H. G. Widdowson © OUP 1974, *English in Biological Science* by I. Pearson © OUP 1978 and *English in Education* by E. Laird © OUP 1977; Cassell Ltd for the extract from *Pleasant Work for Busy Fingers* by Maggie Brown (1896); Edward Arnold Ltd for the extracts from *Think and Link* by J. Cooper (1979); Longman Group Ltd for the extract from *Communicate in Writing* by Keith Johnson (1981); George Allen and Unwin for the extract from *What We Know About Cancer* by R. J. C. Harris (1970); William Heinemann Ltd and Pantheon Books for the extract from *The Night Lords* by Nicolas Freeling (1978); A. D. Peters & Co for the extract from *The Data Bank Society* by M. Warner and M. Stone (George Allen and Unwin) (1978); The Holgate School, Nottingham for the photograph from the *Times Educational Supplement* (24 April 1981); Heinemann Educational Books Ltd for the extracts from *The House on the Hill* by E. Laird (1978) and *Reasons for Reading* by E. Davies and N. Whitney (1980); The British Council for the extract from *Foundation Reading II Vol. 3* by the Chulalongkorn University Language Institute.

1 What is Reading?

This book is about reading a foreign language (FL) and particularly about reading English as a foreign or second language (EFL/ESL). Since it is a book for teachers, we shall be dealing mainly with the place of reading in a teaching programme, though whether it is possible to teach people to read is a vexed question, as we shall see.

A great deal has been written about reading, though most of it does not relate to the reading of a FL; and a great deal of research has been done, though its classroom applications are not always clear. I cannot attempt complete coverage of such a vast topic, but we will discuss some of the current ideas about reading and see how they can be applied in the FL classroom.

I shall make practical suggestions for the classroom, but many people would say that in the reading class it is the teacher's understanding of the reading process that is more important than anything else. It certainly seems to be true that some of the things that happen in the classroom may interfere with reading rather than promote it. So in this first chapter we will consider the process of reading. The conclusions we reach will supply the basis for the rest of the book.

1 Defining reading

Different people use the term *reading* in different ways, and much confusion can arise from consequent misunderstandings. So we had better start by making sure that we are thinking about the same thing when we use the term.

As a first step, it would be useful to find out what preconceptions you have about reading. Will you therefore please take a piece of paper and write down a brief definition of the term *reading*? Don't take more than five minutes over this.

Don't turn the page until you have written your definition of reading.

What sort of definition did you give? It is likely that you used words from at least one of these groups:

(a) understand   interpret   meaning   sense   etc.
(b) decode   decipher   identify   etc.
(c) articulate   speak   pronounce   etc.

If you used the ideas reflected in group (b), you have probably wanted to include the first thing of all about reading: namely that unless we can correctly recognize the words we meet in print, we cannot even begin to read. The process of identifying written words is mainly the concern of the teacher of early reading and will not be dealt with in this book. We are concerned with developing the skills of readers who have already passed this elementary stage.

If you used words similar to those in group (c), you are probably drawing on your own experience as both a student and a teacher. In a great many classrooms the reading lesson is used as an opportunity to teach pronunciation, encourage fluent and expressive speaking, and so on. For early readers, reading aloud is of course an important aid; beginners have to discover how writing is associated with the spoken words they have already learned to use. But the early reading stage does not last long – two or three years at most, normally. What is the function of reading aloud after that? I will return to this question shortly.

Before we deal with words in group (a) and others with similar meanings, it would be helpful if you would now jot down on your piece of paper a list of the kinds of things you have read during the last few days, in any language.

> Take five minutes to list all the different kinds of things you have read recently.
> Don't forget to include things like these:
> telephone directory
> label on medicine bottle
> street map
> timetable
> notices
> statistics
> engagement diary
> letters
> instruction leaflet
> application form

How many of the things on your list were written in English (or whatever FL you are interested in)?

2   Reasons for reading

2.1   Reading in different ways for different purposes

Now think about the things you have listed. Why did you read each one? What did you want to get from it? Was it information only? What about the letters from home? The detective novel? You will find that you had a variety of reasons for reading, and if you compared notes with other people, you would find different reasons again.

How did your various reasons for reading influence the way you read? Did you read the telephone directory in the same way as the newspaper? What was the difference? How about street maps, diagrams, graphs or statistics? We speak of reading these, but it is very unlike the reading of a book: there may be very few actual words in reading of this kind.

You will probably have concluded that the way you tackled the task is strongly influenced by your purpose in reading. The quick scanning of a page in the telephone directory to find a single name is very different from the careful attention you paid to each word in a legal document. The difference in the speeds you used was no doubt very noticeable. Did you also find that for some tasks you read silently while for others you read aloud? What were the reasons that led you to articulate what you read?

For most of us, once we have passed the early reading stage, reading aloud is not common outside the classroom. Most of our reading is done silently, unless there are special circumstances such as reading to someone who has lost their spectacles. Since you are a teacher, reading aloud will be a skill you use quite a lot; but how much do you use it outside your job? And how many of your students are going to need this skill? If you think of the percentage of time most adults spend on reading aloud, compared with the time spent reading silently, you may feel you should adjust the proportion of class time spent on each.

2.2 Authentic reasons for reading

To return to the list of things you have read and your reasons for reading them: whatever the reasons were (and excluding any reading that was directly concerned with language learning), it is unlikely that you were interested in the pronunciation of what you read except in a tiny minority of cases, and it is even less likely that you were interested in the grammatical structures used. You read because you wanted to get something from the writing: facts, ideas, enjoyment, even feelings of family community (from a letter): whatever it was, you wanted to get the message that the writer had expressed. You were interested in what the writing meant; hence the sort of words we found in group (a) turn out to be the most important ones if we are thinking of a definition of reading that covers the most usual authentic reasons for reading. (We use the term *authentic* to mean reasons that are concerned not with language learning but with the uses to which we put reading in our daily lives outside the classroom.)

2.3 Why do you read the FL?

At this point we must face a major problem. If none of the items of reading on your list were written in the FL, it may be that you, and your students too, do not really need to read in the FL at all. If so, you may feel that the discussion that follows is irrelevant to you. But let us analyse the nature of the difficulty.

If your students have no need to use the FL outside the classroom, then the only function of the FL for them seems to be: to be learnt. Similarly, the only reason for reading it is: to learn to read it. This is sterile and self-defeating and we ought not to be surprised if student motivation is low. But it remains true that the FL exists because it is used, just like any other language. And FL users read their language for the same sort of reasons that you had for reading the items on your list.

Your problem is not that nobody reads the FL for authentic reasons, but that your students do not. And this is a problem of motivation. We cannot simply dismiss it, for it is the central problem for many language teachers, but it is a problem of educational policy and organization and therefore largely outside the scope of this book. Later on we shall be making various suggestions that may help to increase motivation by making FL reading interesting in itself; but nothing can replace the motivation supplied by needing to read. If you can, therefore, draw to your students' attention the sort of purposes for which they might conceivably find FL reading useful outside the classroom. And you can try to give them reading materials that reflect the authentic purposes for which people do read. This will help them realize that reading is not just a linguistic exercise but is involved with the getting of meaning out of a text for some purpose.

3 Getting a message from a text

It is reading of this kind that we are concerned with in this book. As we have seen, other meanings of the word *reading* exist, but we shall exclude from consideration any activity that does not have as its main purpose the extraction of meaning from writing. Our business is with the way the reader gets a message from a text. So we should establish what we mean by a message.

4 The communication process

Figure 1 gives a very simple model of the process of communication. On the left is the writer; but since he could equally well speak his message, we will use the more general term *encoder* for his role. The encoder has a *message* in his mind (it may be an idea, a fact, a feeling, an argument, etc.) which he wants somebody else to share. To make this possible he must first put it into words: that is, he must *encode* it. Once it is encoded, in either spoken or written form, it is available outside his mind as a *text*. The text is accessible to the mind of another person who hears or reads it, i.e. who *decodes* the message it contains. Once it is decoded, the message enters the mind of the decoder and communication is achieved.

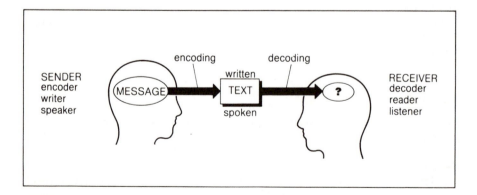

Fig. 1   The communication process

Obviously this model is too simple, for things can go wrong at any stage in the process. That is why I have put a question mark in the decoder's mind, for we cannot be sure that he has received the message that was intended. However, the process is clear enough for us to say that reading means getting out of the text as nearly as possible the message that the writer put into it. We shall need to consider in a little more depth the part played by the writer, the reader and the text itself in this process; and we will start with the reader.

4.1 Is the reader's role passive?

Figure 2 illustrates one fairly widely held view of reading. The text is full of meaning like a jug full of water, and it can be poured straight into the reader's mind which soaks it up like a sponge. In this view, the reader's role is a passive one; all the work has been done by the writer and the reader has only to open his mind and let the meaning pour in.

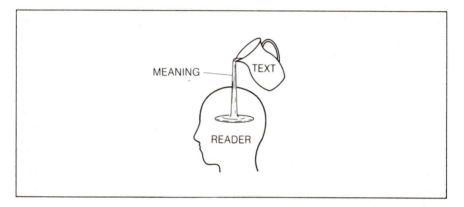

Fig. 2   One view of reading

Why do we reject this? One obvious reason is that it seldom happens like this. Not all the meaning in the text actually gets into the reader's mind; the figure should show at least some of the water trickling – if not streaming – down the reader's face. The fact that the meaning is in the text is unfortunately no guarantee that the reader will get it out, for we know from personal experience that a text that seems easy to one person may seem difficult to another.

4.2 What makes a text difficult?

To throw some light on the question, we will examine some texts that many people would find difficult.

Text A

Istuin eräänä tammikuun loppupäivänä Tiitin kanssa Kokkolasta Jyväskylään kulkevassa linja-autossa. Oli kirpeä pakkasilma, taivas oli kirkas, ja aurinko heitti lumihangille ja tien poikki puiden pitkeä sinisiä varjoja.

Y. Kokko, *Ne Tulevat Takaisin* (Werner Söderstrom OY, 1954)

If you found this text difficult, it is because you are not familiar with the *code* in which it has been expressed; you do not know Finnish, the language in which it is written. So one of the prerequisites for satisfactory communication is that writer and reader should share the same code. The implications for FL teaching do not need pointing out. But this is not the only reason for finding a text difficult.

Text B

In the first example, a carbon anion is formed that is stabilized by resonance (electrons delocalized over the carbonyl group and the α carbon atom). In the second case, a carbon anion is formed that is stabilized by the electron withdrawing inductive effect of the three chlorines.

The Language Centre, University of Malaya, *Reading Projects: Science*
(University of Malaya Press/Nelson, 1979)

This text is difficult to someone, who, like me, knows nothing about science. It would not help me if I looked up some of the words in a dictionary, because I should not understand the definitions. The only thing that would help would be a course in chemistry, starting from basics. So the difficulty here depends on the amount of previous knowledge that the reader brings to the text.

Text C

Ideas imprinted on the senses are real things, or do really exist, this we do not deny, but we deny that they can subsist without the minds which perceive them, or that they are resemblances of any archetypes existing without the mind: since the very being of a sensation or idea consists in being perceived, and an idea can be like nothing but an idea.

G. Berkeley, *Principles of Human Knowledge* (Nelson, 1949)

The vocabulary used in this text does not seem particularly difficult, but many people find that its message eludes them. Even if you have a vague idea what it is about, you will probably not be able to explain it clearly unless you have read a good deal more by Bishop Berkeley (who wrote it) and thought carefully about his arguments. For here the difficulty lies not in the language, and not in the amount of knowledge the reader requires, but in the complexity of the concepts expressed.

Text D

Cavorting in the vicinity of the residential area populated by those of piscatorial avocation, the minuscule crustacean was enmeshed in a reticulated object with interstices between the intersections.

The vocabulary is the only source of difficulty here, since you can 'translate' this into extremely simple English and the message is not challenging intellectually. For readers whose vocabulary is limited, this is more like the problem of text A than B or C: the writer's code is only partly the same as the reader's.

4.3 Shared assumptions

From these examples of different kinds of textual difficulty, we can see how important it is that the reader and the writer should have certain things in common, if communication between them is to take place. The minimum requirement is that they should share the same code: that they should write and understand the same language. Text D shows us that they should also have in common a command of that language that is not too widely different: if the reader has a far smaller vocabulary than the writer, for example, he will find the text hard to understand. In FL reading, this problem is basic and familiar.

A more interesting requirement is that the writer and reader should share certain assumptions about the world and the way it works. We saw that if the writer expects his reader to have a basic understanding of chemistry, the text will not be readily understood by anyone who lacks this; the writer does not tell the reader what he assumes is already known. So problems in understanding arise when there is a mismatch between the presuppositions of the writer and those of the reader.

Naturally there always is a mismatch of some kind; no two people have had identical experiences of life, so the writer is always likely to leave unsaid something that he takes for granted, but that the reader does not.

Figure 3 is a simple way of showing how, for any two people, certain kinds of experience will be shared, while others will not. The shaded area where the two circles overlap represents the things the two people have in common. In this area will be included all the knowledge – including knowledge of language – that they share. But it will also include more intangible things like attitudes, beliefs, values, and all the unspoken assumptions that are shared by two people who have been brought up in the same society. In the unshaded areas are the things that are not shared: the experiences and knowledge that are unique to each individual.

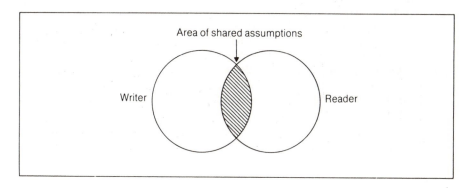

Fig. 3   Presupposition and communication

4.4 Identifying presuppositions

You may find it helpful to see how this works with some actual examples of texts. Study the following extracts and try to write down for each one the presuppositions that the writer has, and the assumptions he makes about his reader. There are some comments below.

(a) Red-wattled Lapwing: In general shape not unlike the European Lapwing and found in similar types of country. (From a handbook of bird identification)

(b) The biggest problem in getting animation accepted has been the idea that 'animation' means Walt Disney. (From an article about animation in films)

(c) Rubber futures closed the morning easier at the lows and mostly from 0.70 to 0.80 pence per kilo down from yesterday. Turnover was 188 lots of 15 tonnes, including 26 kerb trades and two options. (From a newspaper business page)

(d) Total movement of the belt should be approximately 10 mm midway between the pump and jockey pulleys when checked with normal wrist effort. (From a car user's handbook)

(e) It was a puppy. A tiny rickety puppy, mangy, starved; a loose ribby bundle on the ground. It made no noise. It tried to lift itself up. It only collapsed again, without complaint, without shame. (From *The Suffrage of Elvira* by V. S. Naipaul)

Here are my comments; you may well find other things.

(a) No use to the reader unless he too knows what a European Lapwing looks like, and in what sort of country it is found.

(b) Relies on the reader's knowing that Walt Disney is one of the best known producers in animated films. Also relies on his knowing what type of films Disney produced, and sharing the writer's implied view that Disney films are in some way undesirable in relation to his theme.

(c) Relies on the reader's understanding of technical jargon (*futures, easier, lows, down, kerb trades, options*), but also on wider understanding of the way rubber (and other commodities) is dealt with; for instance, is 0.70 to 0.80 a big drop or a small one? Is 188 lots a big turnover or not? Are lots always of 15 tonnes? – presumably not, since the writer has mentioned it; in that case, what is the significance? And so on.

(d) Trivially, the writer expects us to understand the code, including the abbreviation *mm* and the technical labels (*belt, pump, jockey pulleys*). He also expects us to know what wrist effort is 'normal', and what sort of movement of the belt is involved. (Where do you put your ruler to measure 10 mm?)

(e) The writer expects the reader to share his attitude to the puppy; readers from some cultural backgrounds have interpreted it as disgust (misled by words like *mangy*, which they themselves react to with disgust), having failed to tune in to the sympathy signalled by *tiny, starved,* and the half-admiring description of its stoicism and determination. This is an example where the assumptions are so deep that they need to receive only the slightest linguistic expression.

4.5 Total understanding?

The final example above indicates the importance of background in understanding. It will be obvious that for people of similar background, the shaded area in Figure 3 will be much bigger than for people coming from different backgrounds, let alone people from entirely different cultures. It is also clear that the greater the size of the shaded area, the easier communication will be. If the writer and the reader are closely similar in background, training, attitude and so on, the reader is likely to interpret the text with no conscious effort. There are still dangers of misunderstanding, however: a careless reader may read into the text meanings that are not there, simply because his sense of having much in common with the writer is so strong. Such a reader is assuming that the extent of the shaded area – the common ground – is greater that it actually is.

When the writer makes a similar false assumption about the extent to which the reader is likely to share his knowledge, beliefs, etc., the reader may be conscious of having to struggle to understand, and sometimes he may fail. But the widely different backgrounds merely make more obvious a fact that we sometimes forget: that we can never understand one another totally. Except in the most severely scientific writing, this seems inevitable, because all of us have had different experiences which make us see things slightly differently, even though we also have a great deal in common.

But of course one reason for reading is that we want to understand other people's ideas; if we were all identical, there would be no point in most communication. Fortunately, for most purposes, the understanding need not be total; but the fact that we cannot get inside the writer's mind is no excuse for not doing our best to understand what he wants to say. If we are in conversation with someone, we can stop him and ask for explanations and examples whenever we need them. In the same way, when we have difficulties in reading, we need to interrogate the text. Since the writer is seldom available for consultation, the text is our only resource: and reading has been described as 'active interrogation of a text'.

4.6 Active involvement of the reader

We can now begin to see why the model of reading shown in Figure 2 was unsatisfactory. The meaning is not merely lying in the text waiting to be passively absorbed. On the contrary, the reader is actively involved and will very often have to work to get the meaning out. A model like Figure 4 may seem nearer the truth: it shows us a view of reading in which the reader can be seen approaching meaning more actively. The reader on the left is finding little difficulty in interpreting the text: the meaning is fairly clear to him all along, he has much in common with the writer and he has few problems with the language used. To the reader on the right, however, the same text appears very difficult. To get at the meaning involves an uphill struggle and he is not at all sure of the route. He can bring to the task so little of what the writer has taken for granted that the way forward is continually blocked by problems of unfamiliar vocabulary, ignorance of facts or intellectual limitations.

Fig. 4   Another view of reading

However, the reader on the right is aware that he is not understanding; this awareness is important if you hope to be a competent reader. Poor readers often do not even recognize that they do not understand; so recognizing that there are problems is the first step towards competence.

The reader on the right is also tackling his problems with vigour and with all the tools at his disposal. He has understood that to reach the message involves his own efforts as well as those of the writer: it is in a way a co-operative task. The so-called 'co-operative principle', as it applies to reading, might be formulated along these lines:

The reader assumes
(a) That he and the writer are using the same code (the same language).
(b) That the writer has a message.
(c) That the writer wants the reader to understand the message.

This applies so strongly that you may have found yourself even trying to make sense of writing which turned out to be nonsense. Generally speaking, we assume that people are telling the truth and have something sensible to say until evidence to the contrary is too strong to resist.

4.7 Reading as interaction

The writer makes similar assumptions, including the reader's willingness to make some effort to get at the meaning for himself. If either lets the other down, communication fails. If the writer is careless, his message may be impossible to recover; if he makes demands that the reader cannot fulfil, the message will not be received, even though to another reader it might be clear. If the reader on his side is careless or idle, the result is similar: an incomplete interpretation or a distorted one. On both sides, lack of shared assumptions is likely to be the worst problem, because it is not always recognized. The reader is likely to try to make sense of the text in terms of his own presuppositions, and it may be a long time before he is forced to recognize that they differ from those of the writer.

From what we have said, you can see that reading according to this view is not just an active process, but an *interactive* one. We are accustomed to thinking of conversation as interactive, because what one speaker says obviously influences the contribution of the other. The interaction in reading is clearly rather different because the writer is not normally available, and this makes the task of both reader and writer more difficult. Since he can get no feedback, the writer cannot know which parts of his text will cause misunderstanding. He has to guess where the problems lie and shape his text accordingly, but since he never knows exactly who his readers will be, he will never succeed completely.

4.8 Making sense of the text

However, the writer has an advantage which the speaker has not: he has time to structure his text effectively, to help the reader by making it as straightforward as possible. The reader also has time at his disposal: he can stop and think, go back to check an earlier reference, reread the most difficult passages. Unless the text takes for granted a body of knowledge that he simply does not have, a careful reader should be able to reconstruct the assumptions on which the writing is based. He has to read with enough skill and care to make the right inferences about what the writer means, and he has to remain objective enough to recognize differences in viewpoint between himself and the writer. To do this he must assess all the evidence – choice of words, selection of facts, organization of material and so on – so that he gets the message intended rather than the message he might have preferred to receive.

All this suggests that a model of the reading process might be more like that shown in Figure 5: the text functions rather like a do-it-yourself construction kit. The message in the writer's mind is the perfect piece of furniture planned by the designer. The process of breaking this down into its component parts and packing them all into a box with instructions for assembly is a little like the process of putting thoughts into words and organizing them into a coherent text. A reader tackling a text resembles the amateur furniture maker unpacking his do-it-yourself kit and trying to work out how the pieces fit together.

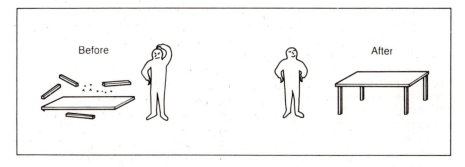

Fig. 5   The text as a do-it-yourself kit

It would not be wise to press this analogy too far, but it does serve to emphasize how much the reader himself has to contribute. We can begin to see the force of the metaphor *making sense*: the reader does in truth have to *make* sense of the text, almost like the amateur making his furniture. Whether his table is rickety, incomplete or more or less as planned depends not only on whether all the pieces were packed and the instructions clear, but also on whether he understands the basic principles involved, whether he follows the instructions properly, and whether he manages not to lose any of the pieces.

4.9 Prediction

A man who knows a bit about carpentry will make his table more quickly than the man who does not. If the instructions are not very clear, or the shape of a piece is baffling, his experience helps him to conclude that it must fit there, or that its function must be that. In the same way, the reader's sense and experience helps him to predict what the writer is likely to say next: that he must be going to say this rather than that. A reader who can think along with the writer in this way will find the text relatively easy: clearly he shares many of the writer's presuppositions.

I am not suggesting that the reader is conscious of predicting his way through a text like this. Usually he is not, but the skill is so useful that you may wish to make your students aware of it so that they can use it to tackle difficult texts. It does seem to be the case that as we read we make hypotheses about what the writer intends to say; these are immediately modified by what he actually does say, and are replaced by new hypotheses about what will follow. We have all had the experience of believing we were understanding a text until suddenly brought to a halt by some word or phrase that would not fit into the pattern and forced us to reread and readjust our thoughts. Such occurrences lend support to the notion of reading as a constant making and remaking of hypotheses – a 'psycholinguistic guessing game'.

If you are interested in finding out how far this idea accords with practice, and how useful it might be in dealing with a difficult text, you may like to try out the text and questions on p.13. To do so, take a piece of card and use it to mask the text (which is printed in roman type). Move it down the page, revealing only one section at a time. Answer the question (printed in *italic* type) before you go on to look at the next section. Check your prediction against what the text actually says, and use the new knowledge to improve your next prediction. You will need to look back to earlier parts of the text if you are to predict accurately, for you must keep in mind the general organization of the argument as well as the detail within each sentence. Try this out before reading further.

If you have tried this out, you have probably been interested to find how much you can predict, though naturally we should not expect to be right every time – otherwise there would be no need for us to read. Conscious use of this technique can be helpful when we are faced with a part of the text that we find difficult: if we can see the overall pattern of the text, and the way the argument is organized, we can make a reasoned guess at the next step. Having an idea of what something *might* mean can be a great help in interpreting it. It can be particularly helpful in leading us to interpret correctly the **value** of an utterance, which we must now define.

5 Text and discourse

5.1 Signification and value

The concept of value is most easily illustrated from conversation to begin with; but, as we shall see, it is equally relevant to the study of written texts. Consider this utterance:

> Aren't you cold?

Imagine for yourself as many situations as you can in which this might be uttered. Who is saying it to whom and why? In all the situations, the utterance will in one sense clearly have the same meaning. But in another sense, the meaning may be quite different: the difference is in the distinction between what we say and why we say it. Said by a mother to her son, the question may express concern for his well-being. It may express surprise at meeting someone unsuitably dressed for the weather. If it is said by someone who is feeling chilly to someone who has just opened the window, it may be a complaint.

Following Widdowson (1978), we shall use the term **signification** to refer to the meaning that would be common to all utterances of the sentence 'Aren't you cold?', and the term **value** to refer to the significance of the utterance for particular

PREDICTING OUR WAY THROUGH A TEXT

Use this text as described on p. 12.
The text is part of Appendix A Text 6.

The Scope of Ecology
What is this text likely to be about?

No living creature, plant or animal, can exist in complete isolation.
The writer starts by making a generalization. What do you think he will do next?

An animal is bound to depend on other living creatures,
What sort of dependence? What sort of living creatures?

ultimately plants,
Do you want to change your prediction about the sort of dependence meant?

for its food supply;
Were you right? What next, do you think?

it must also depend upon
Upon what? Why?

the activities of plants
Were you right? What else must it depend on plants for?

for a continued oxygen supply
Why does it need oxygen?

for its respiration.
Will the writer move on to a new point now? How is he likely to go on?

Apart from these two basic relationships
Do you want to change your prediction?

it may be affected directly
What word will probably come next?

or indirectly in countless different ways
Did you expect this? What must come next? (Note punctuation)

by other plants and animals around it.
What is the most likely to follow: a hypothesis, a definition (of what?), an example, several examples (of what?)

Other animals prey on it
Which was it? What will follow now?

or compete with it for the same food;
What does the semi-colon tell you?

plants may provide shelter,
Will the next statement refer to plants or something else?

concealment or nesting material,
Will the next words refer to plants, animals, or both?

and so on.
Which was it? What next?

Similarly,
Which of the preceding sections does this relate back to? What will follow?

the animal will produce
Produce what sort of thing?

its own effect
What word will come next? How will the sentence continue after that?

on the surrounding plants
What next?

and animals:
What does the colon signal?

some it may eat or destroy,
What will follow, reinforcement or contrast?

for others it will provide food;
What will the writer do next?

and through its contribution of manure
The word 'through' signals what? (purpose? location? result?)

it may influence the texture and fertility of the soil.

speakers in a particular situation – i.e. the reason why it was said. The concept of value is important, because it is quite possible to understand the signification of an utterance without interpreting its value correctly. The distinction is often used for comic effect:

> 'Waiter, waiter, there's a fly in my soup!'
> 'Hush, sir, not so loud, they'll all be wanting one.'

The customer intended to make a complaint; how did the waiter choose to misinterpret his utterance?

A skilled reader grasps not merely the signification of what he reads (though that is the necessary first step) but also its value. This involves understanding the writer's presuppositions sufficiently to recognize what he means by a particular statement: not just what he says, but why he says it. A further example, this time not particularly identified with spoken language but likely to be found in written texts, may be helpful. Suppose we take this sentence:

> Warm air rises.

It is easy to think of contexts in which this sentence can occur with a variety of values:

> As a *reason*, e.g. in a description of how to position a heater.
> As an *illustration* or *example*, e.g. in a simple account of scientific laws.
> As an *objection*, e.g. to refute the suggestion that a heater should be positioned high up.
> As a *conclusion*, e.g. the culmination of an experiment to prove this fact.
> As an *assumption*, e.g. one of the given facts in an experiment to prove something else.
> As an *explanation*, e.g. of why one part of a room is at a different temperature from another.

You may like to take a sentence and see how many contexts you can think of for it, in each of which it will take on a different value.

It should be clear that to understand a text properly involves understanding the value of each utterance that composes it: if you interpret as a conclusion something the writer intended as a hypothesis, you are not likely to understand his argument. The difference between signification and value corresponds to the difference between a sentence in isolation and the same sentence in use. Until a sentence is used in a certain context, it has only signification. It acquires value when it is used. For example, the question 'Is "Warm air rises" a reason or an example?' does not make sense unless it refers to an occurrence of the sentence in a specific context. (Note that once a sentence is in context and is thus used rather than merely cited (i.e. has value as well as signification), it is usual to refer to it as an **utterance**, whether it is spoken or written.)

It is the reader's job to make sure that he understands both the signification and the value of every utterance in the text, and he needs to be actively aware of his responsibility for the meaning he gets out of the text. But no matter how skilled he is, he will have problems unless the writer, on his side, has done his own job competently. The writer's task is to create the outward representation of his thoughts, and this involves him not only in selecting the best words, but in organizing them into a structured sequence: i.e. producing a satisfactory text.

5.2 Text and non-text

The text is the core of the reading process, the means by which the message is transmitted from writer to reader. So we need to study its characteristics and find out what other features, besides presupposition, make a text easy or difficult to follow. We might start by examining this sample:

> There was no possibility of a walk that day. Income tax rates for 1984 have already been announced. What is the defining characteristic of the ungulates? Surely you did not tell her how it happened?

What is wrong with this? The lack of relationship between the sentences is obvious. They go together only in the accidental sense of being together on the same page, misleadingly laid out as if they were part of a text. It is difficult to imagine any context in which they might occur together like this, and we cannot work out what their value, relative to one another, might be. They do not constitute a text at all.

However, a common context is not by itself enough to define a text, as the following example will show:

> A man put some perfume into a drawer.
> James Brown forgot about some perfume.
> A man bought some perfume for Mrs Brown.

We can detect that these sentences might all relate to the same situation, but if so, in a number of ways the situation is not clearly expressed. For one thing the sequencing is unclear. A rearrangement may help; at the same time we will set out the sentences to show another feature that makes them unlike a text (layout based on an article by Gerry Abbott).

A man	bought	some perfume	for Mrs Brown.
A man	put	some perfume	into a drawer.
James Brown	forgot about	some perfume.	

Now the sentences are ordered in a way that suggests they are telling a story; but no reader would accept this as a normally coherent text. What is lacking? The best way to find out would be to rewrite the sentences yourself to produce an acceptable text. As you do this, notice what you have to do to achieve the result you want.

If you have completed this task you will have realized that the sentences can most easily be interpreted as a story if we assume that the 'James Brown' and 'a man' refer to the same individual in each case, and that the perfume is also the same each time. You will probably have changed the sentences to show this, but you may have made other changes too. Perhaps you have produced something along these lines:

One day,	James Brown	bought	some perfume	for his wife.
However,	he	put	the present	into a drawer
and	–	forgot about	it.	

5.3 Coherence and cohesion

This now reads like a normal text; we can see that it is **coherent** because we have made use of **cohesion** to indicate the relationships between the various elements in the story. This will be discussed more fully in Chapter 7, but we can observe a number of ways in which connections are made by linguistic means:

(a) Instead of repeating nouns, pronouns are used.
(b) We use *the* instead of *a* for any subsequent mention of something already referred to.
(c) Words that would be redundant are omitted.
(d) Connectives (column one) are inserted to show how parts of the text are related and also to give some indication of the value to be assigned to them.
(e) Lexical choice may also contribute to coherence: we now know that Mrs Brown is James's wife (and not his mother, etc.). And we have an example of what is sometimes called 'elegant variation' in the use of 'present' to refer to the perfume; writers often prefer not to repeat words so readers have to be on the look-out for different words relating to the same referent (thing referred to). In this case, the use of 'the' signals that this is not the first reference to this object, so an experienced reader will infer that the present and the perfume are the same. So we have been indirectly told that the perfume was a present (and not something his wife had asked him to buy with her own money).

This example demonstrates only a few of the cohesive devices a writer can use to help the reader to see the coherence of his message, but it should be enough to show you the difference between a coherent text and a mere collection of sentences. Strictly speaking (if we again follow Widdowson), it is the **discourse** that has coherence while the text has cohesion; we can think of coherence as a quality of the underlying thoughts and the way they are organized into a message. The way the message is expressed will reflect the coherence by means of the linguistic devices of cohesion.

5.4 Coherence without cohesion

Coherence depends on the value of the utterances that compose the discourse: not on the use of cohesive devices, although these are customarily used to make things easier for the reader. In theory it is therefore possible to have a coherent discourse that is expressed by a text without cohesion, and in fact examples of this can be found in conversation:

'I'd love a cup of tea.'   'It's half past two already.'

On the surface these sentences seem totally disjointed; there are certainly no observable linguistic connections between them. Yet we all know that such exchanges frequently take place and are readily understood in the context of the situation in which they are uttered. In this example, the context presumably is that the second speaker is anxious not to be late for something, or has some similar reason for discouraging the other from having tea.

While examples of coherence without cohesion may not be quite so frequent in written discourse, they are not uncommon:

Suddenly from the dark road ahead came a terrible screaming. Gerard's hand tightened on his dagger.

We read coherence into this because we share the writer's presuppositions about screams being associated with danger, danger requiring a man to defend himself, and so on. None of this is made explicit in the text, but because the two sentences are in sequence, the reader assumes there is a relationship and seeks it. We should be surprised if, for example, Gerard were to take out his dagger and idly carve his name on a tree.

Here are some other examples where coherence has to be interpreted without the help of cohesive devices:

(a) It is possible to walk across the sea bed of 400 million years ago. In the flat desert land of a cattle station in Northwestern Australia, close to a place called Gogo by the aborigines, rises a line of strange steep-sided rocky bluffs, 300 metres high.
(b) When the male meets the female in the mating season, the two intertwine. The process looks rather laborious but at least it is not dangerous. Millipedes are entirely vegetarian.
(c) An external skeleton is an unexpandable prison. The insect's solution is moulting.

(All extracts from D. Attenborough, *Life on Earth* (Collins/BBC, 1979))

Perhaps you did not even notice the lack of cohesion in these examples; as an experienced reader, your mind would supply the connections that are not explicitly made in the texts. You know that a sea bed is generally flattish, so you can identify the 'flat desert land' and the sea bed in example (a). Example (b) is more complex; you will assume that the male and female must be millipedes, but what has being vegetarian to do with it? To see the connection, you need to know that mating in some species is followed by one mate eating the other; so it can be a dangerous process in non-vegetarian species. In example (c), you need to grasp that a solution implies a problem, and look at the first sentence to locate one: if something is described as 'unexpandable', this implies that expansion would be desirable, while 'prison' speaks for itself.

To make these connections, we had to make use of presuppositions in the way described earlier. But an unskilled reader may be unable to cope with such texts; to him, they might appear incoherent. Apparent incoherence ought, therefore, to be tested for possible mistaken interpretation of the value of some of the utterances. Even if the signification has been correctly understood, the message of the text will be incomplete or obscure if the reader does not give each utterance its intended value.

The coherence of a text depends on many things, including obviously the sequence in which sentences are arranged. In addition to cohesive devices such as reference, substitution, ellipsis and lexical relationships (see Chapter 7), a writer will use explicit discourse markers such as *thus, and, however, although,* which point out the intended value of the utterance in which they occur. Hence if we read the word *thus* we expect to find a result; if *however* occurs, we look for a contrast to follow.

Markers like this are often not needed if the text is straightforward enough for the value of its utterances to be fairly obvious; the reader can be trusted to identify the value without their help. But where the text is complicated or deals with an unfamiliar field, markers are likely to be frequent. Whether the writer uses them frequently will depend on the audience he has in mind.

6 Reading and meaning

Even if the reader has explicit discourse markers to guide him, he will have to make use of the other skills we have mentioned if he is going to make sense of the text successfully. Not all relationships can be unambiguously signalled by markers: the reader will always have to draw on his interpretive skills to reconstruct the writer's presuppositions and draw appropriate inferences. He can never sit back and expect to absorb meaning effortlessly unless he restricts himself to pulp fiction or to subjects over which he already has total command: but we have assumed throughout this chapter that the student will read in order to find out things that he does not already know. That always involves some effort.

The view of reading that we have offered sees it as essentially concerned with meaning, specifically with the transfer of meaning from mind to mind: the transfer of a message from writer to reader. We have excluded from this book any interpretation of the word *reading* in which meaning is not central. We have also noted that the writer, the reader and the text each have a unique contribution to make if communication is to take place, and we have stressed particularly the possibly unfamiliar view of the reader as actively responsible for making sense of the text.

This view of reading is valid at any level. A concern with meaning, and with the reader's responsibility for getting meaning out of the text, is not out of place even in the earliest reading lessons from a primer, although some primers make such an approach difficult by providing texts in which meaning is distinctly lacking. Equally, the skills of interpretation which we see as required by every reader are, when fully developed, precisely the skills required for a sensitive appreciation of literature.

However, we shall not be dealing specifically with either the earliest reading lessons or the reading of literature. We shall concentrate on ways of developing the reading skills of students at an intermediate level.

2 Reading for what Purpose?

1 Reading in the FL classroom

In FL learning reading is often used for purposes which are different from those found in mother-tongue learning. For example, we noted that reading aloud is often used (mistakenly, most experts agree) as one form of pronunciation teaching. But the most typical use of reading in a foreign language class is to teach the language itself. The typical text in a FL course book is one that helps the teacher to present or practise specific linguistic items – vocabulary, structures and so on.

1.1 Reading and language improvement

As we pointed out in Chapter 1, this is not an authentic use of a text. It is perfectly true that reading widely is an effective means of extending our command of a language, whether the first language (L1) or the FL: but outside the classroom most of our reading is not done with this purpose, and it is certainly not the purpose for which most writers are writing.

For the FL student, the authentic purposes of reading are often submerged by the purpose of language improvement. Of course, language improvement is the central purpose of the language learner; but why does he want to improve his command of the language? The answer to this question is usually something like 'to deal with overseas customers' or 'to keep up to date with current research in nuclear physics': that is to say, his purpose has nothing to do with language as such. For him, the language is merely the means of achieving a non-linguistic purpose.

If this is the case, i.e. if he needs to read the FL for an authentic purpose, are we doing him a service if we spend our time on texts intended to improve his command of the language? Texts of this kind are certainly very convenient for teachers, but they have serious limitations as material for practising the skills of reading. We need to be aware of this so that at least we may supplement the course book with other material that is more suitable for this purpose.

1.2 Characteristics of FL textbooks

It may be helpful to point out some of the ways in which FL course books make unsatisfactory reading texts. One common feature of the early stages of a course is that the material does not consist of texts at all, even short ones, but is rather a series of disconnected sentences. These may be used to practise the skill of decoding but they are useless for practising any higher level skills.

Even when the course book contains continuous texts, they are often very different from the reading materials we meet outside the classroom. Fortunately, writers are becoming more aware of the need to supply texts that convey a message; but there are still many courses in use with some of these defects:

(a) Texts are often contrived and distorted because of the desire to include numerous examples of a particular teaching item (e.g. a tense).
(b) Texts often reflect spoken rather that written usage. This is not a serious

problem in itself, though the two styles of language are different; but the spoken language presented in class in the early stages is often limited to describing the obvious, and this carries over into the texts. A common kind of text at this level is one that describes an adjacent picture, giving the reader hardly any information that he has not already obtained from the picture itself.

(c) Also common in FL courses are texts which deal with over-familiar topics, such as the 'The clothes we wear' or 'Transport', recounting facts that have long been part of the reader's general knowledge. At their most extreme, texts of this kind are clearly intended, not to convey a message, but to indicate how certain facts are expressed in the FL.

(d) Many FL texts are over-explicit: they say too much, spell out too many details, so that there is no room for inference and hence no chance for the learner to practise this important skill.

(e) Many FL texts are guilty of having virtually nothing to say: the writer is so absorbed by the need to include certain language items that the need for the text to have a message is overlooked. You often feel that the writer is playing with words rather than trying to convey meanings.

These characteristics of texts for FL learners are largely the result of the central problem of early FL teaching: that the language has to be taught to beginners by expressing for them information which they already have. For example, they learn the meaning of the utterance 'John is writing' only because they already know the fact that John is writing. But of course the typical use of language is to express information which the reader or listener does not already have: we do not spend our time telling people things they already know – except in the FL class. So it is not very surprising that the FL seems boring and unnecessary to the students who are obliged to learn it. Only highly motivated students will tolerate these defects.

In the early stages of FL learning, it is probably impossible for the language to be presented in a naturally informative way, given the constraints of the classroom. But once the initial stage is over, there ought to be little need to subject learners to language that carries no message for them. Texts even for early stages can be made a great deal more informative than many of them are at present; and by the intermediate stage, you should be demanding for your students texts which, however simple in language, have a message that is fresh and interesting. (Selection of texts is discussed at greater length in Chapter 3.)

1.3 Language lessons and reading lessons

In this book, we are interested only in the authentic purposes of reading. Language improvement is a natural by-product of reading, and a highly desirable one, but it is not our concern. We have discussed it only because it frequently has such unfortunate effects on the quality of texts used with FL learners. We also need to be aware of its effects on the procedures used in lessons based on texts: they are more often lessons on pronunciation, vocabulary or structure than reading lessons. We need lessons like this, of course, but we need reading lessons too, if our students require the ability to read in the FL.

It is necessary to stress the difference because reading lessons are so often overlooked, especially in the early stages of FL courses. Giving a lesson based on a text is not the same thing as giving a reading lesson: most of the skills practised are probably not reading skills at all. In what way is a reading lesson different?

First, it is different because the type of text used is likely to be different. In a reading lesson we need to use texts that have been written not to teach language but for any of the authentic purposes of writing: to inform, to entertain and so on.

Even if the language has been modified to suit the level of the learners, the purpose of the text must be first and foremost to convey a message (in the widest possible sense, as defined in Chapter1).

Second, the procedures have to be different, because the aim of the reading lesson is to develop the student's ability to extract the message the text contains. So, unlike a language development lesson, we are not trying to put something into his head, but instead we are trying to get him to take it himself: to get him to make use of the knowledge he already has in order to acquire new messages.

Since different kinds of text make different demands on the reader, the procedures used in reading lessons will also have to be varied. Moreover, different readers may respond in different ways to the same text: they are entitled to do so, provided they base their responses on a correct literal understanding of the writer's message. The reading lesson needs to make allowances for both the variety of texts and the variety of readers.

2 Aims of a reading programme

But if every text and every reader require different treatment, can we state any general aim for a reading development programme? We might try something along these lines:

> *To enable students to read without help unfamiliar authentic texts, at appropriate speed, silently and with adequate understanding.*

Inevitably this seems too general to be helpful, but if we examine each phrase of it, we shall discover that it carries some fairly specific implications for teaching.

(a) *to enable students:* The teacher can only try to promote an ability in the student; he cannot pass on the ability itself. This is true of all FL teaching but applies particularly to comprehension, which is a private process over which even the student himself has no real control, though he may struggle to achieve it. In the reading lesson, it is what the student does, not what the teacher does, that counts.

(b) *to read without help:* We can seldom expect help with the reading tasks we undertake in real life outside the classroom; the teacher does not remain at our side. Therefore students have to develop the ability to read on their own. Your job as a teacher is to make your own help unnecessary.

(c) *unfamiliar texts:* Being able to read the texts you have read in class is not enough; part of the work of extracting the message was done by the teacher or fellow students. An independent reader must be able to tackle texts he has never seen before, and you will have to equip your students to do so. This implies that it is more useful to read two texts once each rather than one text twice (though the reasons for rereading may sometimes justify this activity). It also implies that if you want to test reading ability, you should use a text that is not familiar to the students.

(d) *authentic texts:* The reading skill is of no practical use unless it enables us to read texts we actually require for some authentic purpose. At least some of the practice given should be with authentic texts, i.e. the sort of text the student will want to read after he has stopped attending FL classes. If the needs of a single class are very varied, the practice material ought to be varied too. However, the stage at which authentic texts are introduced will need to be decided according to the students' command of the language. Where the level the students have reached is seriously below the level required to read the necessary texts, problems are unavoidable; they are discussed in Chapter 3.

(e) *appropriate speed:* It is not always appropriate to concentrate on reading fast; a flexible speed is the sign of a competent reader. But of course we should prefer to read fast if we can do it without loss of effectiveness. You need to train your students to use different rates for different materials and different purposes, instead of plodding through everything at the same careful speed. Unless you encourage them to skim and scan and read some texts with appropriate irreverence, they may never dare to do so. At the same time, they need practice in assessing what type of reading is suitable for various texts and various purposes.

(f) *silently:* We have already noted that people seldom need to read aloud except in the classroom. But because reading aloud is useful in the early stages of FL learning, it becomes an established part of the lesson and commonly persists far longer than is desirable. This usually means that too little time is given to developing the skill of silent reading; yet all readers need this skill, and most would benefit from help in developing it. (For teachers and others who do need to be able to read aloud well, specific training is necessary; but it should not be equated with the teaching of reading nor the teaching of pronunciation: it is a distinct skill and not an easy one.)

(g) *with adequate understanding:* It may cause surprise that we do not say 'with total understanding'. As in the case of reading speed, however, flexibility is required. We need to understand enough of the text to suit our purpose in reading, and this means that we frequently do not need to read or understand every word. Certainly students must be able to understand completely when necessary, but they must also learn that it is wasteful to read with the same amount of care for every purpose. This implies that various kinds of reading task must be given in class, not all of which require the precision of careful study reading.

But I do not want to give the wrong impression: understanding is central to the process of reading and must be the focus of our teaching. If we settle for less than complete understanding in certain reading tasks, the reasons must be clear. It must be the result of a conscious decision, not the result of incapacity to understand.

3 The role of the teacher

We have emphasized that reading involves skills that the student must learn for himself, and that the measure of the teacher's success is how far the student learns to do without his help. Some people would go so far as to say that reading cannot be taught, but only learnt. This does not, however, mean that there is nothing for the teacher to do: there is, in fact, a great deal.

The trouble is that it is easy to give too much help, or help of the wrong kind. Reading problems can be caused by providing so much help that it becomes a crutch the student cannot do without. What sort of help should we give?

The rest of the book attempts to answer that question. Briefly, it sees the teacher's job as providing, first, suitable texts and second, activities that will focus the student's attention on the text. The student must develop his own skills, but we must make him aware of what he is doing, and interested in doing it better.

Conscious development of reading skills is important because it is obviously impossible for us to familiarize our students with every text they will ever want to read. Instead we must give them techniques for approaching texts of various kinds, to be read for various purposes.

Unless we do this, we are not doing our job. Teaching students just how to read Text A is not teaching them how to read. However, the generalized skills of reading can only be acquired through practising the specific skills required for reading Text A, Text B and so on. One of the teacher's jobs is to make sure that the bridge is built between the specific and the general. And one way of helping the student to generalize his skills it to make sure that he reads a lot and has a lot of practice in using the skills with varied materials.

4 Intensive and extensive reading

Most of the skills and strategies we want our students to develop are trained by studying shortish texts in detail. But others must be developed by the use of longer texts, including complete books. These two approaches are described traditionally as **intensive** and **extensive** reading, and we will retain these labels. Brumfit (1977) points out that better labels might be **reading for accuracy** and **reading for fluency**; these are certainly more informative but still do not reflect all the purposes served by each type of reading.

Of course there are not just two contrasting ways of reading but an infinite variety of strategies which are interrelated and overlapping. Intensive and extensive reading are complementary and both are necessary, as well as other approaches which perhaps fit into neither category.

The labels indicate a difference in classroom procedures as well as a difference in purpose. Intensive reading involves approaching the text under the close guidance of the teacher (the right kind of guidance, of course, as defined earlier), or under the guidance of a task which forces the student to pay great attention to the text. The aim of intensive reading is to arrive at a profound and detailed understanding of the text: not only of what it means, but also of how the meaning is produced. The 'how' is as important as the 'what', for the intensive reading lesson is intended primarily to train students in reading strategies.

It is of course easier to handle work on short texts, which can be studied in a lesson or two, than long ones. It is also generally supposed that in order to understand the whole (e.g. a book), we must be able to understand the parts (the sentences, paragraphs, chapters) of which it is made up. However, it is also true that we are often able to understand a book without fully grasping every part of it; we ought to make the most of this ability and encourage our students to build on it. This suggests that we ought to pay attention to extensive as well as intensive reading.

Moreover, we must not ignore the demands made by longer texts, which are liable to get forgotten in the classroom. The whole is not just the sum of its parts, and there are reading strategies which can only be trained by practice on longer texts. Scanning and skimming, the use of a contents list, an index and similar apparatus, are obvious ones. More complex and arguably more important are the ability to discern relationships between the various parts of a longer text, the contribution made by each to the plot or argument, the accumulating evidence of the writer's point of view, and so on. These are matters which seldom get much attention except in the literature class, but they apply to the reading of any kind of book, not merely works of literature. We cannot afford to ignore them if we want our students to become competent readers, not merely of brief extracts, but of books.

We need an extensive reading programme that will actively promote reading out of class. Class time is always in short supply and the amount of reading needed to achieve fluency and efficiency is very great – much greater than most students will undertake if left to themselves. Some suggestions about how such a programme might be organized are given in Chapter 12.

But some class time ought to be devoted to extensive reading, both to maintain interest in it and to train students how to deal with full-length texts. Students who have not acquired the reading habit are often daunted by books and need the guidance and encouragement that an organized extensive reading programme can provide. Moreover, as there is no absolute divide between intensive and extensive reading, the same text can usefully be employed for training in both, key passages from it being used for intensive study and in turn illuminating the book as a whole.

For these reasons, we shall try to bear in mind the requirements of both intensive and extensive reading, because both are important and each complements the other.

3 Selecting a Text

The drawbacks of the texts generally offered in language course books have already been discussed. Books of comprehension passages are more likely to provide satisfactory material and they may have the added bonuses of (1) being carefully chosen to give practice in particular reading skills and (2) being accompanied by well conceived questions or other exercises. But not all collections offer both bonuses, and even the best do not offer all that is needed for a full reading course.

So you will need to supplement, even if not to replace, the material in the set books. In this chapter we shall consider how to choose supplementary material for the reading lesson. You will need to look at possible material from three points of view:

> readability,
> suitability of content,
> exploitability.

1 Readability

Obviously a text should be at the right level of difficulty for the students, but assessing the right level is not straightforward.

Our concern here is with linguistic difficulty only, ignoring for the moment the questions of conceptual difficulty and interest. The combination of structural and lexical (i.e. vocabulary) difficulty is *readability*.

1.1 Assessing the students' level

Lexical difficulty is fairly easy to assess if you know your students. You can list or mark all the new words or phrases, remembering to include new uses of familiar words and new idiomatic combinations (such as phrasal verbs) whose meaning is more than the sum of their parts.

If you do not know your students well, you will need to find out about them as soon as possible. You must find out how much language they know if you are to select suitable texts. If your students have all previously used the same set books or syllabus, a little research on your part will be worthwhile. Make use of any vocabulary lists supplied in the syllabus or the earlier textbooks. But remember that the presence of a word in the list does not guarantee that your students have learnt it, any more than its absence guarantees that they do not know it.

If the class comes from a variety of backgrounds, a period of trial and error is unavoidable. An idea of their level (or levels) can be got by giving a series of graded cloze texts (see p. 183) but the results can only be approximate in view of the limited number of items in a cloze text. The more advanced the class, the less reliable the conclusions, but even limited information is better than none during the first weeks with a new set of students.

Of course no class is ever entirely homogeneous. In an ideal world, every student would be given material appropriate specifically to his own needs; but most of us teach in circumstances where this is not possible, so we shall assume that the teacher has to compromise by choosing material that suits most of his class.

1.2 How much new vocabulary?

What proportion of new lexical items (words and idioms or compound phrases) is acceptable? The answer is partly a matter of opinion and partly depends on the reader's purpose: if you only want to get the gist of a text, you can skip unfamiliar words in a way that you could not risk if you needed a thorough understanding. On the other hand, for intensive reading – which will be slow and careful anyway – it may be acceptable to have quite a lot of new words. 'A lot' is a relative term: two or three per cent is a lot in my view (it represents about ten to fifteen words on a page of this size), but might be acceptable provided they were well spread out. Obviously it also depends on the nature of the new items.

Another point of view is put by Bright and McGregor (1970, p. 80). They argue that the ideal text for intensive work would contain no new words at all, since the student cannot respond fully to unfamiliar words. Take your choice: probably a compromise must be made: some texts can include only familiar words, so that the fullest possible response can be demanded; while others can include new words, so that students can develop the very necessary skills for dealing with them.

For extensive reading, however, the object is that the student should read a great deal; he will only do so if he can read with tolerable ease. This suggests a rather smaller proportion of new words – one per cent, perhaps; that is, about five on a page of this size. If there are more, the reader will be continually distracted and will very likely slow himself down by referring to a dictionary (even if you have told him not to).

You may be surprised that the suggested proportion of new words is so low; but to pursue the extension of vocabulary by choosing texts with a high proportion of new lexical items will defeat the aims of the reading programme, and is not an effective way of teaching vocabulary either.

1.3 Structural difficulty

Readability is not a matter only of vocabulary, however. Structural difficulty is also important, but is harder to assess. Obviously, new grammatical forms (tenses, structural words, etc.) may cause problems. But a more likely cause of structural difficulty beyond the elementary levels is sentence length and complexity, which can make the relationships between the various parts of the text difficult for the reader to sort out. How can you establish whether a text is structurally about the right level for your students? One way is to work out its **readability index**.

1.4 Measuring readability

Many measures of readability make use of counts of word length and sentence length; neither is a completely reliable indicator but the results give a rough guide which is useful if you have to assess the text yourself. More elaborate methods would take more time than most of us can afford.

To make use of a readability index, you first need to work out the index of texts that you know are about right for your students; this gives you a yardstick against which to measure the readability of texts you are considering using. There are many ways of measuring readability; we will look at just two simple ones.

(a) The SMOG index

This was devised by G. H. McLaughlin ('SMOG grading – a new readability formula', *Journal of Reading* 22 (1969), pp. 639 – 46) and is computed as follows:

(i) Choose three passages of ten sentences each from near the beginning, middle and end of the text.

(ii) Count all words of three or more syllables in the 30 sentences. The total is DW (= difficult words).

(iii) Calculate the square root of DW.

(iv) Add 3 to the square root: the total is the SMOG index.

The SMOG index was devised for use with L1 learners, but some FL teachers have found it and similar readability measures useful. You may wish to experiment, for example by defining 'difficult words' in a way that is more clearly relevant to your own students. But it is said that for L1 learners, attempts to be more rigorous (e.g. to try to measure grammatical complexity as well as mere length) did not achieve spectacularly better results in return for the much greater work.

(b) The Fry readability estimate

This was devised by Edward Fry (see Fry (1963, 1964, 1977)) specifically for use with ESL texts. It is computed like this:

(i) Choose three typical passages of 100 words each from near the beginning, middle and end of the text.

(ii) Count the number of sentences in each passage to the nearest 0.1 of a sentence (i.e if the last five words are the first part of a ten-word sentence, you would count them as 0.5). Add the three totals and divide by 3. The answer is A, the average number of sentences in 100 words.

(iii) Count the number of syllables in each passage. (This depends on pronunciation, not spelling: *picked* is one syllable, *radio* is three.) Add the three totals and divide by 3. The answer is B, the average number of syllables in 100 words.

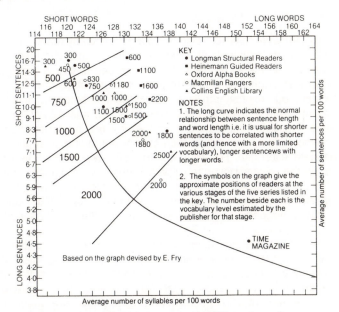

Fig. 6   Fry's readability estimate applied to some graded EFL reader series

(iv) Plot the answers, A and B, on a graph like that shown in Figure 6; one axis shows the average number of sentences per 100 words, the other the average number of syllables per 100 words.

To make use of the estimate, you plot on the graph the A and B figures for a number of books that are known to be suitable for your students. You can then plot the figures for any unfamiliar text and judge its suitability by noting its position in relation to the familiar texts.

You can see that the graph is divided into broad areas (1000, 2000 etc.) by bars along the normal curve. Between those bars you can expect to fall most texts that are roughly in the 1000 (or 2000, etc.) word level, though you can see from the series of graded readers plotted on the graph that these bars can indicate the range only approximately.

Some teachers find it easier to interpret the visual information from the graph than the numerical index produced by the SMOG method. However, any measure of readability takes time to get used to; you will not be able to use it effectively until you have had some experience in interpreting it. At best, it will provide only a rough guide (because it can never take account of the reader's knowledge and interest), but treated cautiously it can be very useful.

The readability index can be written into class library books, and you can work out the index of texts you want to use as supplementary material and file them accordingly. In this way you can quickly tell whether the material is at about the right level. (For the Fry estimate, you can write in the two co-ordinates – i.e. the A and B figures – always putting the A figure first; you need not actually plot everything on the graph.)

A further advantage, if the language you teach is used as the medium of instruction, is that textbooks in other subjects can be checked for readability by one of these methods. By this means textbooks can be avoided if they are written in language more difficult than the level reached in the language class.

1.5 Cloze as an indicator of readability

The kinds of measure we have just discussed are particularly useful because they enable you to compare new texts with familiar texts of established readability. An alternative measure is the *cloze test*. It does not permit you to make comparisons, but it is often favoured because it requires no computation.

The cloze technique may be familiar to you in the field of testing. It involves the deletion of words from a given text at (usually) regular intervals of between five and ten words. No deletions are made in the first few sentences, so that the reader can get some idea of the topic; thereafter he is required to supply a suitable word to complete each gap. (There is an example on p. 143.) It is a matter of dispute whether the word supplied must be the identical word used in the original text, or whether a suitable alternative should be accepted as correct; but to insist on the identical word produces adequate results, and is less laborious to administer (since no decisions about whether an alternative is suitable are involved).

Recently people have started using cloze as a guide to readability. Choose a passage from the text, 100 words or so in length, which seems typical of the text in terms of difficulty. Prepare it as for a cloze test, i.e. deleting words at regular intervals after the first few sentences. Type the cloze version on a card to be kept inside the book. A student who is considering reading the book should be asked to attempt the cloze and check his own score by referring to the original text.

You will need to work out from experience what score is needed to make it reasonable for a student to embark on a book. A 100 per cent score obviously means that he can probably cope with the text, a 50 per cent score suggests that it would be better to look for something easier. A 38 per cent score is said to indicate 'frustration level', i.e. that it would be wise not to attempt the book (see K. R. Cripwell: 'What is a cloze test? How do I use it?' in Moorwood (1978)). For independent reading, a score of 60 per cent or more is recommended; for class use, about 45 per cent (see Harrison, 1980).

However, no mechanical test of this kind – readability index, cloze or any other – can be completely reliable. (See Alexander Adkins: 'Cloze tests and extensive reading material', *MET* vol 7 no. 2, November 1979.) For one thing, the sample chosen may turn out not to be typical. For another, readability is not a matter only of grammatical complexity and lexical difficulty. It depends also on the interest of the text for the reader. A text that grips the reader will carry him along in spite of its difficulty. The opposite is also true: dull material will produce plodding readers and is not likely to contribute much to the development of reading competence.

2 Suitability of content

One criterion for a class library therefore should be the inclusion of a variety of books on subjects known to appeal to the students. Various studies have been made of students' reading tastes (see for example: R. R. Jordan, 'The reading interests of lower secondary school children in Africa and Asia' in *ELTJ*, vol 32, no. 2 (January 1978); P. d'Arcy (1973b) section 2). But it is dangerous to generalize when there are so many variations of age and nationality to be taken into consideration; you really need to carry out an investigation of what your own students like before you order many books or select class reading materials.

2.1 Finding out what students like

If you do plan a survey of reading tastes, it is as well to bear in mind at the design stage:

(a) In some countries, the classics (Shakespeare, Dickens and so on) still retain a strong position. Students may name such writers because they consider it the proper thing to do, but they seldom get much out of reading these writers (especially in abridged or simplified versions) apart from a feeling of virtue. The classics have their place, but it is much later than students think, when they are able to read unsimplified modern prose with ease.

(b) If you can, base your enquiry on what students have actually read as well as on what they say they would choose to read. If there is a school or class library, try to discover which books are borrowed most often; books read in the L1 may tell you more about reading tastes than those in the FL, if there is a reasonable collection. Information of this kind is more reliable than a questionnaire telling you what they think you would like to hear.

(c) You can also keep an eye open for the sort of reading matter that is found in students' possession. If it does not include works of major merit, there is no need to be surprised (let alone disappointed). But you might consider laying in a stock of similar reading material in the FL. Never mind what you feel about its quality: if students want to read it, half the battle has been won. You can wean them on to worthier material later. (A courageous tutor in a women's training college had great success in promoting the reading habit once she realized the appeal of Mills and Boon romances.)

You may not want to study in class the sort of material that has the most immediate appeal for your students. Comics, romances and thrillers have all been used successfully by some teachers, but others prefer to keep these for the library and to choose less controversial texts for actual lessons. Nevertheless, it is very difficult to do good work with a dull text. Look for a book that is going to interest the greatest number of students, and that will not actually bore the others. And (as Bright and McGregor wisely advise) look for a text that interests *you*.

Much of what has been said applies particularly to the selection of books – i.e. of extensive reading material. For intensive reading, many of the same criteria apply but for this purpose you will want to choose material that is not only interesting but worth spending time on. Most teachers use short texts for intensive work; if you can, try at least sometimes to choose extracts from class readers for this purpose. To study short passages in context contributes many dimensions of study.

2.2 Guidelines for text selection

You will want to choose passages from many sources to give your classes a wide range of material: in particular, texts of the kinds the students will later read for themselves, for study or other specific purposes as well as for pleasure. You may find the following guidelines useful:

(a) Will the text do one or more of these things?
   (i) tell the students things they don't already know
   (ii) introduce them to new and relevant ideas, make them think about things they haven't thought about before
   (iii) help them to understand the way other people feel or think (e.g. people with different backgrounds, problems or attitudes from their own)
   (iv) make them want to read for themselves (to continue a story, find out more about a subject and so on).
   (Take a critical look at your current comprehension passages. It is astonishing how many do not fulfil any of these criteria.)

(b) Does the text challenge the students' intelligence without making unreasonable demands on their knowledge of the FL? (It is not necessary to express trivial thoughts just because you are restricted to simple language.)

(c) If there are new lexical items, are they worth learning at this stage and not too numerous? (If not worth learning, or if there are too many, consider replacing them with words already known.) Are some of them understandable by means of inference from the context? (If not, can you build in some additional clues to make this possible?) (See Chapter 6.)

(d) Does the text lend itself to intensive study? Does it enable you to ask good questions (see Chapter 9) or devise other forms of exploitation? For example:
   (i) making a map, diagram, graph etc. based on information in the text
   (ii) reprocessing of information from the text, e.g. functional summary ('Write up the incident for the local newspaper'), dramatization
   (iii) debate, discussion, role play.
   (See Chapter 10 for fuller examples and discussion.)

3 Exploitability

Of all the qualities above, exploitability is arguably the most important after interest. A text that you cannot exploit is no use for teaching even if the students enjoy reading it. We are using the term *exploitation* to mean *facilitation of learning*. When you exploit a text, you make use of it to develop your students' competence as readers. What do we want them to learn in the reading lesson? For what purposes should we exploit the text?

3.1 The purpose of the reading lesson

Of course as they read the students will improve their knowledge of the FL. But this ought to be considered an incidental bonus: it is not the purpose of the reading lesson. We are not saying language must not be taught, of course, but simply that this is not the kind of lesson we are talking about. *In a reading lesson we are not setting out to teach language; alternatively, if we are setting out to teach language, we are not giving a reading lesson.*

Certainly we want students to understand the content of the text, otherwise they cannot be considered to have read it in any real sense. Yet when we use a text for intensive reading, is it chosen because we want the class to learn more about the topic? Not really: the texts may deal with history, biology, economics, but we are not teachers of these subjects, and when we use these texts, any increase in the students' knowledge of the subject is another incidental bonus, not our primary aim. We are interested in the understanding that results from reading because it is evidence that the students have completed the reading process satisfactorily. We choose texts that give practice in the process; but to improve students' knowledge of the content is not our aim.

The focus of interest in the reading lesson is neither language nor content, but the two together: we want our students to learn how language is used for conveying content. We want them to develop the skills needed to extract the content from the language that expresses it. These are the skills they need in order to become effective independent readers.

An ideal reader would be able to extract the content from any text at all; but of course such a reader does not exist; he would have to have not only complete command of the language but also enough knowledge of every area of study to be able to tackle every text ever produced. We do not expect to produce this ideal reader, but we cannot be satisfied with a reader who can tackle only a single text. We have to push him as far as possible towards becoming an ideal reader (or an ideal reader of, say, science texts, if our aims are specialized): that is the target towards which we move, even if we do not reach it. Every text we handle in the reading course helps to move the student towards the goal: but that particular text is not itself the goal, it is just a step in the right direction. You have not exploited a text effectively unless you have used it to develop interpretive skills that can be applied to other texts.

When you choose a text, therefore, you need to be clear what sort of interpretive skills it demands, and what methods you will be able to use to help your students to develop them. But don't forget that the first requirement is that the text should interest the students.

4 Reading skills and strategies

Here in broad terms are the skills and strategies of reading that we hope will be learnt through our exploitation of texts:

(a) Skills involving flexibility of technique: variations in reading rate, skimming, scanning, study reading, etc. (see Chapter 4).

(b) Skills of utilizing information that is not strictly speaking part of the text itself: reference apparatus, graphic conventions, illustrations and diagrams (see Chapter 5).
(c) Word-attack skills: how to tackle unfamiliar lexical items by using morphology, inference from context, etc., or by using a dictionary (see Chapter 6).
(d) Text-attack skills: the process of interpreting the text as a whole, using all the clues available including cohesion and rhetorical structure (see Chapters 7 and 8).

Of these four categories of skills, the last is by far the most important. The text-attack skills are central to the reading process, and are complex and under-described, in spite of a revival of interest in this field. To pursue these skills, it is of course first necessary to have a text which exhibits the characteristics of true discourse: it has something to say, is coherent and structured. This requirement must lead us to examine with some suspicion the quality of the texts we use for intensive study. It is less difficult to find texts to practise the other categories of skills.

5 Simplified or authentic texts?

A text that is linguistically difficult for your students is unlikely to be suitable for the development of most of these skills. If it is loaded with new vocabulary and complex structures, it is probable that your students, if not you yourself, will resort to translation as the only way of coping. This is not a good solution. If they cannot understand without your explanation or translation, they will be slow to achieve independence. Translation not only slows down their reading speed but also interposes the L1, instead of letting the FL speak directly for itself.

A text that demands substantial intervention from the teacher is therefore not well chosen. Far better, if you cannot find a suitable original text, to simplify to the level of your students a text that is suitable in other respects. You can then reasonably expect them to do most of the work of understanding its message.

However, simplification for this purpose needs to be done with discretion. As you simplify, you are of course removing many of the barriers to understanding offered by the original. But if you are not careful, you may also be removing its basic qualities as discourse. So when you simplify, it is important not to go too far.

If you make everything explicit, you will not be able to develop the students' capacity to infer. Retain things that will challenge their intelligence so that you can ask interesting questions. Retain new words if their meaning can be inferred from the context – this is an important reading skill. Do not insert explicit connectives (*because, although*, etc.) if the reader will be able to deduce the relationships between sentences without them.

In short, preserve whatever in the original will appeal to the intelligence of your students, while removing those elements (new words, complex sentences) which intelligence alone cannot deal with. Above all, retain as much as possible of the textual quality and discourse structure of the original.

But however good the simplification, something is always lost. Some teachers feel this so strongly that they avoid all simplified versions, and one has to sympathize with their views. If you can find unsimplified material at the right level, clearly that is the best answer. If you cannot, think carefully before choosing material which is impossible for your class to tackle independently. You will almost certainly have to use simplified materials to begin with.

4 Increasing and Varying Reading Speed

1 Speed and comprehension

There is no doubt that reading speed and comprehension are closely linked. A very slow reader is likely to read with poor understanding, if only because his memory is taxed: the beginning of a paragraph – or even a sentence – may have been forgotten by the time he has struggled to the end of it. But it is not clear which is cause and which effect: do people read quickly because they understand easily, or do they understand easily because of the speed with which they read?

2 Eye movements and sense groups

A great deal of work has been done on the improvement of reading speeds, stemming at least in part from the discovery that good readers do not read word by word; for an account of the research involved, see Banton Smith (1966). We now know that a good reader makes fewer eye movements than a poor one; his eye takes in several words at a time. Moreover, they are not just random sequences of words: one characteristic of an efficient reader is his ability to chunk a text into sense units, each consisting of several words, and each taken in by one fixation of his eyes.

So a good reader may chunk:

The good old man/raised his hand/in blessing.

or he might manage with only two fixations for this short sentence. He would certainly not chunk:

The good/old man/raised his/hand in/blessing.

nor would he read word by word.

It is quicker to take in the sense of two or three chunks and fit them together than to do the same with a larger number of smaller chunks. So the larger the sense groups a reader can take in, the more easily he will turn them into coherent messages.

The FL student's problem is that he does not know the language well enough to chunk effectively. He tends to read word by word, especially if the text is difficult. So to encourage good reading habits, it is necessary to give a lot of practice with easy texts. The amount of practice needed is too great to give in the classroom; this is one purpose of an extensive reading programme.

If we could get our students to recognize sense groups and take in longer groups with each eye fixation, it would obviously help. Opinions differ about whether such skills can be trained; but materials have been developed for this purpose and are claimed to be useful. Among them are:

(a) Texts already divided into sense groups, set out in narrow columns with only one group on each line. The student is asked to force himself to make only one eye fixation for each line, for example by moving his finger down the centre of the column and making his eye follow it.

In this way
it is hoped
he will accustom himself
to taking in
increasingly long chunks of text
at a single eye fixation.

(b) The use of projected material (films, slides, OHP transparencies): one sense group of the text is shown at a time, the rate of presentation being steadily speeded up as the student's ability to take in a sense group improves.

However, the physical act of taking in a sense group visually is not the same as assimilating its meaning; we shall come back to this point later.

3 Flexibility

Speed is useful, but it is not the main criterion by which we judge effective reading. There are occasions (for example, enjoying literature or studying a legal document) when speed may even seem inappropriate. Most people can improve their reading speed and should be encouraged to do so, but insistence only on faster reading may do harm.

Research has shown that one of the main characteristics of a good reader is his flexibility. He will vary his speed, and his whole manner of reading, according to the text and according to his purpose in reading it. For students who have read little (even in their L1, perhaps) except in the lock-step of reading aloud in the classroom, the concepts of speed and flexibility are both unfamiliar. You will need to start any reading improvement course for such students by explaining these concepts and why they are important in reading development. The course will not be successful unless the students understand the reasons for what they are doing, especially when some of the activities will seem strange and may contradict their earlier views of reading.

4 Scanning and skimming

The idea that some words in a text may be ignored or skipped will certainly seem strange to students accustomed to plodding word by word; but the techniques of skimming and scanning require this. These terms are sometimes used indiscriminately, but we will distinguish them as follows:

By *scanning* we mean glancing rapidly through a text either to search for a specific piece of information (e.g. a name, a date) or to get an initial impression of whether the text is suitable for a given purpose (e.g. whether a book on gardening deals with the cultivation of a particular vegetable).

By *skimming,* on the other hand, we mean glancing rapidly through a text to determine its gist, for example in order to decide whether a research paper is relevant to our own work (not just to determine its field, which we can find out by scanning), or in order to keep ourselves superficially informed about matters that are not of great importance to us.

The distinction between the two is not particularly important. In both, the reader is not reading in the normal sense of the word, but is forcing his eye over the print at a rate which permits him to take in only, perhaps, the beginnings and ends of paragraphs (where information is often summarized), chapter headings, subtitles and so on.

Skimming and scanning are useful skills. They do not remove the need for careful reading, but they enable the reader to select the texts, or the portions of a text, that are worth spending time on.

5 What sort of text shall we use?

The time required to read a text carefully depends on its linguistic difficulty and on the density of the information it carries. (A text is 'dense' when the minimum number of words expresses the maximum amount of information. A dense text is usually more difficult to follow than one which presents information in a more extended way.) If students are to read faster and develop the skills of skimming and scanning, they must practise on simple material.

This is particularly important for the FL student, because he may feel insecure when you want him to stop giving equal attention to every word. The material you choose for work on speed, scanning and skimming must be well below the level of the current textbook. To begin with, it should contain no language difficulties at all.

Once the students have accepted that they really can get the gist without reading every word, you can move on to similar exercises using more difficult (but not much more) material. You will next have to prove to them that occasional unfamiliar vocabulary is seldom a major bar to comprehension. At this stage you will have to deal with their feelings of guilt at skipping unknown words and not looking them up in the dictionary.

If a text contains more than a few new words, or if it is difficult in other ways, it is dangerous to make students try to read it fast. You may have to help your students learn how to scan and skim such material, if they are going to have to study difficult texts in the FL for professional purposes; but it is simply not possible to read fast and also with understanding, if the text is full of new words, complex sentences and difficult ideas.

6 What speeds should be expected?

Since it is obviously much more difficult for the FL student to improve his reading speed than for an L1 reader, and much riskier, you may wonder whether it is advisable to attempt it.

The days have passed when people were prepared to accept uncritically claims of reading speeds of several thousand words a minute. Such speeds must be seen as extreme forms of scanning rather than reading proper. They are useful for people burdened with masses of documents, but not for study purposes nor for recreational reading: who would want to finish a good novel in twenty minutes?

It is right to be healthily sceptical, but we should not reject the idea of improving reading speed just because exaggerated claims are sometimes made. FL students can usually make and maintain significant improvements in their reading speed once they understand that it is useful and possible to do so. Progress may be particularly striking and satisfying where initial speeds are very low, as they often are in students from countries with a strong tradition of reading aloud.

Secondary school pupils in countries where English is a second language may read at 120-150 words a minute before training. University students in similar areas may read at about 200 w.p.m. but have been found to study at a rate of as little as 60 w.p.m. (presumably the texts were difficult and had to be understood thoroughly). University students in countries where there is little tradition of reading have been found to read at as little as 40 w.p.m. even in their L1. All these students can make very significant advances in speed after training; doubling the rate is not uncommon. An average increase would be about 50 per cent.

Comparisons are meaningless unless you know what exactly is being compared. (For instance, in the figures above, it is not at all likely that university students in ESL countries read more slowly than school children; there must have been differences in the way they were tested.) But it is useful to know that for an L1 speaker of English of about average education and intelligence (e.g. a student at a technical college), the reading rate is about 300 w.p.m. The range among L1 speakers is very great; rates of up to 800 w.p.m. and down to 140 w.p.m. are not uncommon.

7 Finding out students' reading speed

Begin by checking the speed your students read at now. You will then know the extent of the problem and later you will be able to measure their improvement.

To do this, choose an unfamiliar text that is not difficult for the students (if possible one with no new words). Count the number of words in it. Prepare a copy for each student, making sure that it is clean and legible.

Explain that you want to find out how fast they read, and why: motivation plays an important part in the improvement of reading speeds. Explain that the activity is not competitive, so anyone who cheats is cheating only himself. Explain how the activity will be organized (see below). Then give out the text and ask them to begin reading only when you give the word.

While the students read, your job is to indicate the time that elapses. You need a stop-watch or a watch with a second-hand. If you have an OHP or a large sheet of paper, you can prepare a chart as follows:

$$\begin{array}{cccccc} 1 & 2 & 3 & 4 & 5 & 6 & \text{(1 min)} \\ 7 & 8 & 9 & 10 & 11 & 12 & \text{(2 mins)} \\ 13 & 14 & 15 & 16 & 17 & 18 & \text{(3 mins)} \end{array}$$

The chart should cover as long as the slowest student is likely to need: the figures represent ten-second intervals. Pin the chart up and stand beside it with your watch and move a pointer along the row of figures as the time elapses.

If you cannot prepare a chart (which can be used again and again), use a blackboard. In this case, instead of pointing to a chart, you write the figures 1, 2 etc. on the board as the seconds pass. At the end of each line of six figures, you write '1 minute', and so on.

Whatever method you use to indicate the time, when the student finishes the reading task he immediately looks up and makes a note of the time you are indicating. He can then calculate his reading speed in words per minute by means of a simple equation:

$$\frac{x}{y} \times 6 = z$$

Here, x is the number of words in the text;
y is the number of ten-second intervals required to read the text;
6 is the number of ten-second intervals in a minute;
z is the reading speed in words per minute (w.p.m.)

For example, if the text contains 250 words and the time taken to read it is 80 seconds (i.e. eight ten-second intervals), the equation will read:

$$\frac{250}{8} \times 6 = 187$$

The reading speed is thus 187 w.p.m.

8 What is adequate comprehension?

Reading speed is worthless unless the reader has understood what he has read; so comprehension must also be measured. It is usual to do this as objectively as possible, using multiple choice or true/false questions. But what score is to be considered adequate? The general view seems to be that about 70 per cent is enough. And which is the better reader: one with a score of 100 per cent and a reading speed of 140 w.p.m., or one with a score of 70 per cent and a speed of 200 w.p.m.?

For most purposes the interpretations of these scores need not concern us: we can accept the rough and ready guide that 70 per cent is about right, and we will have to point out to students that for many purposes, 100 per cent accuracy is not necessary. If in your opinion 100 per cent *is* necessary for the sort of reading your students have to do, then set that as your target instead.

What matters is that speed should not be emphasized so much that comprehension is forgotten.

9 Reading habits in the L1

We noted that students from some educational traditions may not read efficiently even in their L1. When this happens, it is a hindrance to the development of efficient reading in the FL, for research shows that there is a strong transfer of reading habits from one language to another.

Normally, we should expect L1 reading to be much better than FL reading, and we should not expect any but extremely fluent readers to bring their FL speeds up to anything like their L1 speeds. But if the L1 is not much read, and if bad reading habits have developed in L1, attention to L1 reading may be a useful preliminary to developing better habits in the FL, at least where a similar writing system is used.

10 Faulty reading habits

Whether you begin with the L1 or the FL, there are plenty of ways of improving reading speed; at the end of the chapter we list a number of books containing techniques that can be adapted to training in other languages if necessary. Some of them were written specially for EFL students, but others had L1 readers in mind, and FL teachers must treat with caution some of the suggestions made about faults in reading technique. Some of these are not accepted by all L1 teachers either.

10.1 Subvocalizing

For instance, several early reading habits are alleged to slow down the reader when they persist into the later stages of reading. One of these is subvocalizing (i.e. forming the sounds of the words you are reading, and even murmuring them aloud). This offers elementary readers the support of the spoken language, with which they are more familiar, when they try to interpret the written code. Children make use of it in L1 reading (where it is encouraged for beginners), and so, understandably, do students learning to read a FL.

It is clear that efficient readers do not subvocalize; reading aloud is much slower than silent reading (our eyes move faster than our tongue) and subvocalization takes almost as long as reading aloud. If you subvocalize you will tend to read word by word instead of in sense groups, and it will be difficult to improve your speed. Reading efficiency specialists urge that this habit should be eliminated, and for an L1 student this may be appropriate. But what about the FL student? We should be more cautious where he is concerned: is it just a pointless defect left over from his early reading days, which should be got rid of without hesitation? Or is it a symptom of his insecure command of the FL, a prop that he still needs?

10.2 Finger-pointing

Similar criticism is made of finger-pointing such as children use to fix their concentration on the word they are deciphering. Again, it is true that this can slow down the reading process if the finger points word by word. The use of a cardboard guide may be more effective, but even fingers can be got to move swiftly over the page if the student realizes that this will help him. Finger pointing in FL students is particularly common when the writing system is not the same as that used for the L1. One way to help them to get rid of the habit is to choose texts with large type if you can. It is a pity that so few are available on the market, but perhaps you can get the use of a typewriter with a large typeface for materials that you prepare yourself. You may be surprised how much more confidently students tackle texts with oversize type.

10.3 Regressions

Another reading habit that is often criticized is the occurrence of regressive eye movements, i.e. the eyes moving back to check previous words instead of sweeping steadily forwards. Naturally this makes reading slower than it would be if movements were continually advancing, but this is not the only factor to be considered. As we saw from Chapter 1, a skilled reader continually modifies his interpretation as he reads, according to whether his predictions about what the writer will say are fulfilled. To do this he may have to return to earlier parts of the text and reinterpret them in the light of what has followed. So regression may be a sign of an active and responsive reader rather than an incompetent or insecure one. Again, it is a question of judgement how far you should urge students to force themselves to move their eyes continually forward. If you can eliminate pointless regression by practice with very easy material, you will be able to relax your demands when using more challenging material where regressions may be evidence of careful reading.

We should make our students aware that efficient readers do not have these habits and explain why. We should not harass students who cling to them because they are insecure; we should concentrate on other ways of developing confidence, and hope that these habits will disappear later.

11 Some approaches to improving reading speed

11.1 Machines

Sophisticated machines (tachistoscopes, pacers and so on) have been designed which force students to read at a given rate, and without regressions, by exposing the text only briefly, a bit at a time. But most of us do not have access to such equipment and it is generally agreed to be unnecessary. A similar effect can be attained by using a cardboard mask which the student himself moves down the page as he reads.

This may be simply a piece of card of about the same width as the page. Many readers find it helpful to place this below the line they are reading, but in fact it is better to place it above the line. The eye can be concentrated equally well, and there is the advantage that the card does not interrupt the sweep of the eye from the end of one line to the beginning of the next, as a card below the line may. Moreover, a card above the line will conceal the preceding text so that regressions are not possible.

Instead of a simple piece of card, you may prefer a cut-out mask designed to reveal the whole of one line and the first few words of the next. This too permits the eye to travel uninterrupted from one line to the next, and prevents regressions (see Figure 7). The eye passes without a break from one line to the next, while the slower hand moves the mask down the page.

Although using a mask means that the student, not the teacher, controls the speed at which the eye is forced to move, it is usually found that the student does in fact move the mask quickly enough to force up his reading rate, and the control that he exerts may motivate him in itself.

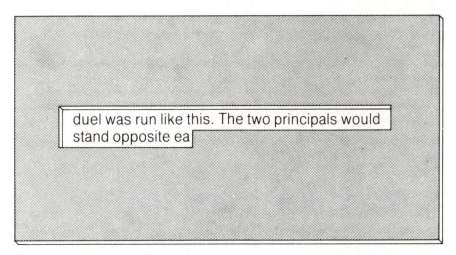

duel was run like this. The two principals would stand opposite ea

Fig. 7   Mask to promote reading speed

11.2 Slides and OHP

Slides or overhead projector (OHP) transparencies offer many advantages for the teacher of reading:

(a) The projected text holds students' attention and improves their concentration.
(b) You may be able to spot students with problems such as those we described earlier − subvocalization, head movements (slower and therefore more inefficient than eye movements, and quite unnecessary; though such movements may be different when reading a text on an OHP and in a book), and so on.
(c) Students have no alternative but to wean themselves from the habit of using a finger as a pointing device.
(d) It is also impossible for them to refer to a dictionary during the presentation of the text. (Using a dictionary slows down the reading speed: see Chapter 6.)
(e) You have total control of the length of exposure and you can, by using a mask, expose as much or as little of the text as you wish. (This applies particularly to OHP transparencies; it is easy to move a mask on the OHP in just the same way as we described in 11.1 above.)

(f) You can control the sequence in which students read. For instance, questions can be read before, after or during the reading of the text. The same text can be briefly exposed for a scanning exercise and later projected for a longer time for other purposes.

In short, get hold of an OHP if you possibly can; it is a most versatile aid for the reading class.

11.3 Scanning

Scanning exercises are easy to devise: the easiest are those requiring the students to scan for a single word, or a specific fact. For example:

(a) Look at page 00 and find out when Shakespeare died.
(b) How many times does the word *this* occur on this page?
(c) (Using a page from an index) On what page is the topic of evolution mentioned?
(d) (Using a page from a telephone directory) What is the telephone number of J. A. Brown?
(e) (Using an article, possibly one with subtitles) Does this article deal with . . .? Where? (Note: if you list a topic that is *not* dealt with, the student will have to skim rather than scan in order to be sure it is absent.)

Scanning exercises can be profitably conducted as races. They must be done fast.

11.4 Skimming

Skimming should probably not be done competitively, as more is involved than mere eye movements. Students can be asked to locate facts which are expressed in sentences rather than in single words; or they can be asked to say briefly what a text is about, or given specific questions that can be answered by glancing quickly through the text. For example:

(a) What (methods of plant propagation) are dealt with in this article?
(b) Which of these titles fits the text best? (Note: the titles should not differ in subtle ways; if they do, the question can only be answered after careful reading.)
(c) Which of these topics are dealt with in the text? (A list of topics is given.)
(d) Which of these pictures/diagrams etc. illustrates the text? (Several pictures etc. are supplied.)
(e) Which text belongs to this picture/diagram? (One picture and several short texts are supplied.)
(f) Which of these texts deals with (methods of plant propagation)? (Several texts supplied; one or more deal with the given topic.)

Although we suggest that these activities should not be done as races, speed is essential, otherwise they are not skimming activities. In some cases, the teacher can fix a time limit, or the students can be asked to see how many such activities they can do in a given time. If they can be prepared for individualized use (i.e. with answer cards available), you can ask students to collect a sheet at a time from your desk and record the number they complete.

12 A reminder

In speed exercises of all kinds, students should be motivated to beat their own records, not to compete with one another. People read at different rates because of variations in purpose, interest, ability, etc; so there is no sense in trying to read faster than someone else. But there is much sense in trying to improve your own performance and almost everyone is capable of this.

Students should keep a record of their progress, especially if you have a regular programme of speed-reading exercises. Both you and the students should be prepared for plateaus which occur now and again, when no progress is made. These are normal, but in general the speed will steadily improve, even if there are occasional falls because of difficult material or an off day. It is the general tendency that counts and this should be a source of satisfaction and continual motivation.

If you cannot organize a programme of reading speed improvement, at least talk to the students about it and give them a little practice in some of the techniques mentioned. Help them to understand how much faster they can read if they try, and to realize that it is not necessary for all purposes to read every word. Above all help them to see that flexibility is a sign of effective reading, and that there is no merit in reading something carefully if you could get the information you need in half the time.

Note: These books and articles, listed in the bibliography, deal with the improvement of reading speed:
Banton-Smith (1966), de Leeuw (1965), Fry (1963, 1967), Hill (1981), Mosbach (1976).

5 Utilizing Non-Text Information

Most of our attention in this book is directed to the interpretation of texts, and most of your attention in teaching reading will be directed to the same purpose. But when we undertake authentic reading tasks, we are frequently helped by information that is not, strictly speaking, obtained from the text itself. We shall consider three broad categories of this non-text information:

(1) *Graphic conventions*: such things as layout, punctuation, type-face, use of symbols.
(2) *Reference apparatus*: all the parts of a book or article that help the reader to locate information or predict what the text contains (including titles, index, blurbs and so on).
(3) *Non-verbal information*: such things as maps, diagrams, illustrations, tables and so on (including any words they may contain).

Making use of this kind of information is not really a reading skill, but a study skill. But the task of reading itself can be made easier or more difficult by these factors.

A skilled reader takes for granted the contribution that is made by information of this kind. For an inexperienced reader, the same information may be unnoticed or, if noticed, may be puzzling. A great deal depends on the reader's background, but even mother-tongue readers might benefit from instruction in these matters. The FL student needs to exploit every source of help he can find; and showing him how to make use of non-text information is a relatively straightforward job.

1 Graphic conventions

If you are teaching sophisticated students, most of this section may seem to labour the obvious. But if you teach people from countries with little tradition of private reading, particularly if their language has a different writing system from that of the FL, you will have come across the difficulties that unfamiliar conventions can cause.

Most of these conventions are things you take for granted, having assimilated them from years of reading, probably without ever having had any sort of instruction in them. But it cannot be taken for granted that the FL student will assimilate them equally easily, if only because he is likely to read far less. Since it is easy to teach people what they mean, it is worth checking to see if you need to teach them.

The graphic conventions that are likely to give difficulty to learners of English as an FL include the following (not necessarily a complete list and not in order of importance).

1.1 Spacing, indentation, layout

(a) *Spacing of letters within a word* is not usually significant in English (and in fact is normally found, without significance, only in newspaper printing). In some printing styles in other countries, a spaced word, e.g. m o t h e r compared with mother, has the same significance as an italicized word in British printing.

(See section 1.2 below on type variation.) This is not likely to give much difficulty.

(b) *Spaces between lines* are significant. Similar spacing is used to show the parts of a text that go together. For instance, when a quotation is introduced into the text, its lines are often closer together than the lines of the text proper, so that you can readily distinguish which is which.

Wider spaces between lines are sometimes used between paragraphs, but the most typical function is to indicate either (a) a shift of topic within a chapter or article, or (b) the passage of time (especially in fiction). Use (a) is often accompanied by a sub-title, where sub-titles are used. Both uses, particularly (b), may be accompanied by one or more asterisks or similar symbols, in the space between the two sections of text.

(c) *Indentation* (i.e. variation in width of the left-hand margin) is always significant.
   (i) It is usual to indent the first line of a paragraph (and necessary if wider spacing is not used between paragraphs).
   (ii) Quotations (i.e. of several lines) are also normally indented, so that the whole quotation has a wider left-hand (often also right-hand) margin than the rest of the text.

(d) Other uses of spacing, indentation and layout in general may be found, especially in specialized texts. If your students need to make use of such texts, you should examine them yourself in order to find out what the conventions are and which ones need to be pointed out or studied.

1.2 Choice of type

(a) Students, especially if their L1 is not written in the Roman alphabet, often fail to understand the significance of variations of type-face that we take for granted.

One problem is that hard and fast rules cannot be given, because every publishing house has its own style, and the styles used in books, magazines and newspapers also differ from one another. Moreover, the choice of type for the main body of the text determines the type variations available. For example, if the main text is itself in italic rather than roman, then italic cannot be used to give special prominence.

It is worth making sure that students realize that a change in type-style is usually significant. The change may involve:

   (i) The choice of type-face – Times Roman, Gill Sans-Serif and so on; for example:
   This is printed in Times Roman.
   This is printed in Gill Sans.
   This is printed in Baskerville.

   (ii) The choice of italic, bold or standard (roman) type:
   This is printed in italic.
   This is printed in bold.
   This is printed in roman.

   (iii) The choice of type size:
   This is printed in 6 point.
   This is printed in 8 point.
   This is printed in 12 point.

(iv) The choice of upper or lower case (capital or small letters): this is printed in lower case.
THIS IS PRINTED IN UPPER CASE.

(b) What are the functions of variations in type-style? First, they help the reader to distinguish different kinds of text or different parts of a text. In newspapers and magazines, type variation is often used simply to provide visual variety and make the text look easy to read by breaking it up. But there are other more useful functions:

  (i) To distinguish between several independent short items which might otherwise look like a continuous text.
  (ii) To distinguish the caption of a picture from the surrounding text.
  (iii) To distinguish between the words of different speakers/writers (e.g. between the questions and answers in an interview).
  (iv) To mark off an introduction, intruded note or tailpiece from the text proper (e.g. a note about the writer, an outline of the background to the article, an editor's comments).
  (v) To mark off different parts of a text (e.g. the ingredients and the method of a recipe; the stage directions and the dialogue of a play).
  (vi) To distinguish headlines, footnotes, etc, from the body of the text.
Many of these variations are also accompanied by variations in indentation.

(c) The above functions of variations in type-face are not difficult to understand and students will be able to explain many of them without help, once they become aware of them. More difficult to interpret are the variations in type found within the body of the text. Typically these involve the use of italics in an otherwise roman text, but different publishers use different conventions. In some kinds of text, bold face and italic may both be used to indicate different kinds of prominence. In textbooks (especially), small capitals may be used to provide a third variety of prominence.
  The main functions are as follows:

  (i) To make words easy to locate, for example:
    A Proper names in *Time/Life* style journalism:
      In Venice yesterday, *President Carter's* helmsman is faced with a bit of tricky navigation.
    B Technical terms at the point where they are defined:
      Sounds may be classified by this *point of articulation*.
    C Text phrases that serve more or less as subtitles or summaries of rules:
      Clearly, *the age of the students* and the things they like to do must influence the choice of materials.

  (ii) To mark the use of a foreign word or phrase:
    A species of viola, *viola calaminaria*, is useful as an indicator of zinc.

  (iii) To cite the title of a book, film, etc.
    If the size of audience is the criterion, *Gone with the Wind* is still among the top ten films.

  (iv) To distinguish a cited word or phrase (i.e. one that is being referred to or discussed rather than used) (cf. 1.3 Quotation marks.)
    What is erroneous about the use of *exact* in this text?
    All the material stuffs on earth possess in their substance an odd but

universal influence which scientists call *inertia*.

(v) To indicate emphasis. This is the most difficult use for FL students to grasp, because it depends so entirely on the writer's spoken style and on the finer points of his meaning. It is more frequent in novels and informal texts, which are closer to spoken style. In formal texts, the same purpose is often achieved by means of choice of words or manipulation of sentence structure. The emphasis may indicate contrast (expressed or implied), or it may simply reflect the writer's view of the importance of what he is saying. Some examples are:

We don't *know* this is so, we only *believe* it.

'There *are* some books in the camp,' he said.

This reaction is quite usual and no cause for alarm *provided the temperature remains normal.*

The amount of liquid *depends on the cooking time.*

1.3 Punctuation

Obviously punctuation has a close connection with meaning, and the student needs to be as familiar with it as possible. There is no space here to discuss the subject adequately, but you should be on the look-out for significant examples in the texts you use in class, and never take it for granted that the students have noticed or understood them.

Listed below are comments on punctuation usages that are not always understood.

(a) *A row of points* (. . .) indicates:

(i) an incomplete sentence:

'I wonder if . . .' she said, but her voice tailed away and we could only guess at her thoughts.

(ii) hesitation (in dialogue):

'She . . . she hasn't come?' he faltered.

(iii) an omission from a quotation:

The principle . . . remained largely unrecognized for half a century.

(The original text reads:

The principle to which Wright had devoted so much of his time and genius remained largely unrecognized for half a century.

The quoting writer has found the omitted words unnecessary for his purposes.)

(b) *A dash* (–) can be used to mean almost anything the writer chooses and so needs particular care in interpretation. Some of its uses:

(i) The same as for a row of points, uses (i) and (ii).

(ii) Indicates an addition to the main idea, often not a complete sentence; often suggests a pause for emphasis.

A They are both drugs – and any drug may harm.

B It is unusual to serve herbal teas in Britain – unlike in France, where you can get them in many cafés.

C 'Let's discuss something else - *please.*'

(iii) Indicates omission:

A John Smith (1893 – —)

(John Smith's death has not yet occurred, or its date is unknown.)

    B In came Mr S — wearing an outrageous hat.
(The writer does not wish to mention the name.)

    C Smith, J   *A Book of Thoughts*
          —   *A New Book of Thoughts*
          —   *A Third Book of Thoughts*
(John Smith wrote all three books.)

(iv) Used in the same way as a colon (see below):

When brass players start play on a cold night, their instruments are always flat —'the notes are lower in pitch than when the instruments have warmed up.

(v) A pair of dashes may serve as a pair of parentheses:

In excess — and the excess may be very little indeed — it is highly toxic.

(c) *Quotation marks* ("..." or '...'): Apart from their basic functions of marking off words spoken by a character, quoted from another writer, or cited/discussed rather than used, quotation marks are sometimes used in rather idiosyncratic ways that may be difficult to explain. In all cases, however, the idea remains that the words used are not really the writer's.

    (i) Indicates a word or phrase which the writer would not use, but which is commonly used:

        A She was afraid he might blame her for her 'guilty knowledge'.
(Who considers it guilty knowledge? Not the writer, apparently.)

        B The so-called 'noble' gases, argon, neon, xenon and krypton.
(The adjective 'so-called' often accompanies this usage.)

        C Never did any woman hate 'writing' as much as I do. (Virginia Woolf)
(Here the quotation marks suggest not only a specialized meaning (writing as authorship) but also the writer's impatience with the occupation.)

    (ii) Indicates a cited word or phrase which is incorporated into the writer's own syntax:

        A A hibiscus was a hibiscus to him 'and it was nothing more'.
(The writer is quoting from Wordsworth.)

        B Boy, 6, 'loved inflicting pain'.
(Newspaper headline, quoting words used in court.)

(d) *A colon* (:) almost always signals a particular relationship between the statements it precedes and follows, namely that the second is an expansion of the first. The expansion may take various forms – an explanation, an example, a listing, etc. – but the relationship is much more predictable than is the case with most other punctuation marks, so it is worth making students aware of it.

1.4 Symbols

Apart from punctuation symbols, a variety of others are commonly used in texts with a variety of functions. You cannot deal with them all, but you can make students aware that symbols do have functions, and give help in interpreting the commoner ones. After that students should be able to continue on their own; of course it is important to make sure they know how to use the symbols in any books they regularly use, and where to find the information that will help them to do this.

(a) Symbols that refer to footnotes (or notes elsewhere).
The use of a superscript number[1] or letter[a], asterisk*, dagger[t] or other symbol to refer the reader to a note may need explanation.

(b) Symbols that tell you something about the continuity of the text.
In magazines, arrowlike or pointing symbols are often used to indicate that you must turn the page; → for the continuation of the article, or ← to show that the beginning of the article is on an earlier page. The end of an article may be signalled by □ or some other blocking symbol.
An asterisk (or a row of them) or similar symbol used between paragraphs usually indicates either a switch of topic or the passage of time.

(c) Other uses of the asterisk.
This is a very versatile symbol, its uses being so various that confusion is possible. We have already mentioned several; others include:

(i) To mark a new item (especially a new technical term) or a particularly important item (similar to one use of italics described above).

(ii) To serve as a marker of items in a list when numerals or letters are not appropriate or not desired; a bullet ● often has this function too. For example:

> Bring with you
> * your old licence
> * the completed renewal application form Q14
> * three passport sized photographs
> * the appropriate fee

(iii) In grammars (particularly those written for foreign learners) to mark incorrect forms, for example:
We can say *the poor* but not **a poor*
And in historical grammars, to mark reconstructed or putative forms:
Kentish **stiocan** from *** stikojan**, *to prick*

2 What we can learn from a book before reading it: reference apparatus

If you teach students from a culture where reading is valued, this section (like the previous one) can perhaps be skipped, although even mother-tongue readers in highly literate societies often make inefficient use of the reference apparatus at their disposal within the covers of the book itself.

The student's first step when setting out on any serious reading task ought to be to define his purpose as closely as he can. This will enable him to judge the relevance of a text more accurately, and so save himself a lot of time that might have been spent on unproductive reading. For someone with a low reading speed and a lot to do, this can be most valuable. In this section, we shall be looking mainly at the information a text provides to help a reader assess its relevance for his purpose.

2.1 The title

Titles are not always very reliable indicators of content, but they are a reasonable starting point in choosing suitable texts.

You can tackle the assessment of titles from two angles:

(a) Getting students to predict from the title what is likely to be the content of the book, article, etc. You might include a few misleading titles to encourage wariness.

(b) Getting students to choose, from the titles alone, the books etc. they would consult first on a given topic. Include a few highly relevant sources with not very informative titles to remind the students that they should look beyond the title towards some of the other sources of information dealt with below.

2.2 The blurb

There is usually a blurb on the back of the cover or, if the book is a hardback with a paper jacket, on one of the inside folds. Some sensible libraries cut off the blurb and stick it inside the book itself, so that it remains even when the jacket has disintegrated.

Blurbs may include press comment – selective, obviously – but they normally consist mainly of the writer's or publisher's own estimation of the book's purpose, principal features and strong points. Despite the probability of bias, blurbs are usually more helpful than titles in guiding readers to select the right books.

Here are some activities to draw attention to the usefulness of blurbs:

(a) Matching items in a list of titles with a selection of blurbs, arranged in random order.

(b) Selecting, from the blurbs, the most likely books for studying a particular topic for a particular purpose.
e.g. Which book would be of most use if you wanted to find out how to repair your car yourself?

(c) Matching extracts from texts with a selection of blurbs + titles.

(d) Matching prospective readers with a selection of blurbs + titles, all dealing with similar fields but at different levels.
e.g. Which book would be suitable for a ten-year-old schoolboy?
A university student? A housewife? A professor?

(e) For advanced students, matching blurbs with a selection of extracts from reviews of the books could be amusing as well as instructive.

(f) For intermediate students, it is instructive to compare the full review of a book with the extract quoted in the blurb.

(g) For any student who needs to use blurbs to guide him, it will be valuable to examine some blurbs in detail, extracting from them:
 (i) matters of fact
   e.g. There is a 200-item bibliography
     Each chapter includes several practical exercises.
     The author is Senior Lecturer in the Philosophy of Science at Oxbridge University.
 (ii) matters of intention (which may or may not have been achieved)
   e.g. Written for those with no previous experience in the field.

Is an attempt to give a readable version of recent research in this area.
(iii)   matters of opinion
e.g.   There is a comprehensive bibliography of current research.
Each chapter contains a wealth of stimulating practical exercises.
Suitable for those with no previous experience in the field.
Offers a lucid and highly readable version of recent research in this fascinating area.

Healthy scepticism in blurb interpretation should not be allowed to obscure the usefulness of blurbs in the selection of texts.

2.3 Biographical information about the writer

Like the blurb, this often appears on the book jacket (usually on the back flap) or, in paperbacks, on the page preceding the title page. In journals, this information may precede the article, but is often found in a separate section of notes on contributors.

Information of this kind can be valuable in indicating the writer's background and position, and thus his qualifications for writing the work.

You might like to ask students to match this bio-information with a blurb from a randomly-ordered selection, or with the needs of a list of prospective readers.

2.4 The summary and table of contents

In scholarly journals, articles are sometimes preceded by a summary of their contents. Occasionally, similar summaries precede chapters in books; more often, a listing of contents in the shape of subtitles, below the chapter title, serves the same purpose. For example:

Chapter Two
THE MINISTRY
The First Sermon – The First Missionaries – The First Retreat – The Return to the Palace – Women Admitted to the Order – The Sutta of the Great Decease – The Cremation and the Relics
(Christmas Humphreys, *Buddhism* (Pelican 1967))

An example of a rather different style of layout:

---

12   THE SYSTEM APPROACH TO INSTRUCTION
  I   Chapter objectives
 II   Introduction
III   What is a learning system?
      A Definition
      B Characteristics
 IV   The strategy of learning system design
      A Basic design strategy
      B Describing the current state of the system
      C Principles of learning system design
(etc.; incomplete)
(R. H. Davis, L. T. Alexander, and S. L. Yelon, *Learning System Design* (McGraw Hill, 1974))

However, such listings of subtitles are nowadays more often found in the table of contents than at the start of the chapter itself.

Students need to be alerted to the existence of summaries like these, and shown how to use them to select texts more speedily and accurately. Matching tasks can be given similar to those described above.

(a) Here are summaries of five articles. Which of them is/are likely to be useful for studying topic X?
(b) Here is a table of contents. In which chapter would you expect to find the answer to each of the following questions?
(c) Here is a chapter heading with its subtitles. Which of the following questions do you think the chapter will deal with?
(d) You want to find out about topic X. Which chapters in this book are likely to contain relevant information? (Table of contents supplied of a book where topic X is likely to be touched on in several chapters.)
(e) Study these two sets of texts: (1) extracts from articles; (2) summaries of articles. Match each extract with the summary of the article it came from.
(f) Study this table of contents and the set of short texts. Then decide: (1) which texts came from the book and which did not; (2) of those which you think came from the book, which chapter each came from.

2.5 Running titles

Sometimes a book has no subtitles listed at the head of the chapter, nor in the table of contents, but still makes use of them as running titles at the head of (usually) the right-hand page of each page opening. The left-hand page usually carries either the title of the book, or that of the current chapter.

Many books do not make use of running titles, and relatively few make use of running subtitles, but when they are used you can get quite a good idea of what the book contains by flicking through the pages and scanning them.

You can draw attention to this possibility by getting at least two copies of the same book and having a group or half-class race to see which team can most quickly locate the page on which a given topic is dealt with. (Use of the index must be banned.) Unless you can find enough copies for everyone, number the team members and have the book passed to the next member for each new topic.

2.6 Preliminary material: foreword, preface, introduction

Different writers use these sections for different purposes, and even position them differently. (A preface and a foreword may precede the table of contents, but an introduction normally follows it.)

A **preface** may be no more than a list of acknowledgements, but it may on the other hand consist of a brief note on the main purpose of the book (rather like the blurb or summary). A **foreword** serves similar purposes. Either may be written by the author of the book or by someone else. If by someone else, it usually includes a note of the writer's qualifications for writing the book, although the reliability of such comment may be difficult to assess.

An **introduction** is typically a longer piece, setting the book in the wider context of other work in the same field or showing its relationship to work in other fields. If it is written by an editor or translator, it often also describes the book's own background and an estimation of its contribution to the field. It may provide an excellent outline of what is to come, but is often too lengthy to serve this purpose and is then best considered as the first part of the text itself.

Only by glancing through the preliminary materials can the reader estimate whether they will help him to assess the relevance of the book. An exercise that might be used is to supply a selection of such materials and ask the students within a fixed (short) time to say of each whether it would be useful or not in assessing the relevance of the book it precedes.

This is however an exercise in skimming and should not be introduced until the students have had practice in the swift selective reading required.

2.7 Non-verbal material: lists of diagrams, illustrations, etc.

If a book contains non-verbal material (i.e. pictures, diagrams, graphs, tables, etc.) a list of the diagrams, etc. may give a useful preview of the contents of the book. In the absence of a contents list, a quick skim through the non-verbal material in the book may offer similar information.

Help students to recognize the value of this information and make use of it in assessing a book's relevance. Most of the following activities would be suitable for group work.

(a) *Supply* five or more specimens of NVM (non-verbal material). These might be Xeroxed or projected by an overhead projector or epidiascope. Also *supply* five or more captions. For weaker students, supply only the captions belonging to the NVM (in random order). For better classes, include some distractors (i.e. captions which do not fit any of the NVM).
Task: Have a look at these examples of NVM. Match each one with the appropriate caption from this list.

(b) *Supply* five lists of NVM taken from the contents pages of five different books. Also *supply* ten summaries or blurbs of different books, five of which relate to the books from which the contents pages were taken.
Task: Here are lists of NVM from five books. Choose from the ten summaries the one you think is most likely to match each list.
or omit the summaries and ask students to predict what the book is likely to be about, and for what readers it is intended, by studying the list of NVM.

(c) *Supply* specimens of NVM including different kinds of maps, tables, diagrams, graphs, flow charts, illustrations, etc.
Task: Say what you would expect to find in the accompanying text (subject matter, intended readership, etc.). (For a weaker class, a matching task could be devised by supplying also a set of descriptions of readers and their needs.)

2.8 The index

Ability to make effective use of an index is worth training. You can use some of the techniques outlined in Chapter 6 below in connection with training in the use of a dictionary; or the race to locate a topic suggested in this chaper (see 2.5). If each student has access to a copy of the same book (or at any rate the same index), you can give him a list of topics with the task of finding out which of them are dealt with in the book.

Make sure students are aware that some books have two or more indexes (proper names, botanical names, etc. in addition to subjects) and that they have practice in locating various terms in the appropriate one.

2.9 Other reference apparatus

Other sections of a book which students need to be aware of, and to be able to use, are:

> appendixes
> notes (footnotes, notes at end of chapter or end of book)
> bibliography/bibliographical references
> lists of symbols, abbreviations etc.
> lists of special terms/glossaries

Again, your job will be easier if you can borrow a set of books for your class to examine. Perhaps their textbooks in other subjects may be used. Failing that, you may have to stencil sample material and base your exercises on that. Some questions that need to be dealt with require access to more than one text. If you cannot base exercises on books in a library accessible to all the students, borrow a collection of books yourself and make them available for long enough for all to use them.

The students should be able to:

(a) understand what sort of material is placed in an appendix;

(b) locate notes indicated by superscript numerals etc. in the text, and be aware that such notes may be located at the foot of the page or elsewhere;

(c) indicate the full details of any bibliographical reference cited in the text (i.e. by referring to the full reference at the end of the chapter or book) and identify the various parts of such a reference (author, title, etc.). Use a bibliography to choose potentially suitable texts for further reading on a given aspect of a subject;

(d) indicate the meaning of any symbol, abbreviation or technical term used in the text by reference to the relevant list or glossary; interpret accurately portions of the text in which they occur.

3 How we make use of non-verbal information

Recently people have become conscious that non-verbal information (such as illustrations, diagrams, graphs and maps) can be of specific help in learning to read effectively. Some of the things we include here, for instance tables, flow charts and many diagrams, do in fact contain language, so our title is not very accurate; perhaps we ought to use *non-text information* or *non-linear information* to refer to this area. The point to remember is that we are speaking of all the kinds of information that accompany a text but are not themselves textual.

It is tempting to say that we are referring to elements that are not integral parts of the text, and in many cases this is true. But people teaching ESP (English for Specific Purposes) will be aware that in some types of text, such as instructions for operating machines or descriptions of biological structures, the non-verbal information is in fact fully integrated with the rest of the text. The text explicitly refers to it and cannot be understood without it.

Even if the relationship is less integral, the non-verbal information is often of great assistance in interpreting the text. Used together, verbal and non-verbal information support each other: an obscure section of the text may be clarified by studying a diagram, or the significance of a diagram may become clear from the text.

Even in the earliest stages of reading, this relationship can be exploited: the learner stumbling over a word ('Janet is holding a . . .') is urged to look at the picture and work out for himself what the word must be. For more advanced readers, the relationship is increasingly complex, but its usefulness is similar.

The ability to interpret diagrams, etc. is largely independent of language, so that skill in interpretation can readily be transferred from L1 to FL contexts. To encourage this transfer is to stress the positive contribution that the student brings to the task of making sense of the new language. (His previous knowledge of language includes so many negative influences when he begins to acquire an FL that it is satisfying to demonstrate that some previous knowledge is a positive help.)

For the teacher, non-verbal information is useful because it makes possible a number of techniques for promoting and checking comprehension. Transfer of information activities (as they have been called) not only are interesting in themselves, but also may enable the student to demonstrate the meaning of the text in ways that do not involve him in the use of words. In this way some of the pitfalls of traditional comprehension questions can be avoided: the student cannot resort to responses which simply rephrase the text or juggle with words. He is obliged to work out the full meaning of the text and to consider the application of what he reads, to look beyond the words and into the real world of facts or ideas.

Transfer of information works two ways. We may have visual information which can be expressed in words, or we may have verbal information which can be re-expressed by means of a diagram, chart, graph, etc. Transfer of information is therefore very useful in devising writing activities too. But since we are concerned chiefly with interpretive strategies, we shall be looking mainly at activities in which the student is asked to provide or complete or label diagrams etc. on the basis of a text, or is asked to study the relationship of text and diagram etc. and note correspondences, mismatches, etc.

3.1 Recipes for exercises

A number of recipes for exercises are given below. They all fall into one or other of these categories:

(a) Matching texts and diagrams (and hence finding out how they support and illuminate one another).
(b) Giving practice in 'reading' (i.e. interpreting) diagrams etc.
(c) Discovering how valuable diagrams etc, can be.

(We use the term *diagram* to include all kinds of non-verbal information.)

Category (a): matching texts and diagrams

(i) *Supply* several texts and several diagrams.
   Task: Match texts with appropriate diagrams. Choose texts that are dissimilar from one another for elementary students; the more similar they are, the more difficult the exercise becomes.
(ii) *Supply* a text and several diagrams.
   Task: Say which diagram illustrates the text. (See Figure 8A.)
(iii) *Supply* several texts and a diagram.
   Task: Say which text relates to the diagram.

Category (b): Interpreting diagrams

(iv) *Supply* a diagram and a set of statements.
      Task: Say which statements agree with the diagram.
(v)   *Supply* a text and an unlabelled diagram.
      Task: Label the diagram by reference to the text. (See Figures 9, 10.)
(vi) *Supply* (a) pictures/diagrams of a process or sequence
            (b) sentences describing the same process/sequence
      Either the sentences should be in the correct order, while the diagrams are in random order, or vice versa.
      Task: If the diagrams are in random order, arrange them in the correct order according to the text (i.e. the sentences). If the diagrams are supplied in the correct order, arrange the sentences in the correct order to form a continuous text.
(vii) *Supply* a text and an incomplete diagram.
      Task: Complete the diagram so that it agrees with the text. (See Figures 11, 12, 13.)
(viii) *Supply* a text and a diagram that agrees with it in some particulars but not in others.
      Task: Correct the diagram by reference to the text, or list all the ways in which it must be changed in order to correspond with the text. (See Figures 8B, 14.)
(ix) *Supply* a diagram and a text with blanks.
      Task: Complete the text by reference to the diagram. (See Figures 15, 16.)
(x)   *Supply* a labelled diagram, graph, flowchart, map etc. which will repay study; and a set of questions (preferably multiple-choice or true/false) on it.
      Task: Study the diagram and answer the questions.
(xi) *Supply* two similar diagrams and a text relating to one of them. A skeleton text relating to the other (based on the model of the complete text supplied) may also be given.
      Task: Write a text, or complete the skeleton text, by reference to the relevant diagram, basing it on the model text. (See Figure 17.)

Category (c): Recognizing the value of diagrams

(xii) *Supply* a suitable text, with comprehension questions.
      Task: Attempt the questions.
      Then supply a diagram that illuminates the text.
      Task: Attempt the questions again and notice how the diagram helps.

Note: Remember that in all the suggestions above, the word **diagram** is used as shorthand to refer to all kinds of non-verbal information. These include:

illustrations (pictures, photographs, etc.)
diagrams proper (of experiments, of operation of machines, of parts of a
    whole, of processes, etc.)
maps and plans
graphs
pie charts
Venn diagrams

tables and charts (e.g. giving information arranged according to some system
  of classification, or in chronological order, etc.)
classification diagrams (showing genus, family etc.)
flow charts
etc.

This is the final paragraph of the text 'The changing earth' p.93:

Based on these findings, some earth scientists have predicted that within the next 60 million years Central America will disappear, the Atlantic and Pacific will meet, Australia will be close to China and East Africa will have broken from the rest of the African continent. This new view of the earth certainly demonstrates the truth of the ancient Chinese belief that the one constant certainty in the world is change.

(Adapted from 'The Changing Earth' by Samuel W. Matthews, *National Geographic Magazine,* January 1973)

This is one of the exercises on the text (p. 94):

4   Which of the following maps shows the predicted position of the continents in 60 million years'
time ?

Fig. 8A   Choosing a diagram to match a text

Here is another text and exercise from p. 5 of the same book:

Activity 1   **Understanding the meanings of word and**
                      sentence patterns

Below is a description of a spaceship by somebody who said he had seen it—an eyewitness. With it there is a drawing of the spaceship. Read the eyewitness's account and write down the sections of it that do not correspond to the drawing. Then rewrite those sections so that they do correspond. Notice what changes in grammar and vocabulary you make in your corrections.

The spaceship was about two metres high. It was round at the bottom and pointed at the top. The craft was supported by three legs which were taller than the main body of the ship. I saw a small green man with two horns who had probably jumped from the ship as there was no ladder. I remember clearly a mysterious sign on the side of the craft. It showed a triangle surrounded by a circle. I am sure this is a message to people on Earth.

Fig. 8B   Correcting a text to match a picture
          (From *Reading and Thinking in English: Discovering Discourse* OUP)

Share performance

This diagram shows the variations in share prices over the last eight years. You can see that, whatever country you had chosen for investment, your shares would have fluctuated very considerably during the period. If you had invested in Switzerland, your shares would today actually be worth less than when you bought them eight years ago. Only in Japan has there been a fairly marked increase; shares there are worth more than twice what you would have paid for them.

Of the others, all have suffered from the oil crisis and its aftermath of inflation and recession. Britain in the darkest days of the crisis in 1974 fell furthest of all, but subsequently made a strong recovery (thanks partly to North Sea Oil revenues) which was maintained until 1979. France, however, has performed even better after a discouraging period during 1976–7; it is now showing a marked upturn and has exceeded even its very successful 1973 prices. Germany, though unaffected by the 1974 crisis (it continued steady throughout the year – the only country not to show a fall at that time) is experiencing a slight downturn at present, in common with Britain and Switzerland.

Study the graph of share performance.
Label the lines with the names of the countries whose performance they indicate.

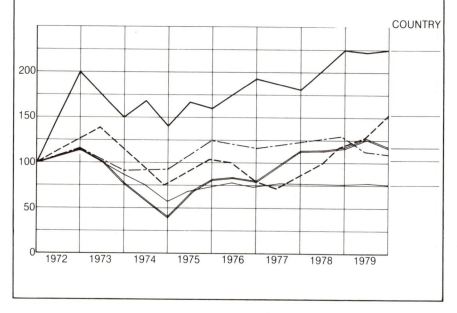

Fig. 9   Labelling a graph to match a text

Making a paper square

Aunt Pollie took a piece of paper and put it on the table.

'The first thing we must do,' she said, 'is to make this piece of paper square. At present this side which I am going to call *a*, is much shorter than this one, which I shall call *b*. I want to make all the sides equal.'

'Cut a piece of *b*,' said Bob.

'How big a piece?' asked Bessie.

'Use the side *a* as a measure,' said Aunt Pollie, 'and fold the paper so that it lies exactly on top of *b*. Then you will find that there is a piece overlapping. I shall call this piece big X, and you must cut it off carefully. Then the paper will be square.'

'I haven't any scissors,' said Bessie.

'Then you can tear it off,' said Aunt Pollie. 'Fold the piece called big X back, and press it down hard with your thumb nail. Then your can easily tear it off.'

Look at the figure. The dotted lines . . . . . . show folds.
Label: the lines a and b and the piece big X.

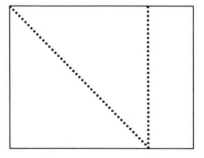

Fig. 10   Labelling a diagram according to a text
(Adapted from *Pleasant Work for Busy Fingers* by Maggie Browne)

2 Bus routes

Here we have a description of two bus routes. Mark the two bus routes on the following map. Use a broken line (– – – –) for the special bus and an unbroken line (———) for the 67 bus. Remember all these are two-way streets, with traffic going in each direction. You do not need to understand all the words in order to fill in the map.

You can see a certain amount of the city by travelling on the 67 bus which goes from the bus station to the museum three times a day. However it is best for the visitor to take a tour of the city on the special bus which is provided by the corporation at a nominal charge especially for the purpose.

Both buses come out of the bus station and turn left. The first place of interest the visitor passes if he goes on the 67 bus is the public gardens, which the bus reaches by taking the first turn left and going to the end of the road. However the special bus continues to the end of the road after leaving the bus station, turns left and drives slowly past the castle. If anyone is

specially interested he can make a special request for the bus to stop at the castle. However such a stop must be arranged in advance so that a guide will be available to conduct the passengers around the castle. After this the special bus takes the first corner to the right and stops at the docks. On the way it passes the station which has an interesting Victorian façade.

The sightseeing bus waits at the docks for about 10 minutes to enable the passengers to get out and walk around. It then goes straight up the road from the docks and takes the fourth corner on the right. Here the routes of the two buses converge for the first time.

Both buses turn right and begin to drive round the outside of the gardens. Then the routes diverge again. The sightseeing bus takes the first road to the left while the other bus continues round the gardens and drives straight to the sea front. The special bus stops at Browns Hill for several minutes to let the passengers look at the view of the city spread out below them. It then goes directly to the sea front. Both buses eventually travel along the sea front, take the third corner to the left and continue along the street until they come to the museum.

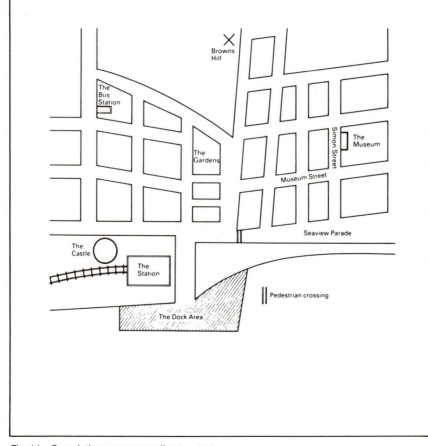

Fig. 11   Completing a map according to a text
(From *Think and Link* by J. Cooper)

A. (1) DIRECTIONS
   Take a tall container of some kind.
   Make several holes at different heights along the side of the container.
   Place the container on the bench next to a sink so that the holes face towards the sink.
   Fill the container with water.

   (2) STATEMENT OF RESULT
   A curved stream of water comes from each hole, but the streams from the lower holes extend straighter and further than the streams from the upper holes.

   (3) CONCLUSION
   This shows that . . .

Draw the diagram below and complete it so as to illustrate the result of this experiment.

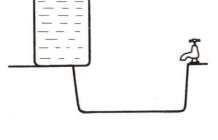

Fig. 12   Completing a diagram according to a text
          (From *English in Focus: English in Physical Science* by J. P. B. Allen and H. G. Widdowson)

9 Water shortage

Read the following passage and then, using the information contained in it, complete the graph that follows it.

The present shortage of water in a growing number of communities in the U.S. is the result primarily of increased consumption of water rather than of any important change in the natural supply. Not only has our population increased but our per capita use of water has risen – and at a much greater rate. In Texas, for instance, while the population increased by three hundred per cent in the fifty-year period ending in 1940, the use of water for industrial and municipal purposes increased about thirty times; for irrigation about fifty-five times and for water power about eighty-five times; for all purposes the average overall increase was almost seventy-one times. Similar increases in the use of water have occurred throughout the nation.

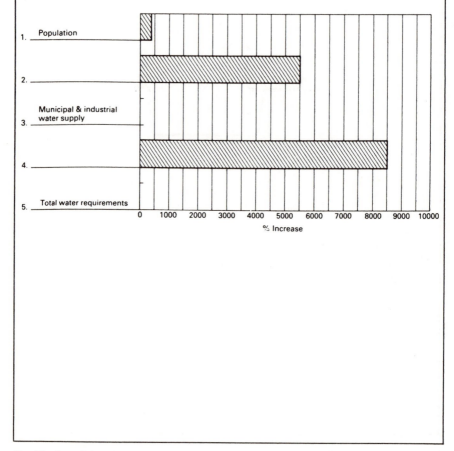

Fig. 13   Completing a bar graph according to a text
(From *Think and Link* by J. Cooper)

1. (a) Look at this diagram showing a threaded sewing machine. Read the instructions given below, and write a list of the mistakes that have been made in threading the machine.

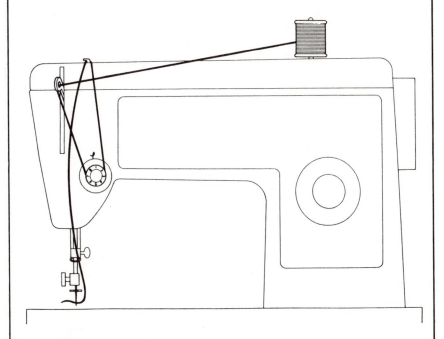

Put the cotton reel on the spindle on top of the machine.
Run the thread over the small hook near the eyeletted arm.
Now loop the thread round the tension reel in a clockwise direction.
Thread it through the eye of the eyeletted arm from right to left, then through the ring below.
Now thread the needle, from left to right.

   (b) Now copy out the diagram. Draw the thread into the diagram showing how the sewing machine is correctly threaded.

Fig. 14   Correcting a diagram to match a text
(From *English in Focus: English in Education* by Elizabeth Laird)

9. 'Morning' and 'evening' types

Some people are more active in the mornings, while others feel and work better in the evenings. Nearly all of us feel particularly tired every six to eight hours, usually at 4.00, 12.00, 18.00 and 24.00.

The following two graphs predict how a 'morning' and an 'evening' type will do an experimental task* at different times of the day. Imagine you are going to do (*but have not yet done*) an experiment on Mr X and Mr Y. Use the table to write a paragraph predicting what will happen.

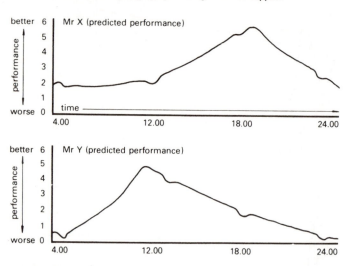

10. Mr X's and Mr Y's actual performance

Sometimes the best predictions go wrong! Here is how Mr X and Mr Y actually did the task. Write part of your report on the experiment. Contrast *prediction* and *reality*.

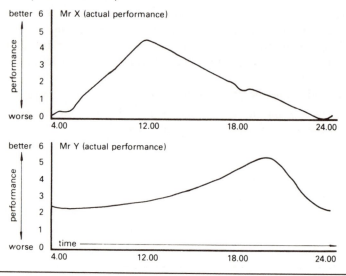

Fig. 15   Completing a text from a graph
(From *Communicate in Writing* by K. Johnson)

EXERCISE G *Describing structure*

In most plants the site of photosynthesis is the leaves. The water that is needed for the process passes up through the stem from the roots. Here is a description of the structure of a typical root. Write it out and complete it by referring to Figure 3.1.

It can be seen from a ... section of a young root that the cells are arranged into different tissues. The outermost layer of cells forms the ..., and if the root is young enough, it can be seen that most of the ... bear elongated ... Inside the piliferous layer there is the ..., which becomes the outermost layer when the ... is lost. Between the exodermis and the ... there is a broad ... that is many cells wide. The last complete ring of cells is the ... It lies inside the ... and it surrounds the phloem, ..., and ...

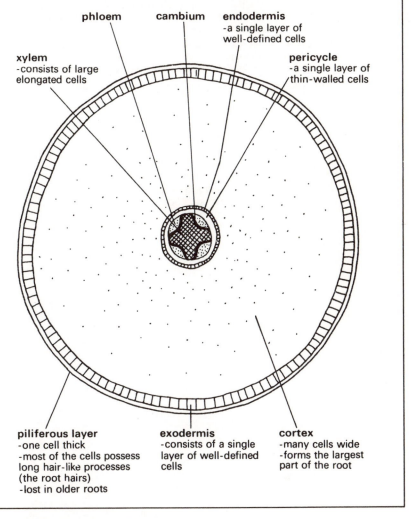

Fig. 16 Completing a text from a diagram
(From *English in Focus: English in Biological Science* by I. Pearson)

EXERCISE F   *Information transfer: definitions and descriptions*

The following diagram conveys the same information as the statement below it.

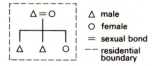

(a) *Definition*   A nuclear family is a group consisting of a man and a woman and their offspring sharing a common residence.

(b) *Description* This is a nuclear family consisting of a man and a woman, their two sons and one daughter.

1. Draw a diagram to correspond with the following definition and description:

   (a) *Definition*   A polygynous family is a group consisting of one man and more than one woman and their offspring sharing a common residence.

   (b) *Description* This is a polygynous family consisting of one man and two women, two sons of the man and one woman and one son and two daughters of the second woman.

2. Write a definition and a description based on the following diagram:

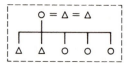

Fig. 17   Producing a diagram from text and vice versa
(From *English in Focus: English in Social Studies* by J. P. B. Allen and H. G. Widdowson)

6 Word-Attack Skills

1 The vocabulary problem

You may feel when reading this book that it evades the biggest problem of all for the FL reader: that his vocabulary is not good enough for the reading he has to do. The size of the problem can be judged by comparing two figures: it is said that moderate readers can recognize about 50,000 different words in L1 reading, while graded reader series prepared for EFL readers seldom go higher than the 3,500 word level. Even granted different interpretations of what we mean by 'a word', this difference is enormous. How is the student supposed to cope with a learning problem of this size?

There is an easy answer to this question: he must read a great deal more. The L1 reader did not learn his 50,000 words by being taught them; most of them were learnt by meeting them in context and assimilating the meaning. An extensive reading programme (such as that described in Chapter 12) is the single most effective way of improving both vocabulary and reading skills in general. You can teach your students to use a dictionary properly, and you can organize a programme of vocabulary building, but greatly increasing the amount of material they read is the best way of all.

This chapter is not intended to tell you what to do if your students' vocabulary is weak. To deal with most of the reading skills, it is necessary to assume that the reader's vocabulary is adequate. Otherwise it would be pointless to write about reading skills at all, because you cannot develop them with texts that are loaded with unfamiliar words.

But naturally we do not expect readers to know every word in the text. How should they deal with the unknown ones? Some can be safely skipped without losing the message. But there may be others that block comprehension, that cannot be skipped. In this chapter we shall consider how the student can tackle words of this kind.

2 Lexical items and attack skills

We shall often refer to 'words' in this chapter, for brevity, but most of what is said applies to *lexical items* of all kinds. A lexical item can be loosely defined as any word or group of words with a meaning that needs to be learnt as a whole. It is more useful to think of new lexical items, rather than new words, as the things the student must learn.

This is because some lexical items consist of more than one word, while there are apparently identical words that turn out to represent more than one lexical item.

For instance, every phrasal verb is a single lexical item, even though it consists of several words: *speak up, switch off, put up with*, etc. On the other hand, the spelling *saw* represents several different lexical items, among them the past tense of *see* and the word that means an instrument for cutting wood.

Discussing what is and is not a distinct lexical item would take us too far from our purpose; it is enough to remember that what students have to deal with is units of meaning, and they should be aware that these may be packaged as one word or several, and that some words that look alike have different meanings.

We did not call this chapter 'lexical item attack skills', though this is really what it is about, because the term 'word-attack skills' is already familiar to many teachers. This usually relates to the skills needed by young children in the process of early reading, but it seems equally relevant to FL students. Both have problems with unfamiliar words, though the problems themselves may be different.

What I like about this phrase is the attitude it suggests the reader should adopt. Instead of allowing new words to frighten him, he should approach them positively and use specific techniques to deal with them. He needs to be shown, most important of all, that many new words can just be ignored: this can be considered the first and basic word-attack skill, and for many students it will be the most difficult to accept. But there are also techniques that can be used to deal with the new words that really stand in the way of comprehension.

3 Phonics

Phonics (not to be confused with phonetics) is the study of the relationship between sounds and spellings, with particular emphasis on the regularities that may help the reader to identify in print words that he knows in their spoken form but has never before seen written.

Even in English, in spite of many irregularities, there are more regular sound-spelling correspondences than irregular ones. You can find them described and exemplified in books for teachers of reading to English-speaking children, e.g. Ball (1977).

The question is not whether phonic rules exist in English, but how useful they are to readers tackling unfamiliar words. Frank Smith (1978) has argued that they are not useful for children learning to read the L1, because there are so many rules, and so many exceptions, that they can only confuse.

You may disagree with Smith, but there is a more important reason for thinking that phonics is not of much use to the FL reader. The purpose of phonics is to enable a reader to identify in its written form a word he already knows in its spoken form. It is assumed that once he knows how it is pronounced, he will associate it with the spoken word and therefore understand it. But from the intermediate stage on, the new words the FL student meets in texts are usually not words that he has heard spoken. So working out how a new word might be pronounced is not going to help him understand it.

For these reasons, I do not think the EFL learner's time should be spent studying phonics unless he is going to be a teacher of young children. He will become a more effective reader if he tries not to worry about the pronunciation of individual words. If he has learnt to read initially in a language that is written with great phonic regularity, he has probably found it very difficult to adjust to the irregularity of English, and it will be more help to him to concentrate on the general shape of a word, and on its meaning in context, rather than on its pronunciation. In fact you need to wean him away from phonics. Phonics will not help him to understand new words. (Learning how to *pronounce* new words is of course another matter. Students who need or want this skill must learn how to use the phonetic symbols in their dictionary.)

4 Structural clues

We can make use of structural clues to establish, not exactly the meaning, but at least the type (grammatical category) of word represented by the new item. This tells us the kind of meaning to look for and is thus a first step on the road to understanding. For example, if you were told that *kneaf* is a verb, then the sequence

　　the sploony urdle kneafed

would begin to make structural sense to you. You would know that either *sploony* or *urdle* must be a noun, because a gap between *the* and a verb must be filled by a noun. Morphological evidence (see the next section) suggests that *sploony* is an adjective; and if it were a noun, *urdle* could only be another noun or an adverb. But it is very unlikely to be an adverb (those that could occur in such a position without ending in *-ly* are a restricted and familiar set). So we conclude that *urdle* is probably a noun.

Explaining this process is laborious, but the process itself is not. Most students who are out of the elementary stage will be able to identify grammatical categories in this way, though they will not be able to explain how they do it. (They can, for example, answer and ask questions like 'What sort of an urdle was it?' or 'What did the urdle do?') The student may not know what an urdle is, but once he has identified it as a noun he is a little nearer to understanding the sentence.

If students are made aware of this process, they can make use of it consciously when faced with difficult stretches of text. Of course new words do not always occur in such straightforward surroundings as the sentence about the urdle. But provided the neighbouring words are familiar, or at least identifiable as verb, adjective, etc., it should be possible to work out the part of speech of the new word; and this is the beginning of making sense of the text.

It is easy to give practice in this technique, either by preparing specific exercises or by developing the skills required when you come across a new word when reading with the class.

It is not essential for students to be able to label the parts of speech correctly (*verb*, *noun*, etc.) but it is certainly useful. What is essential is that they should be able to disentangle the structure. Getting them to ask and answer questions based on the sentence containing the unfamiliar item, like the questions given above about the urdle, is the best way of checking that they have understood the structure.

You can give practice in this skill by using sentences containing nonsense words like *urdle* as a starting point and moving on to authentic sentences containing unfamiliar lexical items. Making up questions can be done in groups and other groups can be invited to answer. Note that this must all be done before the new item is checked in the dictionary: the purpose is to demonstrate its part in the structural pattern, its structural meaning rather than its lexical meaning.

Of course this is not enough for an accurate understanding of the word, but it may enable the reader to understand the text sufficiently for his purpose. If not, when the reader looks up the word in the dictionary, he will be able to slot the meaning straight into its place.

5 Morphological information

Most of us would dislike the idea of preparing lists of prefixes and suffixes to be learnt by students. But understanding the meanings of affixes and the way they are used to build words is extremely useful in tackling new lexical items.

This cannot easily be practised with elementary students, although you can start making students aware of affixes as soon as they meet the simple ones found in early texts, such as *UNhappy*, *teachER*, *DISagree*, *examinATION*. Serious work will have to be left until the students have a substantial vocabulary to provide other examples of the same affix (*UNwilling, UNkind, UNwrap, UNdress,* etc.) and a stock of bases (i.e. the words or parts of words to which affixes are attached). Once this stage is reached, you can use exercises found in books or some of those below.

(a) *Supply* an affix (e.g. *UN-*) and a number of bases (e.g. *happy, slow, tidy*).
Task: Indicate (or find out from a good dictionary) which of the bases can take the affix.

(b) *Supply* a base (e.g. *sharp*) and several affixes (e.g. *UN-, -LY, -EN, -MENT, -NESS*).
Task: Indicate/find out which of the affixes the base can take.

(c) *Supply* a list of affixes of similar function (e.g. the adjective-forming suffixes *-FUL, -OUS, -Y, -ISH*) and a list of bases.
Task: Indicate/find out which basewords take which affixes, and if more than one is possible, what variations in meaning are involved, (e.g. *manful, mannish, manly*).

(d) *Supply* an incomplete table of forms consisting of basewords with various affixes.
Task: Complete the table by filling the gaps. Here is an example.

1	2	3	4
educate	education	educable	ineducable
. . . . . .	variation	. . . . . .	. . . . . .
. . . . . .	. . . . . .	observable	. . . . . .
define	. . . . . .	. . . . . .	. . . . . .
. . . . . .	. . . . . .	. . . . . .	unpronounceable
. . . . . .	. . . . . .	recognizable	. . . . . .
etc.			

(e) *Supply* sentences containing words of a particular form, e.g. verbs.
Task: Rewrite the sentences in a specified way entailing the use of a different form of the given word (e.g. nouns instead of verbs). Here are some examples:

Fill in each blank with a noun related to the verb in the preceding sentence.

(i) The enemy *attacked* at dawn.

The . . . . . . was completely unexpected. (*attack*)

(ii) They *bombarded* the walls with cannons.

The . . . . . . finally gave them the chance to scale the wall at one point. (*bombardment*)

(iii) The city was *destroyed*.

The . . . . . . of the city caused the deaths of 15,000 inhabitants. (*destruction*)

Affixes are one thing, roots are another. Many English words contain roots which are not themselves English, for example *educ-* (or more properly *-duc-*) in the table in suggestion (d) above. How far your students need to be aware of the root itself depends on its significance in their field of study. A student of science might find it useful to know the approximate meaning of *cyt*, for example (*cytoplasm, cytology, leucocyte,* etc.).

If possible, get students to deduce the meaning of a root or an affix by studying several well-known words in which it appears: what they find out for themselves will be better remembered. Give further practice by asking students to infer the meaning of words in which the newly acquired form is combined with familiar affixes or bases.

As well as examining the structure of **complex** words (i.e. those produced by affixation), your students will need to understand the patterns of **compound** words (i.e. those formed by combining two normally independent words). As well as drawing attention to compounds when they occur in texts, it is worth studying the ways compounds are formed. Compound patterns which are permissible in one language may be impossible in another; if your students' L1 has adjectives following nouns, they may produce forms like *watch wrist* instead of *wrist watch* and may not distinguish a *house plant* from a *plant house*. Practice in interpreting and forming compounds, as well as complex words, can be found in a number of books, including: R. Mackin, *Exercises in English Patterns and Usage 5; Forms of Words* (OUP, 1966); T. McArthur, *Patterns of English, Book 1 Building English Words*; *Book 2 Using English Prefixes and Suffixes* (Collins 1975).

6 Inference from context

We have seen how far phonics, sentence structure and word structure can help a student to deal with a new word. It is clear that on their own they are not enough. If a student meets a word that he cannot interpret by these methods, his instinct is to ask what it means; and if his teacher or class-mate cannot supply the answer, he consults a dictionary.

This is perfectly natural. Nevertheless, one of the first things to be said about a dictionary is **don't use it**. Of course this advice is exaggerated and we shall deal with the proper use of a dictionary on pages 78–79. But many students use the dictionary far too much. Sometimes they are encouraged in this by their teachers, urged to look up all new words and to make vocabulary lists to learn by heart.

Are these methods wrong? Like most things in language teaching, there are arguments for and against. It would be idiotic to ban the use of dictionaries or the learning of vocabulary lists; any ways of building vocabulary should be welcomed.

But vocabulary has traditionally been the major component in language teaching programmes and still retains this position in some countries. Too much attention to vocabulary can have a harmful effect on the student's reading habits. If he keeps stopping to look up new words, it may actually make him a less effective reader.

Every time you break off your reading to consult a dictionary, you not only slow down your reading speed because of the time involved, but – more seriously – you interrupt your own thought processes, which should be engaged in following the continued development of thought in the text. A competent reader can cope with occasional interruptions of this kind, but constant need to refer to a dictionary makes effective reading very difficult. This is why I urge that training should be given on texts that do not present too many vocabulary problems, even if ultimately the students must read difficult texts.

In addition, there is the practical consideration that the reader does not always have a dictionary or an informant at hand when he needs them. It is therefore expedient to develop ways of dealing with new vocabulary without these aids, as well as desirable because we want our students to become more independent.

If you wish to free your students from dependence on the dictionary or on your own help, how are you to set about it? In addition to any specific vocabulary teaching you may wish to undertake, much more time should be given to:

(a) promoting extensive reading, through which the students' vocabulary can grow naturally;
(b) developing the skill of inferring the meaning of a word by considering its context.

It is the second of these with which we are concerned at present. (Extensive reading is dealt with in Chapter 12.)

Inferring meaning is a skill we all have to some degree in our L1. We learnt most of our L1 vocabulary by using it: meeting the words frequently and in concrete situations, we gradually assimilated their meanings. We have of course also used the dictionary to increase our L1 vocabulary when we began to meet in books words that we had not previously encountered in the spoken language. But if we are experienced L1 readers, we have learnt from our reading the meaning of a great many words that we have never looked up in a dictionary and never had explained to us. We are able to do this by making use of the context in which the word occurred to give us a rough idea of its meaning; and with every subsequent occurrence the meaning became a little more precise. Here is an example of the way the process works. Cover the numbered sentences below with a piece of paper or your hand. Now read them one at a time; after you have read the first one, consider how much information you have about the meaning of the word *tock*. Then go on to find out how much more you know after reading sentence 2, and so on.

1 She poured the water into a tock.
2 Then, lifting the tock, she drank.
3 Unfortunately, as she was setting it down again, the tock slipped from her hand and broke.
4 Only the handle remained in one piece.

You were no doubt able to complete this easily, partly because you are an experienced reader, partly because the word was a simple one, partly because the sentences were devised for the purpose. In real life reading, inference may not be so straightforward, and even L1 readers are not always good at using the skill. For FL readers, it certainly requires specific training. To some extent, this is because they have much less exposure to the language than L1 readers, and therefore have to make more conscious effort to learn words. But there are two other reasons:

(a) As Bright and McGregor (1970) point out, most students are not aware that it is possible to understand new words without being told what they mean. So the first thing is to show them that it is possible.
(b) The second thing is to encourage the student to adopt a positive attitude ('I can work it out if I try') to new lexical items, instead of the negative one ('Help! Where's the dictionary?') he instinctively adopts.

6.1 Training students to infer

Training students to infer meaning from context gives them a powerful aid to comprehension and will ultimately greatly speed up their reading. And one of the nice things about this training is that it can be enjoyable. It has the problem-solving characteristics that appeal to most people and challenges the students to make use of their intelligence to an extent that is not always common in language classes.

One way of beginning would be with sentences containing nonsense words, like the one about the urdle. It is easy to show students that some kind of understanding is possible even in such cases, in that questions can be asked and answered. They will soon realize that they can get a good deal of information from the sentence even though they do not really understand it.

A second step might be to get students to suggest what range of words could be used to complete given sentences such as:

In order to repair the car, I shall need . . .

Ridiculous suggestions (a glass of milk, a camera, a comb) and borderline ones (a plastic bag, a rubber band) can be discussed. We can consider what difference it would make if we knew what was wrong with the car, and so on. In this way, the students will begin to recognize that the possibilities are not limitless.

The next step is to show that this fact (i.e. that possible fillers for any particular slot in a given sentence are limited) makes it possible for us to work out the sort of thing an unknown word must mean, by careful study of its context. You could use for this purpose sentences in which a nonsense word replaces an ordinary English one. An example is the series of sentences using the word *tock* on p. 70. In class, the sentences would be discussed along these lines (with the teacher asking a few leading questions and the students doing most of the work):

Q What can we learn from sentence 1?
   A That a tock can hold water? (Probably – but what about a sieve? Would you say *poured into a sieve*, or *through a sieve*?, etc.)
   Q Suggestions?
   A A bucket – a bowl – a hole, etc.
   Q Do we know what she was pouring from? How would it affect our ideas about what a tock might be if she was pouring from a bucket? a kettle? a test tube? etc.
Q How does sentence 2 narrow down the possibilities?
   A We know a tock can be lifted (so it isn't a hole, for instance) and that it can be drunk from.
   Q Do we know whether it is intended to be drunk from?
   A No. Perhaps she's drinking from a shell – a hat – some other makeshift container in an emergency.
Q What new information do we get from sentence 3?
   A We know a tock is fragile – it broke when she dropped it.
   Q All tocks?
   A This tock, anyway.
   Q What might it have been made of?
   A Glass – china – perhaps very thin metal, but unlikely – it would dent rather than break. Clay? Stone? The shell again?
Q And sentence 4?
   A If it has a handle, it's probably a cup.
   Q Can we exclude a jug? Other things with handles?
   A No, but in the absence of other evidence, we choose what seems the most likely.

A sequence of this kind is ideal for presentation on an overhead projector, which makes it easy to deal with all the possibilities of sentence 1 before the students are shown sentence 2. Alternatively, you can write up the sentences one at a time, or use a masking sheet of paper to reveal only one at a time.

In this way you can produce a sense of the gradual accumulation of evidence which is central to inference from context (and which is moreover the way we learn much of our L1 vocabulary). You can also impress on students the need to read on to make sure their inference is supported by all the evidence: if they had spent a long time puzzling over sentence 1, think of all the time they would have wasted, in view of the valuable clues in sentence 2. This is a very important lesson which applies not only to made-up examples, but to authentic texts: don't stop for a new word, but read on and return to it later if necessary.

You also need to point out that inference is about probabilities as opposed to certainties. It would be wrong for students to feel that sentence 4 'proves' that *tock* = *cup*. It is important for them to understand that for most purposes, probability is all we need; the demand for 100 per cent certainty is of course what drives them to their dictionaries. But frequently we do not need to understand every word exactly; this depends on our purpose in reading, and on how crucial the word is to the text. The more we read, however, the more exact our understanding of words becomes, so that probabilities gradually turn into certainties without our being aware of it.

6.2 Recipes for exercises

Once the students have been convinced that they are capable of developing this skill, you can give them some specific training by means of activities similar to those we have just described. Here are some suggested variations:

(a) *Supply* a short text, or several short texts as in the *tock* example, each containing the same nonsense word replacing the same FL word in the original version. To make the exercise easier, offer several FL 'translations' for it, i.e. FL words which might be substituted for it, but only one of which fits all the contexts exactly. All the suggested translations should be words familiar to the students.

Task: Choose the substitute that seems most appropriate. Here is an example:

> *Read the text and decide what the word* FLET *means.*
> *Choose the best answer.*
> FLET *means*:
>
> (a) shadow   (b) reflection   (c) colour
> (d) spectrum   (e) rainbow
>
> Flets are solar spectra formed as sunlight passes through drops of water. Flets may be seen when a hose is adjusted to a fine spray. The drops act like prisms, refracting sunlight to produce the spectrum. A single, or primary, flet has red on the outside, violet inside. Its arc, 40 degrees in radius, is always on a line with the observer and the sun. When you see a flet, the sun is behind you. Sometimes a secondary flet forms outside the primary. It is fainter, with colours reversed – red inside, violet outside. The secondary flet is formed from light reflected twice within drops.

(b) Similar to (a), except that instead of nonsense words you use genuine but unfamiliar FL words. Now the concept, as well as the word, may be new. Instead of substitutes, offer a choice of explanations/definitions, or of L1 translations if suitable. In the elementary stages, the explanations etc. can be kept very simple and general. For example if the text contains the word *coelocanth*, the student might be asked to choose the correct alternative from this gloss:

A coelocanth is a type of reptile/fish/rock/plant.

At a later stage, when students are able to handle more elaborate clues, glosses which are more specific, and meanings which are more complex, can be introduced, for example:

Read the text and answer the question:

By exercising immense self-control, he was able to *simulate* death until the bandits had stripped him and finally departed, and thus escaped further injury.

The meaning of simulate *is*:
(a) suffer   (b) hope for   (c) pretend   (d) resist

(c) You can use this method also with longer texts, where the wider context of the text, as well as the immediate context of the surrounding words, will help the student to infer meanings. Here is an example from the University of Malaya's *Reading for Academic Study* (1979); the student is asked to read the text right through before attempting to say which of the suggested words is nearest to the italicized word in the preceding portion of text.

Some of the green plants we have mentioned live on the land and others *dwell* in the waters of the earth, but usually live fairly close to the surface where they are in contact with the all important sunlight.
(a) live   (b) fight   (c) breathe
The purple sulphur bacteria and the chemosynthetic bacteria, on the other hand, *are inhabitants of* swampy and marshy areas.
(a) live in   (b) cannot be found in   (c) do not live in
All other organisms are directly or indirectly dependent upon them for their *sustenance.*
(a) homes   (b) food   (c) air
The bacteria paramecia, for instance, are eaten by tiny fish and crustaceans and the crustaceans, in turn, may be *devoured* by small fish.
(a) chased   (b) protected   (c) eaten

(d) For many exercises of this kind, but (obviously) particularly for those involving longer texts, or sequences of sentences such as those in the *tock* example (p. 70) or the *flet* example (p. 72), you will find that an overhead projector is of great help. Even in activity (c) above, where you want the student to make use of the whole text in forming his inferences, you may like to project the text section by section first, so that the students come to recognize that they should look beyond the immediate environment for their evidence.

6.3 Clues and lexical density

In order to infer meaning from context, we must have clues. It is unproductive, as well as unfair, to give exercises where the clues are too few to make any but the most trivial inferences possible.

This must be kept in mind when you choose items in a text for practising the skill of inference. After initial training along the lines suggested above, you will want to promote the skill by continual practice whenever the text makes it possible. So when you prepare to deal with a new text, instead of assuming that all the important new words must be taught in advance, select some which you can use for practising inference.

You will need to be sure:

(a) that there are enough clues to make the inference possible. If you are editing a text for class use, you may like to build in a couple of clues for this purpose if it can be done unobtrusively.

(b) that there are few or no other new words in the context that will interfere with the attempt to deduce the meaning.

The second point relates to the *lexical density* of the text, that is, the proportion of new words it contains. If the sentence contains several new words, or if there is a high proportion of new words in the text as a whole, the accumulation of uncertainty may be too great for inferences to be drawn.

7 Active, receptive and throw-away vocabulary

Texts with a high lexical density are naturally difficult to deal with. However, many students have to face them if they need the FL for academic purposes, and it is necessary to equip them to do so. In addition to the programme of vocabulary development that we suggested earlier, getting the students to adopt a sensible attitude to vocabulary problems is necessary.

If you examine your knowledge of your own L1 vocabulary, you will find that there are roughly two categories of known words: those that you know well enough to use yourself, and those that you recognize and more or less understand, but are not yet sufficiently sure of to use. This is equally true of FL learners and the FL vocabulary: all of us, in any of the languages we know, can respond to words that we would never use ourselves and may not completely understand.

This is a fact that students are generally not aware of, but it is important that they should be made to understand it – perhaps by getting them to consider their own command of their L1 vocabulary. Once they accept that it is natural to have an **active** vocabulary (words we know well enough to use ourselves) and a **receptive** one (words we understand approximately when we meet them, but cannot use), their attitude to new words may become more relaxed.

You can reduce the tension by not asking students to 'make sentences' with newly learnt words. (Unless the words are very straightforward indeed, you are likely to get a sentence that is either trivial or wrong, so it is not a very productive activity anyway.) Especially in the case of words encountered while reading, it is really not necessary that the student should be able to use the word himself. If it is important enough, he will meet it again and again (this is where the extensive reading programme is so important) and eventually he will be confident enough to use it himself without prompting. By that time he will also know how to use it properly, with luck. Only continued exposure to the language will successfully transform receptive words into active ones.

But there is also a third category of words that students will meet once they move on to unsimplified material; these constitute what I label **throwaway** vocabulary. Not all the words we meet are worth learning, even to the receptive level; students with a vocabulary of, say, 3,000 words, cannot afford to clutter up their minds trying to remember the meaning of words like *boost* or *epicene*. Instead they need to develop a cavalier attitude to vocabulary, ignoring what is not important for their immediate purpose.

Of course it is nonsense to label any word as throwaway of itself; it all depends on the context, the student's level and his reasons for reading. Perhaps an electrical engineer in training would find *boost* an essential item, perhaps for a specific text *epicene* would have to be understood, but that does not make it worth while to write it down in a vocabulary list.

We make the problem worse ourselves by often spending time in class paying a great deal of attention to every detail of a text. Intensive reading is likely to strengthen the student's belief that he ought to pay this sort of attention when he reads on his own. And so he ought, if his purpose requires close and accurate understanding. But we must remember also to give him strategies for dealing with texts which he does not need to master so completely.

8 Learning to ignore difficult words

One mark of a skilled reader is his ability to decide what he can safely ignore. This is something many students have never contemplated; it may seem to them wrong, because it is not done in class. Therefore it needs to be done in class to make it respectable. It may also seem dangerous, and it is, which is why it needs to be practised under your guidance.

When he is tackling a difficult text, the reader should have these questions in his mind:

Before reading Why am I going to read this? More specifically, what do I want to get from it?

While reading Do I need to stop and look up the meaning of this word, or can I get the gist without it?

After reading Have I got what I wanted? If not:
where in the text is the information hidden?
can I get at it by looking up any of the unfamiliar words? If so, which?

This procedure is not of course so simple to put into practice; if the text is very difficult, the reader may not be able to answer most of the questions. It takes a competent reader to be aware that he is not understanding, and it sometimes takes a very skilled one to be aware *why* he is not.

Helping students to recognize that they do not understand must be one of our tasks; helping them to locate the sources of difficulty is another; and a third is giving them strategies for coping with the difficulty when they have found it. This includes strategies that will help them not to waste time on words they don't need to know.

It is impossible to give hard and fast rules about which words can be ignored, but we can do two things to help. The first is to make students aware that this approach is respectable and, in fact, necessary. This is the biggest hurdle, and having crossed it we can then go on to give practice in identifying the sources of difficulty, and in judging whether a word is worth attending to or not. Here are some suggestions:

(a) To prove that it is possible to get the gist without understanding every word, *supply* a text that is incomplete (words and phrases omitted here and there, with the omissions indicated) and some simple questions on it, which it is possible to answer from the incomplete information. The *task* is to answer the questions; if the students can do so, you will have proved your point.

(b) After practice with texts that are incomplete, try the same sort of exercise with texts that are complete and include some difficult words which are, however, not essential to getting the gist and answering the questions. The *task* is again to answer the questions, in this case without looking up any words. Success should prove the point that some words can safely be ignored.

(c) Now try to help students to identify the words they really must look up. *Supply* a short text containing a number of new words, and a number of simple questions testing direct understanding of some of them. The *task* is to see how many questions can be answered without looking up any words, and to make the students think very carefully before choosing to look up a word. This task may be done competitively, the individual or group who has looked up fewest words being considered the winner.

(d) As an extension of the exercise in (c), you can *supply* a text in which you consider that a certain number of new words must be looked up in order for the text to be understood well enough to answer the questions. The *task* is then: You are allowed to look up the meaning of only *x* words. Decide which *x* you most need to understand in order to answer the questions. List them, then look them up and prepare your answers.

Of course in all exercises of this kind discussion of the task by the students will be an important part of the activity.

9 What makes words difficult?

Not all new words are difficult. However, here are some kinds of difficulty that effective readers have to be able to deal with.

9.1 Idioms

We use the term *idiom* to mean a lexical item consisting of several words, with a meaning that cannot be deduced from the meaning of the individual words.

While students are quite aware that phrases like *seeing red* are idiomatic, they often do not recognize that they have a problem when they come across sentences like these:

> He was beside himself.
> I can't go through with it.
> They solved it once and for all.

The problem idioms are the ones composed of simple words, each of which the student believes he understands. He may not realize that he does not understand the sentence unless you ask him a question which he cannot answer.

Like all lexical items, idioms have to be dealt with individually as they occur (and only learnt if they are worth learning). You can help your students to become aware of the deceptively simple ones by *supplying* a short text containing an idiom of this kind. Devise a question that can only be answered if the idiom has been understood. Then give this *task*: Read the text and answer the question. If you cannot, locate the source of your difficulty. Do you need to find out the meaning of any word or words? If so, which?

After practice with texts of this kind, students should at least be conscious of the pitfalls and equipped to identify idioms when they meet them. When idioms occur in texts you are using in class, make sure that the students have noticed them and understood them; don't be satisfied with just asking 'Do you understand?'!

9.2 Transfer of meaning

Metaphor, metonymy and similar kinds of transferred meaning are always potential problems. Like idioms, they do not mean what they at first glance seem to mean. The difficulty is not faced only by students of literature: when he reads of a tapeworm budding off sections from its tail-end, a student may wonder if it is botany or zoology he is studying. A student of accountancy will have to know what is meant by *soaring rates, galloping inflation, profits wiped out, fringe benefits* and so on.

Metaphor is likely to provide most of the problems because it occurs so frequently. Since it always involves an implicit comparison between A and B, one way of handling metaphor is to analyse what A and B have in common that is relevant to the context. For instance, *galloping inflation* suggests comparison between inflation and a horse. What characteristics of a horse are relevant? Sometimes the first step is to establish what the two terms, A and B, are: for instance, what are they in *profits wiped out*?

This approach need not be pedestrian. It offers a method the students can apply for themselves:

(a) identify the two terms of the comparison, A and B.
(b) identify the characteristics of A and B that are relevant.
(c) check that your interpretation makes sense in the context.

9.3 Words with several meanings

Any word that has more than one meaning is bound to cause trouble to the inexperienced, and we are all inexperienced in some fields – some of the most dangerous misunderstandings arise when apparently everyday words are used in specialized senses by writers in specialized fields. The mathematician's use of *argument*, the statistician's *random*, the communications expert's *noise*, are all very different from the layman's.

You can only alert your students to the occurrence of unexpected meanings and train them to use common sense in deciding whether to accept a familiar meaning or to check whether another is possible. Some specific practice may be helpful: supplying sentences in which words are used with unfamiliar meanings, and asking the students to select the appropriate one from several definitions; studying a technical text and listing all the words used in ways that differ from the usual ones. Training in the proper use of a dictionary (see p.78) will also help, because it involves selecting the meaning that is appropriate to the given context.

9.4 Subtechnical vocabulary

If you have taught a language for specific purposes, English for technologists for example, you will be aware that students often have difficulty not so much with the specialized technical jargon (which usually has a unique L1 equivalent and is familiar to them from their specialized studies), but with the common core of semi-technical words that occur in most specialized disciplines.

The sort of words that give trouble are words like *average, approximate, effect, combination, determine*. Words like these are needed in most fields of study and are therefore worth attention even if you are not teaching a homogeneous class. The problem, however, is conceptual rather than linguistic, so you will have to make sure, for each word, that the concept it expresses has been grasped.

9.5 Superordinates

Superordinates are words of more general meaning viewed in relation to other words of more specific meaning which could also be referred to by the more general term, for example:

SUPERORDINATE   building

HYPONYMS   house   school   factory   cinema   hotel

You can see that the superordinate (*building*) could replace any of the hyponyms in many contexts. Such words can give difficulty if the reader fails to realize that the general and the specific term may both be referring to the same thing:

Mrs Hill came in slowly. The woman looked tired, I thought.

Here the general word *woman* must be assumed to refer to Mrs Hill; if the student does not realize this, he will not make sense of the text.

The example is trivial, but interpreting superordinates is not always so simple. Sometimes the superordinate and its hyponym are different parts of speech; or the hyponym may be expressed by a whole sentence or an even longer stretch of text:

A six-year-old boy recently gave a performance of the Beethoven violin concerto. This feat was reported in the press.

The feat, of course, is not playing the concerto, but playing it at the age of six.

The second example illustrates another difficulty with superordinates: they may embody judgements or opinions. You may not consider it remarkable that a child of six should play the concerto, but the writer evidently does. Students have to be trained to watch out for such evidence of the writer's attitude.

(A cloze exercise on superordinates is given on p. 144)

9.6 Synonyms and antonyms

Fondness for lists of these seems to be a characteristic of students. It is not in fact that the words themselves are difficult (almost any word can fall into one or other category in some context), but the attitude to them which is wrong. Unfortunately rubrics like 'Choose the word that means the same . . .' often promote this misconception.

The point is that a sophisticated reader must look for distinctions between words rather than — or at least as well as — similarities. If two words mean the same, is it just chance that the writer used one and not the other? The answer is seldom 'Yes'; two words seldom do mean exactly the same thing, and the writer probably selected with care the alternative he thought most appropriate.

Students, especially if they are going to appreciate works of literature, need to understand what difference it makes if we say A rather than B, and therefore, why the writer chose the alternative he did.

9.7 Irony

In this case too it is not the words themselves that are difficult, but the use the writer makes of them. The difficulty lies in the mismatch between the words and the intention of the writer as it appears from the text as a whole.

Word-attack is involved to the extent that irony sometimes hangs upon a single word; Wilfred Burchett, writing movingly of famine in China, is expressing fury, not nonchalance, when he refers to 'mere starvation' and the reader is expected to pick up this indication of mood. It would be total misinterpretation to criticize him for not taking starvation seriously.

Irony is probably the most difficult of all uses of language for the student to interpret; even though it is not very common in non-literary writing, advanced students should be helped to deal with it.

10 Using a dictionary

Earlier we noted that it is advisable to discourage students from making use of dictionaries. But this is only because the usual tendency is to use them far too often. Any student reading for a serious study purpose will need to be able to look up key words.

If he has to use a dictionary at all, he had better be able to do so efficiently. So once you have convinced your students that they are able to cope without a dictionary, and that it is wasteful to look up every new word, it will be necessary to show them how to use a dictionary effectively and with discretion.

We have already discussed the need to decide which words must be looked up, and indicated that they should be as few as possible. This is the first step towards using the dictionary as a tool, rather than a crutch. Make sure that you give students practice in it.

Having concluded that a word must be looked up, we want to be able to do it quickly and to make the best use of the information the dictionary supplies. Both skills need training.

It is surprising how long it takes some students to find a word in the dictionary. You can help by giving exercises on alphabetical order if they are needed (which may be the case, especially if the L1 is not written in the same alphabet as the FL), and on making use of the guide words that appear at the head of each page opening. Even practice in opening the dictionary as nearly as possible at the right page can be useful. Many exercises of these kinds can be done as races.

Dictionaries vary in the amount and kind of information they offer, so your students need to familiarize themselves with the characteristics of their own. As far as reading is concerned, by far the most important is of course the semantic information provided, together with examples if any. In view of the problems noted earlier in this chapter, it is important to give practice in selecting, from the several meanings offered, the one that is relevant in the given text.

You can do this by, for example, supplying short texts including unfamiliar terms, and asking which of three or four different definitions will be the most appropriate. Or supply several short texts, each containing the 'same' words used with a different meaning, together with all the alternative definitions of the word. The task is to match each text with the relevant definition.

Specific training of this kind is a useful first step, but continual insistence on the use of this skill is even more important. This means that it should be the students, not you, who select the appropriate definitions whenever it is necessary to resort to the dictionary in class. It also means that you must make sure practice of this kind is routine, and resist the temptation to give the meaning yourself, even though it is quicker.

Note: Several books are available to train students in dictionary skills. This is a selection:

R. Border, *Working with Words from a Learner's First Dictionary* (Macmillan, 1979).

R. Border, *Working with Words from the New Basic Dictionary* (Macmillan, 1979).

A. S. Hornby, *Oxford Student's Dictionary of Current English Student's Guide* (OUP, 1978).

A. S. Hornby, *Using the Advanced Learner's Dictionary of Current English* (OUP, 1977).

K. Methold, *Junior Dictionary Exercises* (Longman, 1972).

A. Underhill, *Use your Dictionary* (OUP, 1980).

J. Whitcut, *Learning with Longman Dictionary of Contemporary English* (Longman, 1980).

7 Text-Attack Skills (1): Signification and Cohesion

1 Text and discourse

In this chapter and the next, we are going to consider the skills a reader needs in order to understand a text. Strictly speaking, a text could consist of a single sentence, but we are more interested in texts composed of a number of sentences organized to carry a coherently structured message. The **message** may be a story, a body of information, an argument and so on; and the way the meanings in a text are organized to convey the message is **discourse.**

Recently a great deal of attention has been paid to **discourse analysis**, the study of how discourse is produced and organized. This relatively new discipline has achieved many insights and a thorough understanding of some elements of discourse, but no comprehensive account of it has so far been given.

However, in order to produce an inventory of text-attack skills, we need some idea of the kinds of meaning that a text embodies and that a reader must understand.

2 Four kinds of meaning

Understanding a text involves understanding different kinds of meaning at the same time. At least four levels of meaning exist:

2.1 Conceptual meaning: the meaning a word can have on its own

Concepts, or notions, can be found at any level, from the whole text down to a single word or morpheme. Every lexical item embodies a concept, sometimes simple (e.g. *blue*), sometimes complex (e.g. *probability*). Whole books can be written on complex concepts like probability or truth. Other concepts can be expressed by the smallest meaning units of all, such as the concept of plurality, expressed in English by the suffix *-s* among other ways.

All other kinds of meaning rest on conceptual meaning: making a text involves putting concepts together to form propositions, which carry the next kind of meaning.

2.2 Propositional meaning: the meaning a sentence can have on its own

This is the same as **signification** or **plain sense**. It is the meaning a clause or sentence can have even if it is not being used in a context, but is just standing on its own. A word on its own, e.g. *misleading*, carries no propositional meaning: we cannot affirm it, deny it, question or doubt it. But as soon as it is put into a proposition, these operations become possible:

> Examination results are misleading.

It is now possible to deny the truth of the proposition (*Examination results are not misleading*), to doubt it, question it, etc.: in short, it has a truth value.

The signification of a sentence (its propositional meaning) is the only kind of meaning it can have when it is cited (as we cited the sentence about examination results), except in a limited number of cases where the form of the sentence itself gives it a kind of value. For example, the sentence we cited could be described as a *generalization*, while this sentence is clearly a *definition*, even though it is not in context:

A thermometer is an instrument for measuring temperature.

Usually, however, the form of the sentence is no guide to its functional value, which comes from the way it is used in context.

2.3 Contextual meaning: the meaning a sentence can have only when in context

This is the same as **functional value** (which we discussed in Chapter 1, p. 12). As soon as a sentence is used in a given situation or context, it takes on a value derived from the writer's reason for using it, and from the relationship between one sentence (utterance) and others in the same text.

For instance, the proposition

Examination results are misleading.

has no value when it stands alone, except as a generalization. But if it were to follow this sentence:

You should not expel my son just because he has failed.

it could be seen to have the value of an explanation or justification. The writer is using it to substantiate the claim that expulsion would be wrong.

Explaining, justifying and so on are often called **rhetorical acts**. In a text, they are sequenced and organized into patterns which display the writer's thoughts. These patterns combine into larger patterns and so on until the overall pattern of the whole is reached: the writer's overall message.

2.4 Pragmatic meaning: the meaning a sentence has only as part of the interaction between writer and reader

This last kind of meaning is not easily distinguished from contextual meaning, but in some examples it can be clearly established that a distinction exists. This is the meaning that reflects the writer's feelings, attitudes and so on, and his intention that the reader should understand these. It therefore includes the intended effect of the utterance upon the reader.

Let us return to our examination results example. Suppose the father is talking to the headmaster who is proposing to expel his son, and suppose he utters the two sentences we discussed above. If the headmaster were to respond to the second sentence (*Examination results are misleading*) only as a logical proposition, he might reply:

How true!

But the father clearly intends the remark as a plea, protest or complaint; the headmaster has not replied to it at all. In any normal conversation, his reply could only be construed as an offensively sarcastic way of refusing to discuss the matter further. If the head did not mean to be offensive, he has got the pragmatics of the conversation badly wrong.

Pragmatic meaning involves interaction and can be most clearly seen in conversation, but remembering that in Chapter 1 we concluded that reading is an interactive process, we can see that this kind of meaning too can be found in texts.

3 The meanings in the text and the reader's understanding

Every sentence has these four kinds of meaning when it is used in a text, though sometimes one is more important than another. If we want to understand a text completely, in the fullest possible way, we need to understand every sentence in it in these four ways. As we have seen, in practice we seldom do need to understand with such total thoroughness.

Sometimes it is possible to get the writer's message when we understand only bits of the text – only some of these kinds of meaning, for example. We can make imaginative leaps from one bit to another, and if we find nothing to contradict the meaning we assume the writer intended, we read on. We only stop and go back to read more carefully if we discover inconsistencies. This is a sensible and effective way of reading provided it is not necessary to understand the text with absolute accuracy. (It is also a good way to approach the initial reading of a text we have to read with care.)

In making the imaginative leaps, the four kinds of meaning are a great help: each supports the others. You may understand a sentence because you understand the one before it and the one after it, and can therefore predict more or less what the middle one means, even if it is difficult. Sometimes you can interpret the value of an utterance without being able to explain its propositional meaning, for instance, if you had been listening to the father talking to the headmaster about his son's examination results, you would probably have known that he was protesting even if you did not know the meaning of *misleading*, and you would recognize that the word had the meaning of an undesirable quality, even though you did not know exactly what.

So although logically we ought to understand the plain sense if we are to understand anything else, in practice the reader of a difficult text will continually shift from one focus to another, now concentrating on the plain sense, now on one of the other kinds of meaning, which will later lead him to understand the plain sense.

Moreover, even the plain sense of each sentence cannot be established by looking at the sentence in isolation. We all know that the exact meaning of a word often cannot be established without reference to its context. But there are some words that cannot be interpreted at all without reference outside the clause where they occur:

However, she naturally did so.

Obviously we cannot establish the meaning of *she* and *did so* by inspecting this sentence on its own; but the force of *however* and *naturally* is equally obscure, since we know nothing of the circumstances and assumptions involved.

In fact, every word in that sentence shows us that the sentence has been taken from a text; it is not meant to stand alone. Every word in it ties the meaning of this sentence with the meaning of other parts of the text. These ties are the ties of **cohesion**, which both contribute to the signification of the sentence and at the same time relate it to other sentences in the text.

4 Problems in understanding texts

We shall concentrate on the features of a text that are known to give rise to difficulties for the reader.

4.1 Concepts

The first of these, *concepts*, are outside the scope of this book. It has often been argued that concept formation is not the job of the language teacher, although many (especially those teaching language for specific purposes) have found themselves willy-nilly teaching concepts as well. We shall assume that the student has a reasonable understanding of the concepts involved within the clause; concepts expressed at higher levels are part of the message that the text expresses and will therefore be taken care of in other ways.

4.2 Vocabulary and sentence structure

It is possible to have a pretty good idea of a writer's message without understanding the signification of every sentence, but it is not possible to be absolutely certain of it, nor to give the fullest response. This entails, first, understanding all the *vocabulary*: we have dealt with this in Chapter 6. In this chapter we shall deal with the problems caused by the *sentence structure*, limiting ourselves to the problems that arise in English.

4.3 Cohesive devices

A further problem arises from the use of the various *cohesive devices*, i.e. the ways of tying sentences together to create a cohesive text. Pronoun reference, elliptical sentences and so on are often so straightforward that their potential difficulty is overlooked, and it is only when he encounters a problem that the student will think them worth attending to. The problems that arise concern the signification of sentences: the reader who does not know what a pronoun refers to, or who cannot supply the full version of an elliptical sentence, will not be able to establish its signification. So cohesion will be handled in this chapter.

4.4 Discourse markers

A particular kind of cohesive device is the *discourse marker*, words such as *however, although, furthermore, namely*. These words serve to mark the functional value of a sentence; they tell you what the writer intends by it. (If he uses *although*, he is conceding something; if he uses *namely* he is specifying something; and so on.) The reason why they are included in this chapter – where we are concerned with propositional meaning, not value – is that they are extremely useful signals to the reader. They do not themselves contribute to the signification of a sentence (except in the case of those which indicate time), but they can help a careful reader to establish the signification.

For example, suppose a reader comes upon a difficult clause following several sentences that he has understood reasonably well. Then suppose this clause is introduced by the word *but*. He realizes from this word that the obscure clause contradicts or in some other way goes against the sense of the previous clause; this realization may be enough to unlock its meaning.

4.5 Problems beyond the plain sense

Even when the plain sense of each sentence has been understood, the reader may still be unable to make sense of the text as a whole. L1 readers experience this problem; FL readers, given their different backgrounds, are likely to experience it frequently. Problems which go beyond the plain sense of a sentence involve the interpretation of value, or the relationships between the utterances in a text, or between writer, reader and text. These will be dealt with in Chapter 8.

5   Training text-attack skills

5.1   The problem of credibility

In normal circumstances, reading a straightforward text, readers are not conscious of the four kinds of meaning or of the other features which give rise to difficulty. But when we fail to understand a text, we have to become aware of them in order to locate the reasons for our failure. Training in text-attack skills therefore involves making students aware of things they normally do not notice at all.

This produces a problem of credibility; some teachers and students dismiss these skills as self-evident and tedious. Unfortunately it is easy to make training exercises seem quite pointless, especially if you do not explain their purpose. You would not be doing these exercises except with students at intermediate level or above, so it should be possible to start by showing them the kind of problems that occur, and the way in which training can help them to deal with them.

The timing is crucial. If you want to give training in some of the duller aspects of text-attack, choose a time when the students have been brought face to face with the relevant problems in a difficult text. If you can manage without such training, so much the better. My view is that a small amount of basic training is necessary, to give students the knowledge required to use the text-attack skills when they need them. If you are not convinced, it is better to skip to training you believe in.

5.2   Identifying the text-attack skills

It is convenient to assume that each feature of a text (cohesion, functional value, rhetorical organization etc.) requires a particular interpretive skill. This makes description easier and helps to focus and simplify the way we approach the complex process of comprehension. The various features can be looked at separately to a certain extent, but of course they are not fully separable and you cannot satisfactorily interpret one unless you can interpret all. So to describe and train the various text-attack skills must be seen as a way of focusing attention, not as an attempt to keep separate skills which are in fact tightly bound up one with another.

In focusing on the analytical skills, we must take care not to overlook the integrative skills required to make sense of the text as a whole. The reader must be able to assess its message, evaluate the writer's success, even (if appropriate) appreciate the text as literature. These skills are more familiar to teachers and will therefore get less attention in this book than they deserve.

5.3   Sources of exercises

Many of the techniques that will be suggested for training the text-attack skills have been developed by the writers of the reading courses mentioned in the Foreword. It is seldom possible to prove that reading exercises work, but most of those described have been used successfully: that is to say, teachers have believed them to be useful and students have got satisfaction from doing them.

Some of the types of exercise described are easily devised, but others are the opposite. If you are too busy to develop exercises that take a long time to prepare, or if you doubt your ability to do so, start by using exercises from the books listed, which adopt an approach similar to that used in this book. After some experience, you will find that you are able to develop similar material of your own.

If you choose to prepare your own material, take your texts from the kind of books your students will have to read (if possible). But even if you are preparing students to read university texts, it is advisable to train them first on something simpler. School textbooks often provide clear models of academic discourse; it will be useful to have a collection of FL school texts on a variety of subjects according to the needs of your class. Some graded readers also offer good material, but choose if possible those which are original, rather than simplified versions.

Writing your own texts is· of course a possibility but not recommended: composed texts are rarely effective even when they are written by experts. You are likely to find it better to use authentic material; this can be modified slightly to make it more suitable for your purpose, but even if you are an L1 speaker of the language you teach you will need to exercise great care. It is easy to make a text sound unconvincing: always have it read by a suitable friend before deciding to use it.

5.4 Displaying a text

When you are teaching text-attack skills, it is often necessary to display the text as a central visual, i.e. so that it is visible to everyone. This is needed when you want the class to see not only the text but your handling of it: you may wish to underline, circle or draw lines from one word to another, use colour to indicate differences in function or structure, block off certain sections, annotate in the margins, and so on. You cannot do this if you only have the text on a set of stencilled copies; everyone must be able to see the copy you are marking.

This presents a great problem. The most effective solution by far is to use an overhead projector. With an OHP, you can write the text in indelible ink and annotate it as much as you like in washable ink of various colours, or you can use an overlay prepared on a separate transparent sheet. In this way you can use the same text again and again for as many different purposes as you wish. It is less wearisome to write on an OHP transparency than on a blackboard or even a whiteboard, and you can prepare it beforehand, store it easily and keep it as long as you like.

If you cannot get an OHP, try writing the text on a large sheet of newsprint in letters large enough to be seen by the whole class. You can use a thick felt pen for this. The paper should be rolled for storage if possible. Get a sheet of strong transparent plastic and display the text by suspending it from bulldog clips, with the plastic covering it. You can annotate the text by writing on the plastic with OHP pens. Use washable ones so that the plastic can be cleaned: thus the text is not marked and the plastic can be used again with other texts.

6 TAS 1   Understanding sentence syntax

When a sentence is not understood although the vocabulary is known, it is often because it is long and difficult to unravel syntactically. Syntactic complexity coupled with unfamiliar vocabulary doubles the problem.

The first advice for a reader who finds a text difficult for these reasons is: read it fast, without stopping, getting what you can from it. Then read it again a little more slowly, looking up key words in the dictionary if you have one. Next stop and ask yourself questions about what you think the text is saying, i.e. questions you think the text might answer. Read it a third time looking for evidence that your predictions were correct. By this time, some of the sentences should be clearer and a picture of the overall message should be emerging. At this point, if some of the sentences still baffle you, and if you need to understand the text thoroughly, use the analytic approach described below to tackle the problem sentences. (There is an excellent account of this approach in Nation, (1979), from which most of these ideas derive.)

There are a number of reasons why a sentence may be difficult to unravel syntactically; we shall examine five of them:

(a) complex noun groups
(b) nominalization
(c) co-ordination
(d) subordination
(e) participial and prepositional phrases as modifiers

Any of these on their own may give trouble; when they combine, things get even more difficult. By adopting Nation's approach, the reader tackles each problem in turn until the bare structure of the sentence is clear, so that he can then put the bits together again and make sense of them.

6.1   Complex noun groups

A noun group consists of a head noun modified by adjectives or other words which may precede or follow it. Generally it is the modifiers that follow which give most trouble:

> One surprising factor is the *willingness* with which the public in most countries accept the by now well-known risk of developing lung cancer in spite of the evidence of its connection with cigarette smoking.

(The head noun is *willingness*.)

Nation's technique is to give the students practice in identifying the kinds of item that can follow a head noun (prepositional or participial phrase, *who/ which/ that* clause, noun in apposition, adjective). The head noun in a suitable example is identified by the teacher and the students then draw brackets round the entire noun group and identify the kinds of item that follow the head, labelling them and analysing them into their constituent parts according to the procedures described below if necessary.

The point is that if a student knows what structure a noun group may have, he is better equipped to identify the structure it actually has in a text where he is having difficulty.

6.2   Nominalization

It is well known that this is a major problem in academic texts. This is an example of the form it can take:

> The implementation of the recommendation that child allowances should be restricted to the first three children was delayed for several years.

You will note that this is also an example of a complex noun group, made more difficult by the nominalizations. There are two: *implementation* and *recommenda-tion*, the second being dependent on the first and being itself modified by a noun clause in apposition (*that . . . children*). How can students be helped to deal with such constructions?

First, they must be taught to recognize nominalizations. When nouns are formed from verbs, only a limited range of forms occurs and they are not difficult to recognize. Students may be able to recognize most of them already, but are unlikely to realize how complex they can make a sentence.

Because nominalizations are formed from verbs, they normally conceal unstated propositions:

A someone recommended that child allowances should be restricted . . .
B someone implemented A

Once you have worked out these implied propositions, it is fairly simple to see that B was delayed for several years.

Hence the procedure for dealing with nominalization is:

(a) Identify the nominalization.
(b) Work out the implied proposition (and give it a label – e.g. A – if the sentence is very complex, so that you can refer to A rather than the whole proposition).
(c) Work out the place of the proposition in the rest of the sentence.

6.3 Co-ordination

Unlike the other items in this group, co-ordination is not usually difficult in itself, but in a complex sentence it may be difficult to isolate the two parallel parts of the sentence that are joined by *and/or/but*. Often it is hard to determine the extent of the parts joined: are they single words, phrases or what? The two parts are always parallel and stand in the same relationship to some other part of the sentence (unless of course they are co-ordinate clauses constituting the whole sentence):

He looked at the child with surprise that he should know such words at his age and indignation that he should be permitted to use them.

Here the item that parallels *indignation* is not *age* (as a student might be tempted to assume) nor *words*, but *surprise*. The two parallel items are:

A surprise that he should know such words at his age
B indignation that he should be permitted to use them

It is then clear that both stand in the same relation to the first part of the sentence:

He looked at the child with A.
He looked at the child with B.

In extreme cases the student might even write out the two parallel sentences produced by repeating the common part, as above.

6.4 Subordination: noun clauses

Subordinate noun clauses are often troublesome because they make it difficult for the reader to identify the subject or object of the sentence.

Here is a rather extreme example:

How difficult it is for the medically trained, and those whose work is based on the current concepts of medical science, to envisage all the barriers that others lower down the social scale will find in the way of their accepting what seems such a simple ordinary test, is seen from some recent studies in the USA.
J. Wakefield, 'The social context of cancer' in R. J. C. Harris, ed., *What we Know about Cancer* (Allen & Unwin, 1970)

For a fluent reader, this is not difficult, and indeed the style is not academic but popular in tone; yet you can see that an FL reader might get extremely perplexed by the complexity of this sentence with its four-line subject.

To cope with difficulties of this kind, use the 'What does what'? approach. When you encounter likely difficulties in a text, identify the verbs affected (in the above example, the key verb is *is seen*) and ask the students to discover the subject (in this case) or object by asking themselves the question 'Who (or what) does (or is) what?' In the example. the student would ask himself 'Who or what is seen from recent studies in the USA?' When the verb is in the passive, it is often helpful to devise an active sentence, and the question would then be 'Who sees what?'; in this particular example this does not help much, and the student will have to supply the subject (the 'who') from his common sense ('we', 'the readers', 'the public', etc.).

6.5   Participial and prepositional phrases

In the case of participial phrases, the problem is generally to know where to attach them. Those which are part of a noun group (*an elderly man standing near the door*) should be handled as under 6.1. But all participles can be handled also by the 'What does what?' method outlined in 6.4, and this is really the best way of finding out where they belong.

As to prepositional phrases, the problem presented is usually not great except when there is a crowd of them, as in this extract:

> It is, for instance, all too easy, in our anxiety to stress the ravages of lung cancer in heavy cigarette smokers, to raise a new bogy in the public mind to add to those nameless terrors of the disease that we are trying to combat by other means.
>
> (Harris, 1970)

In cases of this kind, the procedure the student should adopt will include:

(a) checking which instances of *to* are genuinely prepositions and which belong to infinitive verbs; circling the latter;
(b) checking whether there are any words in the text that regularly go with a preposition (e.g. *easy*, *add*) and linking them with the preposition if it is there;
(c) for the other prepositions, finding out which two nouns are joined by each one (*ravages of cancer; cancer in heavy cigarette smokers; bogy in the public mind*, etc.) and linking them;
(d) dealing *ad hoc* with any prepositions that do not fall into the above categories, e.g. *for* (*for instance*), *in* (*in our anxiety*), *by* (*by other means*).

For the last category (and for the others), a variation of the 'What does what?' technique seems to be useful: take the nearest noun (it usually will be the one that follows) and ask the question 'What – preposition – noun', for example, 'What in the public mind?' or 'A new bogy in what?' However, this will not help the student to interpret the phrase *in our anxiety*, and one is driven to conclude that (as with so many prepositional problems) the only solution is to learn the meaning as one must any other lexical item.

6.6   Simplifying sentences

Nation points out that by combining the various techniques suggested, it is possible to simplify complex sentences sufficiently to make the structure clear. The procedure to be followed is this:

(a) Find the reference words in the sentence and find out what they refer to. (This is explained in TAS 2 below.)

(b) Re-write the sentence as two or more sentences by removing *and*, *but* and *or*.

(c) Find the nouns and remove any items following them which are part of the same noun group.

(d) Identify the nominalizations and if necessary establish what propositions are implied.

(e) Find the verbs and use the 'What does what?' technique to find the subject and object of each.

(f) If any participial or prepositional phrases are still unaccounted for, use the 'What does what?' technique to find out where they fit in the structure.

6.7   Caution

This is an efficient and systematic way of dealing with complex sentences but obviously laborious and interesting only to students who are highly motivated. It is not suggested that training of this kind should be given in long stretches in the reading lesson. If your students need a lot of help of this kind, it should be given in a lesson labelled 'Grammar', because that is what it is.

But do not dismiss the usefulness of the techniques just because they are laborious. They offer a struggling student a reasonable chance of making sense of a difficult text, and he should have practice in using them. As far as the reading lesson goes, the practice should come when it is needed, i.e. when you come up against a sentence that needs to be disentangled before even its signification can be understood.

7   TAS 2   Recognizing and interpreting cohesive devices

Subskill 1	Interpreting reference and substitution	(7.1)
Subskill 2	Interpreting elliptical expressions	(7.3)
Subskill 3	Interpreting lexical cohesion	(7.5)

We shall deal in this section and the next with some of the elements of cohesion that seem most likely to give trouble, or to be helpful, to the reader. It is not possible to give a full account of cohesion here; it has been described fully in Halliday and Hasan (1976) In their book they deal with cohesion between different sentences of a text: this is the accepted meaning of the term. However, most of the relationships described can occur within the boundaries of a single sentence as well as between sentences, and can cause similar problems for the reader in either case. Both will be treated here.

We shall consider the discourse markers separately, in TAS 3, because their position seems rather different, from the point of view of the reader. The other devices, which will be considered in TAS 2, all directly affect the signification of a sentence; they impose on the reader the task of retrieving some of the parts of the sentence from elsewhere in the text. A sentence that includes reference, substitution or ellipsis, does not itself express all the information required to convey its message. We can only fill the gap by referring to other parts of the text, identifying the missing information and using it to supplement the information actually expressed.

Lexical cohesion, which is also dealt with briefly (p. 94), in most ways is very different from the other cohesive devices; but its cohesive role is similar to that of reference in one major respect: both require the reader to re-cognize that two different words refer to the same thing (have the same referent).

7.1   Subskill 1   Interpreting reference and substitution

This subskill involves identifying the meanings of words like *it, he, our, this, those, then, one,* (as in *the wrong one*), *so/not* (as in *I think so, It appears not*) and comparatives (*smaller, same, additional, such, other,* etc.). When such words are used, they are signals to the reader to seek a meaning for them elsewhere in the text. In using such devices, the writer avoids burdening his text with needless repetition. Instead he signals to the reader: 'I have referred to this person, object or idea before; you should be able to identify it, if necessary by searching the adjacent text until you find the required referent.'

Experienced readers often find it hard to believe that anyone has difficulty interpreting these devices, but a short check is likely to convince you that many FL students do have problems. Of course not every occurrence causes difficulty; more often than not, they will identify the referent easily. It is the occurrences where it is not easy that interest us and make it useful to draw attention to possible misinterpretations. We can illustrate some of the problems in this short text:

> James glared at his brother, took the money from the box and threw it angrily into the fire, where it crackled swiftly into flame. This appeared to amuse him, for he burst out laughing and walked towards the door, which did not improve matters. Mary marvelled that he could be so nonchalant. Surely its loss could not leave him unmoved?

Problem one is that the writer has been careless, so that his references are ambiguous. What did James throw into the fire? The box or the money? Who was amused? James or his brother? Only a greater knowledge of the context would resolve these questions.

The second problem is that with the reference words *this* and *which*, we are not sure how much of the preceding text to include when we interpret them. Presumably 'he' was not amused because the object burst into flame, but was amused by the whole incident; only a closer knowledge of the context will tell us. We can be fairly sure that it was not the door that 'did not improve matters', but it is less easy to know whether *which* refers only to the second action (walking towards the door) or to the whole of the preceding part of the sentence.

Thirdly, what about 'its loss'? We must assume that *it* refers to the money, or the box, but the reference is so far away that for a slow reader it might be quite difficult to recover. Similarly, if the referent occurs in a complex sentence, it may be difficult to find because the reader is unsure how to interpret the sentence in which it occurs. Finally, since reference may be either anaphoric or cataphoric, the reader may be unsure whether the referent occurs before or after the reference word; in the great majority of cases it will be anaphoric (i.e. found in the preceding part of the text), which makes it all the more unexpected and disconcerting when occasionally it follows:

> Explaining why *he* had headed the group in charge of explosives,
> *Lu Yin* replied . . .

(Appendix A, Text 3.)

To cope with reference and substitution, the reader must be able to recognize that it is the reference word that is causing the problem; since words like *it* and *this* are so common and look so harmless, the first step is to make the students aware of the potential difficulties by drawing attention to them when they occur in texts you are reading.

Once you know the source of your trouble, you can take steps to cure it. The student should ask himself questions like those exemplified below:

(a) *He gave her a letter. This gave her food for thought.* What made her think: the letter, or the fact that he gave it?

(b) *They all said the same.* The same as who, or what?

(c) *Such a contingency must be avoided . . .* What event is referred to as a contingency? What kind of contingency is it?

(d) *In other cases different rules apply.* Other than what? (i.e. from what case are these others distinguished?) Different from what?

(e) *The Greeks believed so.* What did the Greeks believe?

(f) *The man pointed.* Which man? Where was he mentioned before?

The answers to these questions have to be found by searching the text and using your common sense and knowledge of the context. It is good tactics, if you find yourself unaccountably puzzled by part of the text, to look for words of this kind and ask about them the kind of questions exemplified above. You may find that a wrongly identified reference has led you to misinterpret.

7.2   Training Subskill 1

To develop this skill does not require complicated exercises; it is sufficient to ask questions of the kind given above. The difficulty is to make students realize the value of this activity and to prevent them from dismissing it as trivial. You cannot prepare exercises precisely for this purpose, since the point is lost unless each example is located in an extended text. The best way is therefore to make use of every opportunity to draw attention to these features in the texts you study for other purposes. Focus attention on the cases where the reference is difficult to identify, and demonstrate how identifying the referent can help when difficult sentences have to be unravelled.

This should be an ongoing activity, but some specific exercises may also be given:

(a) More advanced students enjoy making their own questions, searching the text for items they think may baffle their colleagues. This gives good practice in focusing their attention on potential problems, a skill they need for tackling texts independently.

(b) *Supply* a suitable text, i.e. one containing varied reference and substitution items. Put boxes round suitable items.
   Task: Students find all other items with the same reference as each boxed item; they circle each one and join them with lines to the appropriate boxed item. Or use different colours: all items with the same referent will be underlined or circled with the same colour.
   Note: This kind of activity is best demonstrated first by working through a text on the OHP. See Figure 18 (p. 92) for an example.

(c) *Supply* a text with the reference items (or some of them) omitted and replaced by gaps. Supply also a list of the omitted items, in random order.
   Task: To insert the items in the correct gaps. More advanced students can manage without the list, and be asked to supply a suitable item for each gap.

(d) You need to give special practice with the word *this*, which is often used to relate to an extended idea, not just a single word. The idea (occurrence, situation, etc.) may have been described in several sentences and may be difficult to express succinctly. When you notice a suitable example, draw students' attention to it, ask what it refers to and, if necessary, give several alternative answers for them to choose from.

Last week, Rahman's wife Leila had an accident. Rahman's youngest child, Yusof, was at home when it happened. He was playing with his new car. His father had given it to him for his third birthday the week before.

Suddenly the little fellow heard his mother calling 'Help! Help!'. He left his toy and ran to the kitchen. The poor woman had burnt herself with some hot cooking oil. She was crying with pain and the pan was on fire.

Rahman had gone to his office. Both the other children were at school. He was too small to help his mother, and she was too frightened to speak sensibly to her son. But he ran to the neighbour's house and asked her to come and help his mother. She soon put out the fire and took the victim to the clinic.

When her husband came home, Leila told him what had happened. Of course Rahman was very concerned about his wife, but he was also very proud of his sensible son. 'When you are a man, you will be just like your father,' he said.

Instructions

1 Read the text
2 Note the three boxed items
3 Find all the other items in the text that refer to the same person as each of the boxed items.
4 Using a different colour for each of the three items, circle each item with the same reference.

NOTE: In the figure, the items with the same reference as Rahman have been circled.

Fig. 18   Exercise to practise the use of reference

7.3   Subskill 2   Interpreting elliptical expressions

It is a principle of efficient communication that we do not give the reader more information than he needs. It is true that there is usually a certain amount of redundancy to cope with human carelessness, laziness or slowness, but dislike of needless repetition is the reason why the reference and substitution systems are used.

For the same reason, we prefer to omit rather than repeat certain kinds of information which the reader's common sense can readily supply from the surrounding text. This omission is called ellipsis.

An elliptical expression is one where something necessary to the sense (and often to the structure) is left unsaid. For example:

The days are hot and the nights cool. (= the nights are cool)

They came although they were asked not to. (= not to come)

The ladies need not stand but the gentlemen must. (= must stand)

I could not find any. (Any what?)

The most expensive was selected. (The most expensive what?)

Like reference and substitution, ellipsis directs the reader to supply information from elsewhere in the text. In short simple sentences like these examples, there is little difficulty; but the dislocated syntax that ellipsis produces can be very puzzling to an unskilled reader:

> Man is seen in perspective as just another piece in this grand jigsaw, and his activities in terms of the effects, good or bad, that they are likely to produce on the communities and soils from which he derives his food.

> (Appendix A Text 6)

Will an unskilled reader recognize how *and his activities* fits into the structure of the sentence?

To deal with ellipsis, the reader must:

(a) recognize that the information is incomplete;

(b) search the text and retrieve the required information.

The problem is that there is no signal to alert the reader. It is the *absence* of something that the reader is required to identify. This is of course harder than noticing the presence of a signal. If we look at some more examples, we can readily see why ellipsis may offer problems:

A   I carried the bag and my friend the suitcase.

B   We agreed that the patient should be taken to hospital and the house locked.

C   He told us where it was hidden and despite the disapproving glances of the others promised to show us the way.

D   She said that her informant had revealed the name but would say nothing more.

Items A and B display the curious syntax often found in elliptical expressions. What will a weak student make of sequences like 'my friend the suitcase' or 'the house locked'? Ask him who, in sentence C, promised to show us the way and the chances are he will reply 'The others'. Will he perceive that in sentence D it is not clear whether the informant or the woman refused to say anything more?

Of course common sense will often come to the rescue, but some students are too lacking in confidence to use it. Most writers are considerate enough to avoid the more extreme forms of elliptical expression, but from time to time it will present problems. So we have to make sure that our students are aware of it and know how to tackle it when they meet it.

7.4   Training Subskill 2

First of all, draw attention to the nature of ellipsis by presenting a series of sentences, similar to the examples above, in which ellipsis occurs. It is better to choose examples of the same pattern to begin with; for example, sentences where the omitted words are all verbs, or all the subjects of verbs. However, you will need to make sure that you give practice in the full range in due course: all parts of speech, single words and more complex expressions (as in B above, where we have to supply *we agreed that (the house) should be (locked)*.

Now direct students' attention to the elliptical nature of the sentences by framing questions that focus on the elided element:

e.g. sentence A: (1) How many things did the writer carry?
　　　　　　　　(2) Who carried the suitcase?
　　　　　B: (1) What exactly did we agree?

At a later stage, *supply* texts in which elliptical sentences occur and signal the ellipsis by means of carets:

I carried the bag and my friend ⋏ the suitcase.

The *task* is to write out the sentence in full (noting how clumsy most of the resulting sentences are; this should help students to see why ellipsis is used).

Later still, *supply* a suitable text and ask the students to locate the elliptical expressions and either expand them or prepare questions to draw attention to them. This is a more difficult exercise but a particularly useful one because the ability to identify ellipsis for themselves is a prerequisite skill for effective reading. It is suitable for group work.

You can also prepare an expanded version of a text in which ellipsis occurs. Ask the students to restore the original elisions, i.e. to rewrite the text omitting redundant expressions. This is of course a productive exercise rather than simply a reading exercise, and would not be suitable for all types of student; but if they are able to cope with it, it will help them to see the point of ellipsis and the way it works.

7.5   Subskill 3   Interpreting lexical cohesion

We are concerned here specifically with the problems that can be caused when a writer uses different words to refer to one and the same thing. Here are the main problems.

(a)   Interpreting synonyms

Writers often avoid repetition of the same word for stylistic reasons. Those who prefer 'elegant variation' will select a word that means almost the same as the word to be avoided; thus, in the same text, you might find *house, home, dwelling* and *residence* all used to refer to the same building. Clearly, if the reader fails to recognize that the words all relate to one single referent, he is going to have trouble understanding the text.

(b)   Interpreting superordinates

This particular kind of synonymous relationship was described on p. 78. Since the relationship between the two terms is not symmetrical (in the sense that, though a *house* is necessarily a *building*, a *building* is not necessarily a *house*), students often have more trouble with this than with symmetrical synonymy.

(c)   Interpreting metaphor

This too has been dealt with in Chapter 6, but not in relation to cohesion. The problem of interpreting metaphor is increased when a metaphorical term is used as a form of elegant variation: not only must the student understand the metaphor as such, but he must also recognize that it is being used to refer to the same object as other non-figurative terms. For example, you might have the metaphor *nest* used to refer to the same building as *house, home,* etc.

The problem in all these cases is the same: to recognize that two or more different expressions have the same referent. The expressions may occur in different sentences or different paragraphs, so the correct identification of one with the other is a skill required for understanding texts.

7.6   Training Subskill 3

The best way to train this skill is to draw attention to suitable examples when you meet them in texts. You may also wish to devise activities to help students recognize the nature of the problem and give practice in handling it. Here are some suggestions:

(a) Devise questions to help students realize that different terms can have the same referent.
E.g. from Appendix A Text 11:
Read the first four sentences of the text. Apart from the word *moth*, what other word is used to refer to the same creature? (***prey***)
From Appendix A Text 8:
Read paragraph three and find another word that refers to the same people as *sufferers* in line 4. (***victims***)
From Appendix A Text 9:
How many different words can you find in the text that refer to the beatings the older boys used? (***whip hit flog blow***)

(b) *Supply* a suitable text, preferably several paragraphs long.
Task: To circle, box or underline terms with the same referent, either joining them with coloured lines or giving them the same number. (This is a good activity to start on, especially if you can use an OHP.)

(c) *Supply* a suitable text and a diagram illustrating a lexical relationship found in it, only partially filled in.
Task: To complete the diagram.
E.g. from Appendix A Text 6:
Complete the diagram with terms A, B, C from the text:

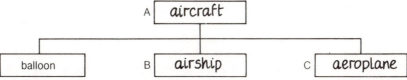

Only the word *balloon* will be supplied; the student has to search for the others. Naturally it will be necessary to do similar exercises in class first so that students become familiar with the conventions used in this kind of diagram.

8 TAS 3   Interpreting discourse markers

The kinds of cohesion dealt with in TAS 2 are all concerned with identifying what the writer is talking about: with signification. We now turn to the interpretation of other discourse markers which are not concerned with reference at all, but which signal the relationships between different parts of the discourse, and often indicate the functional value of the sentence in which they occur.

Most of these markers fall into the category labelled *conjunction* by Halliday and Hasan. (Their use of the word differs from its use in traditional grammar.)

However, we shall also include words that signal similar relationships within the sentence, whereas Halliday and Hasan deal only with relationships between sentences. From the point of view of the reader, they operate in similar ways.

As we noted earlier, these markers are not in themselves difficult to understand, though for a few of them exercises that draw attention to their meaning may be useful. But the main reason for studying them is not so much for their own sake as for their usefulness in helping the reader to work out the meaning of difficult sentences. These words are signals that tell you the kind of relationship the writer intends between two parts of his text: if you can understand one part, the discourse marker serves as a possible key to the other part. Frequently the marker explicitly signals the functional value of the sentence, which otherwise has to be inferred. We need to be aware exactly how these markers work so that we can use them to help elucidate difficult texts.

From the point of view of the reader, these relationships that the markers signal fall into three main classes:

A   Those which signal the sequence in which reported events occurred.
B   Those which signal the writer's manner of organizing his discourse.
C   Those which indicate the writer's view of the facts etc. about which he writes.

The groups are very dissimilar in function, even though the markers in each operate in similar ways; and some of the same words serve as markers in more than one group, according to the way they are to be interpreted.

Since my treatment differs slightly from that in Halliday and Hasan, I shall outline the main features of each group.

8.1   Group A markers: signals of sequence of events

E.g. *then, first, at once, next, the following day.*

This is the most straightforward group, and differs from the others in that these markers contribute to the signification of the text: they answer the question 'When?'. But they answer it not explicitly (e.g *on Monday*) but by reference to other events mentioned in the text. Hence the reader has to interpret the marker by establishing the time relationships between the events. To that extent, these markers are search signals, like the ones we have already discussed.

The use of markers like this is not of course the only way of indicating time sequence. In addition to the use of explicit time phrases such as *in 1981* and so on, time sequences can be signalled by lexical items like *precede, ensue*; by means of verb tenses; by means of subordinate time clauses; and by means of co-ordinate clauses or merely a sequence of unjoined sentences:

> The guests arrived. Then the sports took place.
> The arrival of the guests preceded the sports.
> The sports took place; the guests had arrived.
> The guests arrived before the sports took place.
> The guests arrived and the sports took place.
> The guests arrived. The sports took place.

The time sequence is the same in each case, but the focus of attention differs; the sentences are not quite synonymous.

8.2   Group B markers: signals of discourse organization

E.g. *in conclusion, that is to say, in this connection, for example, to resume, in short.*

These discourse markers serve a completely different function. They are not, like group A, part of the report (or other text content); they are outside it. They serve to inform the reader about what the writer is doing at the given point in the text, drawing his attention to the function of this sentence etc. in the overall pattern of the discourse.

These markers, then, indicate relationships between one part of the discourse and another: this is a repetition of that, *a* is an example of *b*, here is the next point to be made, now I will summarize my argument, etc. It is possible to group these markers according to the type of function performed:

Sequencing	*first of all, next, at this point, in conclusion,* etc.
Re-expressing	*that is to say, or rather, to put it another way, i.e.,* etc.
Specifying	*namely, that is to say, viz., to wit,* etc.
Referring	*in this respect, in that connection, concerning this, as we said, ignoring this, apart from this,* etc.
Resuming	*to resume, to return to the previous point, getting back to the argument,* etc.
Exemplifying	*to illustrate this, thus, for example, e.g.,* etc.
Summarizing	*to sum up, in short, to recapitulate,* etc.
Focusing	*let us consider, we must now turn to, in this chapter we shall, I shall begin by,* etc.

This list could be expanded or subdivided. But it serves to indicate the kind of functions these markers perform.

As in the case of group A, the writer may signal his text organization not only by using markers of this kind, but by using lexical items or sentences involving meta-statements (i.e. a statement *about* the discourse rather than part of the discourse). In fact it is hard to draw a line between them; the list above includes lexical items such as *conclusion, illustrate, ignore,* etc.; phrases like *to return to the previous point*, and the beginnings of sentences like *We must now turn to . . . .* Whether we choose to call these 'markers' is not so important for our purpose: what matters is that we should recognize that they are all performing similar functions.

Most of these markers do not occur in either of the other groups, with one major exception: as discourse itself is sequenced, it is not surprising that its sequence can be signalled by many of the same markers that we use to signal a sequence of events, i.e. those in group A. The difference is usually easy to see:

> First she plucked the chicken. (The first thing she did was . . .)
> First, let us consider the legal aspect. (The first thing this discourse will do is . . .)

8.3 Group C markers: signals of the writer's point of view

E.g. *moreover, incidentally, similarly, however, as a matter of fact, in any case, therefore, in order to, if, although.*

These markers are again quite distinct from the other two groups. They show us relationships perceived by the writer between the facts or ideas about which he is writing, e.g. the relation of cause and effect. But they also show us the relative importance that the writer attaches to each, and they show us other things about his attitude to them: whether he considers them unexpected (or feels that his reader will do so), whether he sees similarities between them, whether he takes them to be hypothetical or factual.

This group can also be subdivided. We follow Halliday and Hasan in the three main divisions, but not in the subdivisions:

Additive   These markers are used to introduce further facts or ideas that are seen by the writer as adding to or reinforcing those already dealt with.

The basic marker in this group is *and*. Others have more specific functions:

Adducing (and emphasizing) further evidence: *moreover, furthermore,* etc.

De-emphasizing a further point: *incidentally, in passing,* etc.

Comparing a further with a previous point: *likewise, similarly,* etc.

Adversative These markers introduce information that the writer sees as contrary to what is expected or hoped or to what has been said. The basic marker may be seen as *but*, though it does not cover the sense of all the subgroups:

Denying expectation: *yet, though, however, nevertheless,* etc.

Admitting the unexpected: *actually, as a matter of fact,* etc.

Correcting from expected to unexpected: *instead, on the contrary, rather,* etc.

Contrasting: *on the other hand, at the same time,* etc.

Dismissing: *in any case, anyhow, at all events, either way,* etc.

Causal   These markers indicate relationships of cause, effect, result, intention; and of condition. These relationships may be (a) between external facts or (b) between parts of the writer's argument; in the second case, the marker will be used in a meta-statement, for example:

(a) She felt extremely tired. For this reason, she did not leave her room.

(b) This matter is extremely complex. For this reason, we shall not go into it further at this point.

The group can be subdivided like this:

General: *so, hence, therefore, for, thus, consequently,* etc.
Reason: *for this reason, on account of this, it follows, because,* etc.
Result: *as a result, arising from this, so . . . that,* etc.
Purpose: *with this in mind, to this end, in order to, so that,* etc.
Condition: *in that case, that being so, in these circumstances, if, unless, otherwise,* etc.

8.4 Training TAS 3

As usual, the main purpose of training should be to create awareness of these markers and how they function. A limited amount of specific training may be useful, and some suggestions are given below. But more important is ongoing training using every opportunity you get when you are studying texts with the class.

Whenever there is a difficulty in a sentence containing one of these markers, make the students examine it to see if the marker will throw any light on the meaning of the obscure part. This should become accepted routine which with practice the students will be able to use on their own. To use the technique successfully involves understanding clearly how each marker operates, and this is the purpose of the exercises suggested below.

Although the three major groups of markers are so different from one another, similar methods can be used to help students to become familiar with the way they are used. Here are some basic ideas that can be adapted for use with any of the groups or subgroups.

(a) *Supply* a text with discourse markers omitted and replaced by gaps. In each gap put two or three markers (multiple choice style).

Task: To choose the alternative that suits the context.

Note: Like any other multiple choice work, this can be deadly if treated as a test. Use it for group discussion as described in Chapter 9 (p. 126) after first doing a similar exercise in class with the text on the OHP. Make sure that it is not treated as a purely mechanical exercise by showing the students how it forces them to think closely about the meaning of what they read so as to work out the relationships between the various parts of the text. Get them into the habit of discussing the differences in meaning produced by choosing different markers.

(b) *Supply* a text as above, but with the gaps left empty. Supply also a list of suitable markers in random order. (See Figure 19 for an interesting layout for this exercise.)

Task: To allocate markers to the correct gaps.

Note: A good variation of this for group work is to supply the markers not as a

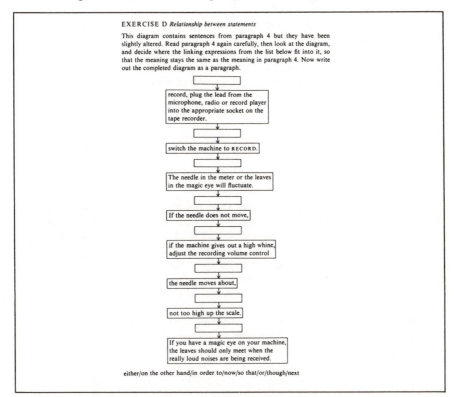

Fig. 19 Practising the use of discourse markers
(From *English in Focus: English in Education* by Elizabeth Laird)

list but written on cards, which are distributed to group members, so that each member may have two or three cards, each with one marker on it. The task should begin by everyone silently reading the text to see where his own markers will fit. Thereafter there will be group discussion until the best allocation is agreed. You can introduce this activity by working with a text on OHP, the marker-cards being distributed among the class.

(c) *Supply* a text as above, but do not list the omitted markers.

Task: To select suitable markers to fill the gaps.

Note: This is obviously a more advanced task and should not be tried until students have shown that they can cope with the simpler tasks described above.

(d) *Supply* a text in which the first few sentences are given in full, but after that a multiple choice text is given, consisting of the discourse markers with two alternative sentences between each one.

Task: To reconstruct the entire text by choosing the alternative that makes the best sense.

Note: This is also good for group work. The students should discuss the different meanings that arise if you choose one rather than the other alternative; they should also be brought to see that in many cases one will be ruled out by the context. The alternatives can be constructed to show that some can be ruled out completely when context and markers are considered together. In this way students should begin to see how helpful markers can be in understanding a difficult text.

(e) *Supply* a text similar to the above, but instead of giving alternative sentences, leave gaps between the markers so that after the first few sentences only a skeleton text remains, containing only the markers with gaps indicating the position of sentences or clauses. Supply also all the sentences/clauses of the text, without markers, each on a separate slip of paper.

Task: To reconstruct the text by deciding which sentences fill which gaps. This is intended to be used as group work.

Note 1

In all the exercises above, it is possible to restrict the type of marker being practised. Even elementary students should be able to deal with sequencing markers (group A) in some of these ways, provided the text is simple.

Note 2   *Instructional language: a warning*

Students being trained in the text-attack skills are often required to perform tasks that sound quite complicated if you try to describe them. Some of them actually are complicated; others are not, but are difficult to describe in simple language.

It is not helpful if the task itself offers more problems than the text it is supposed to illuminate. The students must at least be clear about exactly what they have to do. You may be able to solve the problem by demonstration; working through a similar task with the class is often the best way of making sure they know what to do.

Another solution is to give instructions in the L1 if you have a monolingual class; you may need to combine this with a demonstration if the task is complex.

If neither demonstration nor instructions in the L1 serve your purpose, have another look at the task. Is it really worth the effort? Can you achieve a similar purpose in a more straightforward way? It is better to reject the task than spend a great proportion of your class time explaining how to do it.

This warning applies even more forcibly to some of the tasks outlined in Chapter 8.

8 Text-Attack Skills (2): Discourse

1 Beyond text and into discourse

TAS 3 took us beyond the area of signification and into the area of intention, point of view, attitude, which the discourse markers signal. To interpret these, the reader has to recognize the functional value of the sentences in the text, and we saw that where discourse markers are used recognition is made easier.

But in many sentences there are no discourse markers to aid interpretation. In this chapter we shall be looking at the skills needed to recognize functional values, implications, presuppositions; in short to understand what the writer means but has not explicitly stated. We shall also deal with the skills needed to trace and interpret the way the writer organizes his utterances into a coherent sequence so that they convey the intended message.

In short, we are here concerned with discourse: the underlying patterns of meaning that are given expression through the medium of text. The meanings we are now most concerned with are contextual meaning and pragmatic meaning; and not only the meanings of individual utterances in a text, but also the way they combine with unstated but implied meanings to produce a coherent message.

The root of understanding discourse is understanding the functional value of the utterances that constitute it. The first skill we shall discuss is this one.

2 TAS 4 Recognizing functional value

The reader may not need to know exactly the signification of every sentence in the text in order to know its functional value, though obviously it helps. But as we saw earlier, we can sometimes recognize the value of an utterance from its context, even though we do not understand its sense clearly.

In any case, understanding the signification is not enough. We must also understand what the writer is doing with the utterance: we must recognize that he is defining something, making a hypothesis, giving an example, etc. Naturally the skilled reader does this unconsciously. It seems useful to make the unskilled reader aware of functional value so that he understands the possibilities of misinterpretation and can handle them.

He has to recognize value in two distinct circumstances:

(a) when this value is explicitly signalled by a discourse marker or other means: *therefore, however, for example*, etc.; or *I conclude . . ., Let us define it as . . ., It can be assumed that . . .*, etc.

(b) when there is no explicit signal and the value therefore has to be inferred. The reader has to work out for himself whether the writer intended the sentence to be a hypothesis, an example, etc.

2.1 Categories of functional value

It is perfectly possible to understand texts without understanding the terminology required to describe functional value and rhetorical organization. It is equally possible to understand the terminology without being able to interpret texts effectively. Nevertheless, if you want to be able to discuss these matters clearly and easily, your students will need to understand the necessary terms (e.g. *generalization, classification, prediction*). This is a nuisance, but unavoidable. You may be able to build on the student's knowledge of how his mother tongue works (in a monolingual class); otherwise you will have to teach the concept along with the term.

There is an immediate difficulty: no widely accepted taxonomy of functions is available. Different writers categorize them in different ways, though there is, not surprisingly, a measure of agreement. The trouble is that functions of different kinds tend to be lumped together, with consequent complexity or even confusion. We certainly cannot solve the problem here, but it may help to recognize three categories of function which are associated with three of the types of meaning we discussed (pp.80–81).

We can identify functions of at least three types, which we will describe in subsections A, B, C:

A   Independent functions. (These are associated with propositional meaning.)
B   Text-dependent functions. (These are associated with contextual meaning.)
C   Interaction-dependent functions. (These are associated with pragmatic meaning.)

The important thing to remember is that a single utterance will have all three kinds of meaning, and can therefore perform (at least) three separate functions at the same time. (As we shall see, it often seems that more than three functions are performed by one utterance.) This should become clearer later, when we look at some examples. First we shall look at some examples of each type of function in turn.

Type A   Independent functions

These examples show that in some cases functions can be identified even in sentences that are out of context; the form of the sentence and its signification are sufficient to signal the function it serves, independently of any context.

Defining	*A thermometer is an instrument that measures temperature.*
Classifying	*There are two types of acid: organic and inorganic.*
Generalizing	*Women live longer than men.*
Naming	*The ridge behind the teeth is known as the alveolar ridge.*
Describing	*The north of Iran is mountainous and well watered.*
Reporting	*Several experiments were carried out successfully.*
Speculating	*It is possible that people from Peru colonized Easter Island.*
Predicting	*If water is added to Dettol, the liquid will become cloudy.*

Of course this is not a complete list of functions of this type, and even these few examples show that there are problems: for example, what is the distinction between a report and a description? In the absence of any accepted list of functions, each investigator is free to decide his own categories and the way they are defined.

It must be pointed out that although some sentences may be identified from their form as, for example, definitions, this does not mean that all definitions must have this form. On the contrary, we commonly find that sentences of varying form may perform similar functions. Certain types of sentence may, in specific types of text, be typically associated with certain functions, but even within the same text we cannot expect to find regular correlations between sentence pattern and functional value. It is important for students to understand this and concentrate on the work the sentence is doing, not on its structure.

Type B   Text-dependent functions
These can be defined only in terms of the relationships between sentences of the same text. They depend on the place of the utterance in its context.

In these examples, the right-hand column contains the sentences of a continuous text, in the correct sequence. Otherwise we should not be able to interpret them in terms of the labels in the left hand column. You can only see sentence 3 as an explanation, for instance, because it follows sentence 2. There is nothing in the form of sentence 6 to indicate that it functions as a hypothesis here; and so on. It is true that the example and the explication contain markers that tell us their value: but it is also true that you cannot have either unless you have had something to exemplify or explicate first.

Asserting	*There is great danger to wild life in the pollution of water.*
Exemplifying	*A good illustration of this is the oil released from tankers at sea.*
Explaining	*It kills all kinds of sea animals, including fish, plankton and other forms of marine life.*
Reinforcing	*Birds are also frequent victims, for they become oiled.*
Explicating	*That is to say, their feathers become covered with oil and they are unable to fly.*
Hypothesising	*Certain tankers are believed to regularly flout the regulations governing the discharge of oil at sea.*
Commenting	*If this could be proved, we should be in a better position to take action.*
Concluding	*As it is, the authorities are almost powerless and the slaughter continues unchecked.*

Type C   Interaction-dependent functions
This is the most controversial category, but I think it is worth trying to distinguish it from the others.

When a writer defines or gives examples or comments (i.e. uses functions of types A or B), he hopes his words will be read and he makes various assumptions about his readers. Sometimes these are explicit, as for example when he directly addresses the reader and shows that he expects a reaction. The writer expects the reader to feel, think or act as a result of having read; that is, what he writes has pragmatic meaning, and this is what concerns us here.

Unlike types A and B, these functions can only be interpreted if we assume that some kind of relationship exists between the writer and the reader. They reflect the aspect of language that Halliday calls interpersonal.

Inviting	*Let us now consider some methods of classifying metals.*
Instructing	*Calculate the difference before proceeding to the next stage.*
Apologizing	*Unfortunately, I cannot at present offer any explanation for this.*
Suggesting	*If time permits, we could consider making the journey by boat.*
Complaining	*The authorities refused to issue the necessary permit, so we were obliged to cancel the show.*
Complimenting	*You will, of course, easily follow the reasons for this.*
Warning	(Example discussed below, p.104–5)

It will be apparent that these lists are incomplete and in other ways imperfect. But perhaps they point the way in which a helpful classification may eventually be worked out. They are useful not as inventories (which they are not), but as examples of the kinds of functions to be recognized and interpreted when we read.

2.2   The multifunctional utterance

It is important to reiterate that any utterance has a value from each of these three categories simultaneously; and may in fact have more than one value from each, since they are not necessarily mutually exclusive. Some examples will make this clear. The first comes from an account of a detective searching for a missing car. He is thinking about where it might be hidden.

> 1 It is very difficult indeed to hide a car at all efficiently in the country.   2 The number of disused quarries, flooded gravel pits, deep pools in rivers, etc., is strictly limited.   3 You have to know about them, meaning you must know the countryside really well, and you will almost always leave tracks.   4 It is much easier to hide a leaf in a forest.   5 In the city.   6 It won't stay hidden very long, but long enough for you to vanish.
>
> (N. Freeling, *The Night Lords* (Heinemann, 1978))

The whole of this short text repays study, but we will look particularly at sentence 4. This appears to be a generalization: the present tense verb and the use of the indefinite article (*a leaf*) suggest this. It is also a comparison, as the word *easier* shows. But what is the force of it? What is easier than what? Why is the writer talking about leaves in a forest? What is the connection between this and the elliptical sentence 5?

To interpret this sentence, we have to be able to think along with the writer (or the detective) until we can reconstruct his chain of reasoning, which seems to be along these lines:

> It is much easier to hide a leaf in a forest than in a place without trees; that is, it is easier to hide something in a place where it is not noticeable, where there are many others of the same kind. So if you want to hide a car, the best place to choose would be the city.

If this reconstruction is correct, sentence 4 is seen to be a metaphor, a generalization, a comparison, an inference (drawn from the detective's reasoning about what the criminal will probably do), a speculation (about what the criminal is likely to do), a hypothesis. And it leads to a more specific hypothesis in sentence 5, upon which the detective in the book then proceeds to act.

Which of these are we to call the value of the sentence? The fact is that it serves a number of different functions at the same time, according to your focus or to the level of analysis you are using. It may be necessary to recognize all of them in order to make coherent sense of the text; this certainly seems to be the case in the example just discussed. It is true that the laconic style of the example makes for difficulty: but similar difficulty can be discovered in many texts. The extreme instances occur typically in poetry.

There is nothing unusual about this; it is not a symptom of poor writing. But it does mean that we cannot always expect a simple answer to the question 'What is the functional value of this utterance?' Another example may make this clearer; it comes from an account of the loss of privacy that results from the widespread use of computers, especially their use by bureaucracy and the consequent availability to many different departments of a wide range of information about an individual.

> In the past, the power of the bureaucracy was in effect limited by the enormous problem of processing enough information about a given subject, and then acting on it in relation to certain policy goals. In the near future, however, this inefficiency will be markedly diminished.
>
> (M. Warner and M. Stone, *The Data Bank Society*, (Allen and Unwin, 1970) slightly adapted.)

In this extract, it is the last sentence that is interesting. It is an *assertion*, and since it refers to the future, it is a *prediction*. The use of the marker *however* shows that we are to interpret it as in some way counter to the previous sentence, and this sentence seems to be referring to a problem. So the last sentence seems to suggest that a solution is predicted (diminished inefficiency = increased efficiency = solution of problem).

So far so good. But of course the reader who gets no further than this will have missed the message. Since inefficiency is usually an undesirable characteristic, it is tempting to view the last sentence as an *auspicious forecast*, a *hope* or even a *promise*. But if the context has been correctly understood, it is clear that the opposite is the case. Inefficiency in the past has operated to protect the individual; now this protection is to be removed. The prediction is thus seen to be a *warning*, and anyone who does not realize this will not be able to make sense of the text at this point.

2.3 Training TAS 4

Naturally the kinds of function in group A, which are to some extent identifiable from the form of the sentence, are worth practising on their own. But even here it will be important to make students realize that there is no single way of expressing any of these functions; you might get a definition a whole paragraph long. So specific exercises based on individual sentences are of only limited use.

The most useful work is to go through continuous texts and see how the functional value of the utterances is determined by their relationship with one another. Since this approach is not likely to be familiar to students, it will need to be done in class to begin with, with the text on the OHP if possible. You may find it helpful to prepare the text so that each sentence begins on a new line, like the examples in B above; this will give you room to write labels or comments in the margin.

To begin with, choose short texts that are simple in pattern. They could be texts involving classification, description of a sequence of actions or of steps in a process, descriptions of the characteristics and functions of an object, and so on. School textbooks in various fields are good sources of texts of these kinds.

Here are some suggestions for activities that can be used in the early stages of training, when the basic terms and concepts are being learnt. As always, the best approach (once these concepts are understood) is to discuss interesting examples when you come across them in a text you are studying.

(a) *Supply* a simple text. Supply also a set of alternative function labels for each sentence, or for key sentences. For example:
Sentence 1 is (a) an assertion (b) a hypothesis (c) a classification.
Task: To choose the appropriate alternative. With more advanced students, you could give more than one appropriate one, to convey the multi-valued nature of a single sentence.

(b) *Supply* a suitable text. Supply also alternative descriptions of it in terms of functions, or alternative text diagrams setting out its functional structure, as shown in Figure 20 which relates to paragraph 2 of Appendix A Text 5, *Airships*.
Task: To choose the description or diagram that best reveals the pattern of functions in the text.

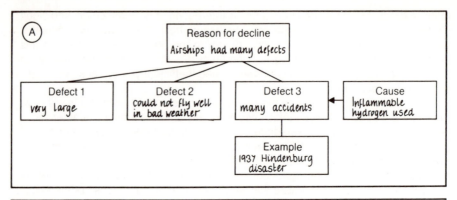

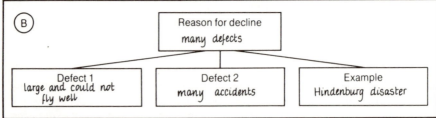

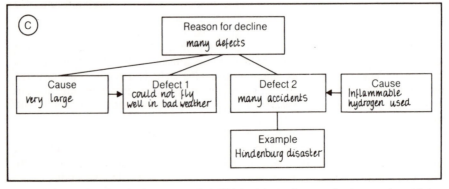

Read Appendix A Text 5, *Airships*, paragraph 2. Which of these diagrams fits the meaning of the paragraph best?

Fig. 20   Alternative text diagrams

(c) *Supply* a skeletal functional description of a short text a few sentences long. Supply also the sentences of the full text, in random order. You may need to make small changes: see note below.
 Task: To arrange the sentences in accordance with the description so that they make a coherent text in which each utterance has the intended function. E.g:

> Arrange the sentences below so that they make a text with this structure:
> ***assertion – example – explanation***
> Make minor changes (e.g. pronouns replace nouns) needed to produce a coherent text. Use *for instance* in your example and *thus* in your explanation.

Sentences:

    Foxes will collect seagull eggs during the nesting season and bury them in scattered places.

    Foxes often conceal the food items they obtain.

    Seagull eggs can be eaten at times when food supplies are scarce.

Answer:

    Foxes often conceal the food items they obtain. For instance, they will collect seagull eggs during the nesting season and bury them in scattered places. These can thus be eaten at times when food supplies are scarce.

(d) This is a variation of Exercise (c).

Supply a skeletal description of a text. Supply also all the sentences of the text, each written on a strip of paper.

Task: Students in groups have to arrange the strips so that they produce a text of the required structure.

Note: This is suitable for slightly longer texts than Exercise (c). In this exercise you supply the actual sentences of the text, whereas in Exercise (c) the sentences have been slightly modified -- nouns instead of pronouns, markers removed and so on. If this were not done in Exercise (c) the form of the sentences would make the exercise too easy, for the students would not need to think much about the work the sentences are doing, which is the whole object of this training.

3 TAS 5 Tracing and interpreting rhetorical organization

3.1 Rhetorical structure

In the previous section we were considering the functional value of utterances in a text; we recognized that in most cases it is impossible to say what value a sentence has until you see it in use in a context. Now we must look at the context itself. It consists, of course, of other utterances, each with its own value; each utterance takes its value from the others and in turn helps to give value to them.

This complex network of relationships within a text is its rhetorical structure. It is the structure of the underlying ideas, and the connections the writer makes between them. Its elements are the rhetorical acts that the sentences perform: not the words and grammar of the sentences but the way each is used, its functional value.

To understand what is meant by rhetorical structure more clearly, we need to think first about the *topic* of the text, the writer's *purpose* in writing it, and the *audience* he had in mind.

If we ask what the topic is, we shall expect answers like 'Cancer research' or 'The threat to privacy created by computers'.

If we ask about the writer's intention, we may be told 'He's telling a story' or 'He's giving us some information' or 'He's explaining his views and trying to convince us that they are correct'.

If we ask about the intended audience, we shall learn that the text is aimed at schoolchildren, perhaps, or intelligent laymen, or academics, and so on.

Taken together, the topic, purpose and intended audience give us a good idea what sort of text we are dealing with and what sort of rhetorical structure to expect. You would not expect a children's story to have the same sort of structure as a university physics textbook.

Once you know the answers to these questions, you can go on to ask 'How does the writer approach his objective?' And answering this question involves tracing the rhetorical development of the text.

3.2   Content and organization

When he begins to write his text, the writer has in his mind a certain body of facts, or a story, or an argument, etc., which he wants to communicate to the reader. He has to decide where to start, what sequence to follow, which aspects to emphasize and so on. He knows what he wants to say; now he has to choose the best way of saying it. The choices he makes are the choices of rhetorical organization.

So tracing the rhetorical development means perceiving how, given his raw material, the writer has selected from it, organized and shaped it and given it coherence, until it suits his purpose and becomes the text we read.

Although the reader does not consciously think about rhetorical organization in normal circumstances, it is desirable to be able to trace it if necessary. If you are reading an involved and difficult text, you may be obliged to study the development carefully in order to find out how its ideas hang together. If you cannot do this, the text may seem like a jigsaw puzzle in which the parts can be identified but the way they fit together is obscure.

3.3   Organization within the sentence

Selection, weighting and arrangement takes place at every level from the sentence to the whole book. We saw on page 96 how the relationship between two events (the guests arriving, the sports taking place) can be expressed in a number of different ways. All of them relate to the same facts, but the emphasis and the point being made differs in each.

Consider these two sentences:

(a) The sports followed the arrival of the guests.
(b) The arrival of the guests preceded the sports.

And now these two continuations:

(c) Now, he felt, his weeks of strict diet and patient practice would be rewarded. He would win, he must win!
(d) Now at last he would see her. Surely she had come? He searched anxiously among the crowds, but she was nowhere to be found.

It is not difficult to decide which continuation is likely to follow which of sentences (a) and (b). This is because, although the facts in (a) and (b) are identical, the way the information is presented is not. In (a), the topic of the sentence is the sports, and we expect the writer to go on to tell us more about them. Hence (c) is a suitable continuation. But in (b), the topic is the arrival of the guests, and we therefore expect to hear more about them, as in (d).

The way the sentences are organized thus influences the progression of the reader's thoughts. A good writer structures his sentences in such a way that the information in one is so presented that its connection with the previous sentence and the one that follows is made clear. He can also show us, by the way he organizes the information, what his attitude to it is. Consider these two statements:

Mary is kind.   Mary is not pretty.

We can join these two contrasting sentences with *although* in two ways:

Although Mary is kind, she is not pretty.
Although Mary is not pretty, she is kind.

Which of these would be written by a friend of Mary's? Why?

Or consider:

I asked him to stand up. He stood up.

Which of these versions indicates disapproval?

He stood up when I asked him to.
He did not stand up until I asked him to.

3.4   Organizing sequences of sentences

Sequences of sentences are generally organized into paragraphs. Sometimes the paragraph is more a way of breaking up a long text visually than a way of organizing information; but usually there is some unity of thought and often (but not always) this is given focus in a topic sentence.

Recognizing the organization of a paragraph means being able to identify the topic, the main point, the minor or supporting points and so on. It means recognizing that, for example, the first sentence makes an assertion, the second and third substantiate it with examples, the fourth modifies it by a reservation, and so on.

Clearly this builds on other skills, particularly TAS 4: in fact the two are interdependent. You need to identify the functional value of each sentence in order to plot the structure of the paragraph. Equally you need to comprehend the paragraph structure in order to assign the value of each sentence.

In addition to this, it is often possible to see some overall principle of organization in a paragraph. It may be organized according to the sequence of events described, or according to a logical progression from general to specific, or from specific to general. Or the structure may be problem – solution; evidence – hypothesis; classification – examples; cause – result; and so on.

Different types of paragraph organization will be found in different types of text. For example, assertion – substantiation (examples, explication, etc.) is a common pattern in textbooks. (Almost all the paragraphs in Appendix A Text 6, *Ecology*, are of this pattern.) For students, it is useful to learn how to handle the paragraph structures that occur most often in their textbooks.

3.5   Organization above paragraph level

The structure of a text is almost always hierarchical: the largest unit is the whole text, which is composed of sections. Each section is separate from the others and has some kind of internal structure and cohesiveness; the chapters of a book, for example. These in turn may be seen as composed of smaller units and so on, down to the level of the clause and even the word.

The hierarchy may be differently structured in different types of text. Looking at a text as a whole, it may be helpful for the reader to find out what principle is used to organize it: is it structured chronologically? Does it begin by outlining a problem, then offer a hypothesis, experiments to test it and finally sum up the findings and what they imply? And so on.

Understanding the structure of the whole text may contribute to an understanding of individual parts of it, just as understanding what a paragraph says is sometimes useful in understanding one of its sentences. But more importantly, tracing the structure of the text will usually result in a clearer understanding of its overall message.

For practical reasons, it is often difficult to deal with organization above the level of a chapter or journal article, because there is seldom time to deal with longer texts in the language class. If your students are using the FL as a study language, it would be worth examining the organization of some longer texts by looking at chapter headings and skimming the contents. Knowing how the text is organized enables a student to read it more selectively if he wishes, and to locate the information he needs for a specific purpose.

3.6   Training TAS 5

Organization of paragraphs into texts
To make students aware of the significance of rhetorical organization, it is probably easier to begin with the organization of paragraphs into texts (rather than organization within the paragraph, which we will discuss later).

Most of the suggested activities below are excellent for group work. Different groups can work with different materials and then exchange with one another. This cuts down the quantity of material to be prepared, though not the number and variety of exercises required.

(a) *Supply* a text several paragraphs long, with one paragraph omitted.
Supply the omitted paragraph separately.
Task: To decide where in the text the omitted paragraph fits.
Note: This can be made easy or difficult by choosing a text with a very clear sequence or one with a looser structure.

(b) *Supply* a text several paragraphs long with the opening or concluding paragraph omitted. Supply separately several possible opening or concluding paragraphs, including the original one.
Task: To decide which paragraph best fits the text.
Note: This entails working out what the purpose of the text is, in the case of the opening paragraph; and what conclusion it reaches, in the case of the concluding one.

   If you choose paragraphs that are different in style, the exercise will be easier, but for the wrong reasons: the idea is to get students to trace the sequence of thought.

(c) *Supply* a text several paragraphs long with the key (topic) sentence of each paragraph omitted and replaced by a gap. Supply separately a set of sentences including the omitted topic sentences (together with others as distractors for advanced students).
Task: To decide which sentence fits into which paragraph.
Note: The topic sentences, if they were arranged in the correct sequence, should provide a skeletal summary of the text organization. So to concentrate on them should make the student aware of the organization.

(d) *Supply* a text, several paragraphs long, with one paragraph in the wrong place (e.g. original paragraph 2 is moved to a later position in the text, or original paragraph 9 is placed earlier).
Task: To decide (i) which paragraph is out of place and (ii) where it ought to be.

(e) *Supply* a text, several paragraphs long, with the paragraphs arranged in random order. This can also be done by cutting up the text so that each paragraph is on a separate piece of paper or card: this method is more fun to use and is particularly suitable for group work. Keep each set of paragraphs in a labelled envelope.

Task: To arrange the paragraphs to make a coherent text.

Note: If you number the paragraphs (in random order of course), you can prepare an answer sheet giving the correct sequence of numbers. Alternatively you can supply the full original text, as for all these exercises.

(f) This is a variation of (c) and (e) combined.

Supply (i) the paragraphs of a text, arranged in random order, with the topic sentences removed and replaced by gaps; (ii) the topic sentences, arranged in the correct sequence, to provide a skeletal summary of the text.

Task: To match the paragraphs with the topic sentences and produce a coherent text.

Organization of sentences into paragraphs

Similar exercises can be done to practise the organization of sentences within a paragraph. This is likely to be more difficult than working at paragraph level, although clues to sentence sequence are supplied by discourse markers, reference system etc. Exercises give useful practice in using signals of this kind, as well as in thinking about the logical sequence of the sentences and so on.

(g) *Supply* a paragraph with the key sentence omitted and replaced by a gap. Supply separately a number of possible key sentences.

Task: To choose the correct key sentence.

(h) *Supply* a paragraph with one sentence omitted (but not indicated by a gap). Supply separately the omitted sentence.

Task: To decide where in the text the omitted sentence should fit.

(i) *Supply* a paragraph with one sentence out of place (cf. (d) above).

Task: To decide (i) which sentence is out of place, (ii) where it should be.

(j) *Supply* a paragraph with one sentence omitted. Supply separately the omitted sentence, plus several others.

Task: To decide (i) where a sentence has been omitted, (ii) which of the separate sentences is the omitted one.

Note: In (h), (i) and (j), by choosing carefully the sentence you omit, you can make the student focus on different aspects of rhetorical structure. Choose sentences where the structural sequence is very clear, otherwise unprofitable discussion can result.

(k) *Supply* a paragraph in which all the sentences are scrambled (i.e. arranged in random order). The most interesting way to do this is to type each sentence beginning on a new line, and then cut the paper into strips bearing one sentence each. Keep the sentences in a labelled envelope indicating how many there should be inside, as they are easily lost.

Task: To assemble the sentences into a coherent paragraph. See notes on (e) above.

(l) *Supply* two or three paragraphs, taken from different texts, prepared as in (k). The sentences, on strips of paper, are all scrambled together.

Task: To assemble the sentences into two or three unrelated coherent paragraphs.

Note: The first time you use this task, number the sentences of each paragraph in the correct sequence. The students will thus have three sentences numbered 1; they must then choose which sentence 2 goes with which number 1, and so on. The more similar the texts in style and content, the more challenging the exercise will be.

Text Diagrams

A text diagram is intended to display visually the structure of the text. It can be designed to show various aspects:

chronological or process sequence
levels of generality
main point/minor point/example etc.
cause and effect
classification
relationship of ideas

Figure 20 (p.106) is an example of a text diagram showing the relationship of ideas. Figure 21 (below) is an example of a diagram that shows sequence of stages in a process; it relates to the text in Figure 10, p.57.

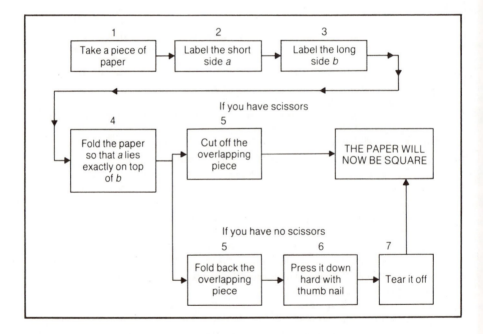

Fig. 21   Sequence diagram relating to *Making a paper square* (see p. 57)

Figure 22 (p.113) is a cause – effect diagram relating to Appendix A Text 11, (*Survival of the Fittest*). The downward pointing arrow means 'causes' or 'results in'. If you compare the diagram with the text itself, you will see that it forces the students to make explicit several relationships that are merely implied by the text, and to relate ideas that are scattered. (This assumes that the student will be asked to supply those words that appear in manuscript on the diagram.) It also enables the teacher to make such ideas explicit if this seems helpful.

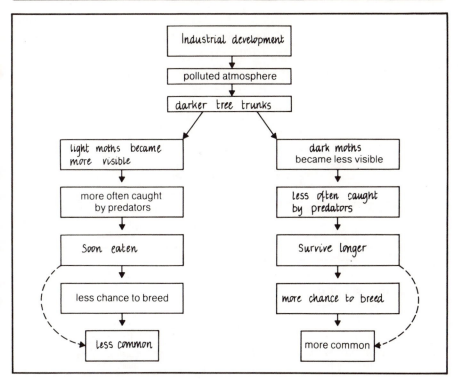

Fig. 22   Why dark moths are more common in industrial areas:
cause and effect diagram relating to Appendix A Text II: *Survival of the fittest*

A number of text diagrams will be found among the exercises in Appendix B:

Classification diagrams:	Text B3 (*Acids*) p. 211
	Text B6 (*Pollution*) p.219
Chronological diagram (table):	Text B1 (*Airships*) p. 204
Levels of generality:	Text B2 (*Ecology*) p. 205
Summary of main ideas (table)	Text B1 (*Airships*) p. 204
Organizing information:	Text B4 (*Malnutrition*) p. 213

It is your decision what to write in the text diagrams you prepare for your class. You can make a diagram relatively easy to complete by filling in most of the boxes yourself, leaving just a few for the student to do. If you want to draw attention to the way the ideas are related, you can give suitable labels to the boxes. Figure 23 (p.114) is a text diagram of this kind, displaying the structure of the first paragraph of Appendix A Text 3 (*Red Flag Canal*) p.196. (Again, the manuscript portions might be supplied by the students.) In diagrams displaying classification, cause – effect, sequence, it is not usually necessary to use descriptive labels, but in those that attempt to trace the argument (as in Figure 23) it is often unavoidable.

A few words of caution

(a) A text diagram made by the teacher imposes the teacher's view of the text.
    Obviously this is the justification for using diagrams, and it can be helpful. (It is also a feature of most teaching.) But having to put the text into diagram form forces decisions and can thus obscure valid differences over interpretation of

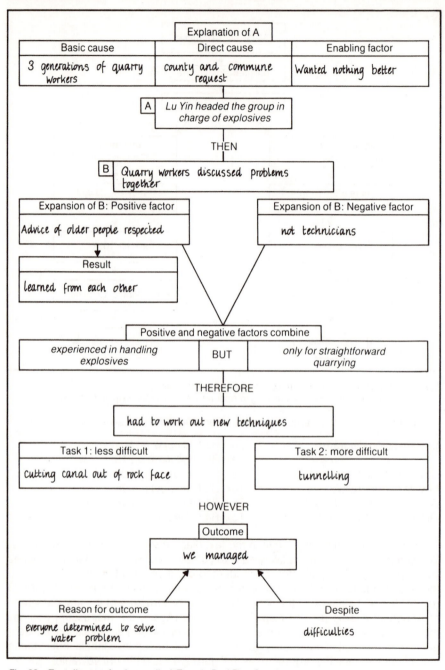

Fig. 23   Text diagram for Appendix A Text 4: *Red Flag Canal*

ambiguous or otherwise doubtful parts. Advanced students can discuss these, but others may be confused.

(b) In the effort to represent the text visually, a structure may be imposed that is not entirely present in the text.

In this case, the diagram may lead to distortion rather than interpretation.

(c) Labelling boxes (e.g. 'positive expansion of B' as in Figure 23) involves the use of abstract terminology that may cause more problems than it solves. But this seems impossible to avoid in studying textual organization by whatever means, as we noted earlier.

(d) It is sometimes difficult to get the student to understand what you mean by your diagram.

Sometimes it is harder to understand a text diagram than to understand the text itself. (You can help the student to understand what you have in mind by filling in for him the boxes that give the key to your perception of the text.) If the task is so dominating that it seems more important than the text, it should be changed or scrapped. Familiarize yourself with the problem by trying some of the diagrams in the textbooks listed in the Preface.

Despite these cautions, text diagrams used sensibly provide a helpful way of looking at text organization. Students usually find them interesting to work on, and able students will enjoy discussing alternative possibilities. All the same, the point of using a diagram is to illuminate the text; if it falsifies or obscures it, it is better to abandon the diagram and seek another approach.

Using text diagrams

Text diagrams can relate to a single sentence (e.g. a classification diagram), a paragraph or a longer text. Some kinds of text lend themselves to diagrammatic representation; for others, there are better ways of approach.

Once they have learned the possibilities, advanced students can be asked to construct text diagrams themselves. This is best done in groups and produces useful discussion focused strongly on the text. There is of course no right and wrong way of representing any text; only ways that are more justifiable than others, or perhaps are equally justifiable.

Work on text diagrams can be varied in these ways:

(a) In whether or not metalinguistic labels are used: (see (c) under *A few words of caution* above).

(b) In the number of boxes that are completed for the student and hence the number he has to fill in himself.

(c) In whether the labels or the contents of the boxes are supplied (in random order) or whether he has to word them himself.

(d) If they are supplied, in whether the student simply has to write the number/ letter of the correct sentence/phrase in the box, or whether the actual words have to be entered.

(If the number/letter is used, the diagram can be much smaller but the text structure is more readily seen when words are used.)

(e) Boxes can be labelled with alternatives from which the student has to choose.

> Hallucinogens defined/classified.

> Purposes/effects of hallucinogens described.

> Explanation of/example of previous point.   etc.

(f) Two (or more) alternative text diagrams may be offered, from which the student must choose the one that best represents the text. (Figure 20 on p. 106 is an example.)

(g) Text diagrams can be used as the basis for written work. While this is not a reading skill, it will add to students' understanding of text structure. For such an exercise, supply a completed text diagram; the task is to recreate the text it represents. This is more successful if the students first study the text diagram of a text with similar structure.

4   TAS 6 Recognizing the presuppositions underlying the text

4.1   Presupposition and rhetorical structure

As you trace the rhetorical development of a text, following the writer's train of thought from one utterance to another, you may find that sometimes you cannot see the connection between two utterances. When this occurs, it is likely that either the writer is expecting you to draw inferences (from other things he has said) to bridge the gap, or he is making mistaken assumptions about your knowledge, or your point of view, in the way described in Chapter 1 where we first spoke about presupposition. We shall deal with inference in TAS 7; here we shall concentrate on presupposition, though the two are very closely related, as we shall see.

Presupposition pervades everything people say or write, but we are aware of it only when our failure to understand forces us to realize that we do not share the writer's presuppositions, because we do not understand him. A housing agent's description of 'a fine bungalow in the Spanish style' is meaningless to a reader who would not know the Spanish style from the Norwegian. There is a well-worn joke to the effect that a camel is 'a horse designed by a committee', which cannot seem very amusing unless you share the view that committee decisions are generally clumsy compromises which try to incorporate bits of everyone's ideas and end up being criticized by all. (This is very unfair to the camel.)

The presuppositions that concern us may be roughly divided into two groups:

(a) the knowledge and experience that the writer expects the reader to have;

(b) the opinions, attitudes, emotions that the writer expects the reader to share, or at least to understand.

In the examples we gave in Chapter 1 (pp.7–8), most of the presuppositions are in the first group, relating to the knowledge the reader is expected to have. But the second example also expects the reader to share the writer's view of Walt Disney, or at least to understand it; while in example (e) (about the puppy), it is the point of view or emotion that must be shared, not knowledge at all.

You cannot tackle a problem effectively if you are not clearly aware of it, and we are often not aware of things that are not expressed. It is easier to overlook unstated assumptions than to ignore the presence of a difficult word or structure. So we need to make students aware of the existence of presupposition and of the problems that arise when the writer's assumptions do not coincide with those of the reader.

Very often, even if we do not share the writer's views or knowledge, we can infer what they are if we read the text carefully. An example of this occurs in the text we cited earlier, on p. 104. The writers assume that the reader will share their view that inefficiency is a desirable characteristic in this context, despite the paradox; and the reader has really no excuse for failing to understand the assumptions made, since the text has made very clear the reasons for this view.

In such cases, clear thinking and the proper use of inference will lead the reader to form the correct interpretation even if he himself does not share the writer's views. So presupposition is very much bound up with inference, the skill we shall describe next, and it is convenient to deal with them together for practice. However, it must not be forgotten that not all presuppositions can easily be inferred from the context, and there are sometimes real problems here, which you and your students should be on your guard against.

5 TAS 7 Recognizing implications and making inferences

We have just seen that presuppositions which are not immediately clear to the reader can often be reconstructed by making intelligent use of the clues the text supplies, and by drawing the necessary inferences. So TAS 6 and TAS 7 are not completely distinct.

We can think of the relationship between them in these terms: inference must be used by the reader in these circumstances:

(a) When the writer makes *assumptions* which the reader is expected to share or at least understand in order to make sense of the text. In this case, as just described in TAS 6, the reader may be able to establish these assumptions by the use of inference.
(b) When the writer is presenting facts or points in an argument, etc., from which he expects the reader to draw certain unstated *conclusions*. In this case, the reader has all the evidence required, but he is expected to take the final steps himself.

There is perhaps no very clear division between these categories in practice, even though the writer's expectations may be different in each case.

Because the art of inference requires the reader to use his intelligence, it is often considered an advanced skill and it tends to be neglected in comprehension courses. This is a pity, because it is very easy to improve this skill by training.

As an example of the way a text can require the reader to infer, we can look again at the text on p. 104 about the detective looking for a car. If we take only the main line of the detective's reasoning, the logical steps of his argument are something like this:

1 It is difficult to hide a car in the country. (We will omit the reasons for this assertion, although they too involve inference.)
2 Therefore it would not be sensible to hide one there.
3 Therefore it is likely to be hidden somewhere else.
4 Where could that be? We need to consider what would make a good hiding place.
5 A good hiding place might be one where it is easy to hide something.
6 It is easier to hide something in a place where it will not be noticed.
7 If there are a lot of things of the same kind in a place, you don't notice any particular one.
8 Therefore such a place is a good hiding place.
9 If you are hiding a car, you might choose a place where there are a lot of other cars, for that reason.
10 Where do you find a lot of cars?
11 In the city.
12 Therefore the city would be a good hiding place for a car.

Of all these steps, only 1, 6 and 11 are expressed in the text; and 6 is expressed figuratively. The others must be inferred, and unless they are, the reader will find the text at this point incomprehensible.

This skill and the previous one are closely connected with TAS 4: the presuppositions the writer makes and the inferences he expects the reader to draw will affect the reader's interpretation of the value of an utterance. For instance, if you have not followed the inferred reasoning of the text just examined, how will you interpret the sentence 'In the city'? How will you recognize it as a hypothesis which the detective is putting forward as a suggestion to himself, and which he will now go on to test?

Inference is a tricky skill, because often it is not clear how much the writer expects you to infer; but you cannot refuse to infer just because you may make mistakes, because inference is essential in making sense of much that we read, from complex argument like the text we have just studied to single sentences like:

> The second of these statements is demonstrably untrue.

Are we to infer from this that the first statement is true? Or just that the writer cannot disprove it? And what about:

> The treatment was later withdrawn. The next day the patient died.

Are we supposed to infer that the death was caused by the withdrawal of treatment? This would certainly be an intended inference in many cases, but perhaps not in all.

Problems of this kind arise continually and can only be solved by caution and common sense, and of course by taking the whole context into consideration. The best way of practising the skill of inferring is to make sure that inferences are spelt out in class whenever they are necessary to an understanding of a text. Similarly, the underlying presuppositions of the text should be identified wherever you feel that the students may fail to recognize or share them.

Some specific training of these two skills may be useful; since they are so closely related, and can be trained by similar means, we will consider them together.

6   Training TAS 6 and TAS 7

(a) *Supply* sentences such as those in Chapter 1 (p.7–8), introduced by this rubric:

> Read the sentence (text) and then read the facts stated below.
> Tick the fact if you think it is true that you have to know the fact to understand the sentence (text).

Example:

The pintailed pigeon is not unlike the orange breasted pigeon, though slightly larger. Coloration is similar, though in the pintailed the green of the back extends to the head and the orange breast band is absent. The slender tail is considerably longer.

> (a) The orange breasted pigeon is mostly green. √
> (b) The orange breasted pigeon has a grey head.
> (c) The orange breasted pigeon measures 29 cm. √
> (d) The orange breasted has an orange breast band.
> (e) The tail of the orange breasted measures about 10 cm. √
>
> etc.

(b) *Supply* sentences or very short texts in which certain facts are implicit, introduced by this rubric:

Read the text and then read the facts stated below. Tick all the facts that you think are implied by the text.

Example:

One of the Archaeopteryx specimens was at first wrongly catalogued as a small pterodactyl, because its feathers were very difficult to discern. This shows how even the experts considered it a reptile.

This implies that:
   (i) Archaeopteryx is a reptile.
   (ii) Pterodactyls do not have feathers. √
   (iii) Pterodactyls are reptiles. √
   (iv) Pterodactyls are large compared with Archaeopteryx. √
   (v) Archaeopteryx has feathers. √

(c) *Supply* a longer text, followed by a set of statements and a rubric similar to the rubric in (b). Practice with a longer text is needed because some inferences can only be made by putting together facts taken from various parts of the text.

Example: Appendix A Text 2

Read the text and then read the facts stated below. Say which facts can be inferred from the text.

   (i) Rahman had three children.   (*Yes*)
   (ii) Yusof was three years old.   (*Yes*)
   (iii) Yusof was playing in the kitchen.   (*No*)
   (iv) Rahman's wife was frying something.   (*Probably – not sure*)
   (v) Rahman was a clerk.   (*No*)
   (vi) Yusof had a brother and sister.   (*No – sex not indicated*)
   (vii) Rahman's house was not isolated.   (*Yes*)
   (viii) The neighbour was a nurse.   (*No*)
   (ix) Yusof's mother needed medical treatment.   (*Yes*)

(d) *Supply* a longer text and a set of statements, as before. This time students must judge whether the statements are presupposed, implied or neither.

Example: Appendix A Text 1

Read the text and the statements below. Mark each statement A, I or O according to this system:
   A = assumed (i.e. you cannot understand the text unless you know this)
   I = implied (i.e. you can infer this from information contained in the text)
   O = not assumed and not implied

You need to know/you can infer:

   (i) that Bavaria is in Europe.   (O)
   (ii) that a centimetre is this length: ⊢———⊣   (A?)
   (iii) that limestone is a sedimentary rock.   (O)
   (iv) that birds have feathers.   (A)
   (v) who the Red Indians are.   (O)
   (vi) that Red Indians use signs to convey messages.   (I)

   (vii) that dinosaurs lived over 63 million years ago. (O)

  (viii) what lithographic printing is. (O)

   (ix) what evidence exists for evolution. (A? I?)

    (x) what a bedding plane is. (I (partly))

   (xi) how a book opens. (A)

   (xii) that pterodactyls have wings. (I)

  (xiii) how big a pigeon is. (A)

  (xiv) that birds do not have claws on their wings. (I)

  (xv) that Darwin wrote *The Origin of Species*. (I)

  (xvi) that Huxley was alive at the time Archaeopteryx was discovered. (O)

Note: Clearly exercises like these provoke a lot of discussion. Often it is a matter of interpretation which answer you consider correct. They are therefore ideal for group work followed by guided discussion.

7   TAS 8   Prediction

Each of the preceding text-attack skills has related to some specific feature of the text; this one does not, except in so far as it relates to the text as a sequenced development of thought. Because the writer organizes his ideas, and because people often think in similar ways, it is possible to predict what a text will contain.

The ability to predict what the writer is likely to say next is both an aid to understanding and a sign of it. If you understand a text, you can say with a fair chance of success what is likely to come next and what is not: you can predict *because* you understand. How far it is possible to use the skill of prediction *in order to* understand is not so clear, but it is a principle of learning that new information is more easily assimilated if it can be fitted into an existing framework of ideas in the learner's mind. In the same way, if you can frame the thoughts the writer is likely to put forward next, it will help you to understand what he does in fact say, even if you predicted wrongly, provided you are prepared for that.

Prediction begins from the moment you read the title and form expectations of what the book is likely to contain. Even if the expectations are contradicted, they are useful because they have started you thinking about the topic and made you actively involved.

If you formulate your predictions as questions which you think the text may answer, you are preparing yourself to read for a purpose: to see which of your questions are in fact dealt with and what answers are offered. If your reading is more purposeful you are likely to understand better.

Naturally your predictions will not always be correct. This does not matter at all as long as you recognize when they are wrong, and why. In fact mistaken predictions can show you the sources of misunderstanding and help you to avoid certain false assumptions.

Prediction is possible at a number of levels. From the title of a book you can predict the topic and possibly something about the treatment. From the beginning of a sentence, you can often predict how the sentence will end. Between these extremes, you can predict what will happen next in a story, or how a writer will develop his argument, or what methods will be used to test a hypothesis.

Because prediction ensures the reader's active involvement, it is worth training the skill.

7.1   Training TAS 8

You could start with exercises on predicting the content of books etc. from their titles; a number of suggestions along these lines were made in Chapter 5. The suggestions that follow are all concerned with textual prediction.

Exercise 1 For this and other exercises below, you will need a text for use as a central visual if possible (on OHP, etc.).

Method: Expose the first paragraph of the text and allow time for the students to read it. Make sure it is understood. Discuss what the paragraph is doing: for instance, perhaps it is making a generalization. Or it may be the beginning of a story.

Next ask what the next paragraph is likely to do: will it give specific examples to support the generalization? Or will it qualify the generalization in some way? If it is a story, what will happen next? The students should look for the clues as to the line the writer is likely to follow, and should be encouraged to propose questions they think the writer will have to deal with either now or later.

When it has been discussed enough, expose the second paragraph and discuss how far it agrees with the predictions, and the reasons for choosing this rather than another way of developing the text. Then repeat the above process with this paragraph, and so on.

Exercise 2 Use the same approach as in Exercise 1, but hand out stencilled copies of the text to group leaders and do it as a group activity. Hand out the text a paragraph at a time; the group signals when it is ready for the next one, and you can discuss briefly what they have predicted before handing the next to them.

Note: For Exercises 1 and 2, the text of a story is particularly enjoyable and enables the technique to be used with less advanced students. It also promotes creative thinking. See Walker (1974) for further descriptions of this and similar techniques.

Exercise 3 Prepare a text for use as a central visual. Arrange to cover the text so that you can reveal only one line at a time.

Method: Expose the first few sentences of the text, allow time for students to read them, discuss if necessary. Then:

either show two or three possible continuations (i.e. the actual sentence that follows, plus one or two possible alternatives, in random order); the students are to choose the most suitable.

or show two or three questions that a reader might ask at this point. The students are to choose which question they think is likely to be answered.

When the students have discussed their responses and agreed on the most likely, expose the next sentence to confirm what the writer actually said and then repeat the process either with the next sentence or after reading a few more sentences, according to suitability.

Note: The text may be written continuously, but be careful to begin on a new line at points where you wish to pause for prediction. The possible continuations or questions could be written separately; they could indeed be cyclostyled on individual worksheets. However, it is probably more effective to interrupt the text at these points, provided you don't want to use it for other purposes, and embed the questions etc. in it, as shown in Figure 24 (p.122).

Exercise 4 Prepare to read a text for which a reasonably informative title is given.

    Task: (a) Write a list of questions that (judging from the title) may be answered
            in the text.
        (b) Read the text and find out which questions are actually dealt with.

A SON TO BE PROUD OF

    Last week, Rahman's wife had an accident. Rahman's youngest child, Yusof, was at home when it happened. He was playing with his new toy car.

> a. It was a plastic one which had not cost much money.
> b. Rahman had given it to him the week before, for his third birthday.
> c. His grandmother lived in a different town.

Rahman had given it to him the week before, for his third birthday. Suddenly, Yusof heard his mother calling 'Help! Help!'

> a. He ran to the kitchen.
> b. He went on playing with his car.
> c. He started to cry.

He ran to the kitchen. His mother had burnt herself with some hot cooking oil.

> a. She was very foolish and Rahman was angry with her.
> b. She was crying with pain and the pan was on fire.
> c. Yusof ran back to fetch his car.

Fig. 24   Text prepared for work on prediction

    (c) Discuss why the others were not dealt with and whether they should have been. (This promotes discussion about the difference between the writer's purpose and the reader's.)
    This is a good way of focusing reading for study purposes.

Exercise 5 For advanced students, two further techniques may be tried.

(a) *Supply* a suitable text and get the students to work through it, individually or in groups, sentence by sentence. (Sometimes even clause by clause may be better; or you can vary the amount covered by inserting two obliques // at every point where you want them to stop.)
    Task: To write a question to which each sentence etc. supplies the answer. This is not in itself prediction, since the student already has the answer in front of him and has to work backwards, so to speak, to make the question. But it does help to show how the text grows.
    Note: Do this in class first before asking for individual or group work, so that students understand what to do.

(b) *Supply* a text and ask students to read it, covering the unread part with a card etc. It should be read sentence by sentence or clause by clause, as appropriate. Advanced students may be able to decide for themselves how much to read at a time.
    Task: After reading the first sentence, frame a question that you think the writer will answer in the next. Then uncover the next and check how accurate your prediction was; repeat with the next sentence and so on.

8   TAS 9   Integration and application

All the other skills are useful because they lead the reader to this point: the understanding of the text as a whole, its overall message. This must include its relationship with external facts, and with the knowledge that was in the reader's mind to begin with.

There are no doubt a whole range of skills here; I shall focus mainly on application, but evaluation is equally important (though more familiar to teachers), and appreciation may also be relevant for some students and some texts.

To understand accurately, the reader must be able to distinguish between:

(a) important and unimportant points, and supporting details;
(b) fact and opinion;
(c) relevance and irrelevance;
(d) sound and unsound conclusions; adequate and inadequate evidence; valid and invalid inference;
(e) hypothesis, evidence, inference and conclusion;
(f) general (*all*), restricted (*some*) and particular (i.e. reference to an individual);
(g) certainty, probability, possibility, necessity and their absence;
(h) causes, effects, purposes, conditions.

And of course much else.

Different kinds of text require different combinations of skills; literary texts require skills of kinds that have not even been mentioned, and will not be dealt with in this book. We shall not deal with any more ways of practising points (a) – (h) above (some have already been included in earlier sections, though not in relation to the text as a whole). This is not because they are unimportant, but because they are so text-specific that they can only be illustrated by working through extensive texts for which we have no space. We must now turn to the ways in which integrative skills can be trained. Many activities are suggested in Chapter 10 and in Chapter 11, section 7. Here we shall limit ourselves to suggestions for training one particular integrative skill only. We often read and think we have understood, without having really considered or registered the practical implications of the message the text conveys. It is important to push students to this final stage if you can. The exercises that follow are intended to do this.

8.1   Training TAS 9

(a) *Supply* several statements of fact or opinion, or several examples.
    Task: To assess whether each one follows from the text, supports it, contradicts it, or is assumed (presupposed) by it, etc.

(b) *Supply* a series of specific examples relevant to theories discussed in the text or general statements made there.
    Task: To categorize the examples in terms of the theories etc. (For instance, suppose the text has talked about various types of motivation: the exercise might describe various people doing things for various reasons; the task would be to say which type of motivation each was demonstrating. Or the text may have discussed the climate and soil conditions needed for cultivation of various different types of crops: the exercise might describe a region and ask the student to suggest which crops succeed there.)

(c) *Supply* a description of conditions, or an experiment, relating to theories discussed or conclusions reached in the text.
    Task: To predict what will happen in the given conditions, or what will be the outcome of the experiment.

    (For instance, suppose the text has described investigations into the effectiveness of certain types of advertising in influencing certain types of prospective customer; the exercise might describe a new product and the intended customers, and might then offer examples of advertisements for the

product and ask the student to predict which one would be most successful.)
(d) *Supply* a problem which can be solved by making use of principles or other information in the text.
    Task: To solve the problem.

Note

Throughout this chapter, there is an underlying assumption that a text will be organized in recognizable ways and that the writer will communicate his ideas effectively. By and large these assumptions are justified, but not always. Some writers make their own rules and structure their texts in unusual ways; when such a text is studied, the reader's job is to ask himself what the writer is doing and why, not to apply stereotypes and complain that the writer does not keep to them. Some writers, being human, are not very good at their job; if they fail to communicate their message effectively, the reader must be capable of recognizing this. It may be worth exposing your students to some imperfect texts so that they can be helped to deal with them and will be reassured to find that it is not always their fault if they fail to understand.

9 Questioning

Reading comprehension lessons have traditionally centred on a passage of text followed by questions. But the questions were usually designed to *find out* whether the student had understood, rather than to *produce* understanding. In other words, they were devices for *testing* rather than teaching.

1 Teaching or testing?

In recent years the feeling has been strong that teachers should spend most of their time teaching rather than testing. This has given rise to concern about how we should teach reading comprehension. If the traditional approach to teaching comprehension is rejected, what is to replace it? Two main lines of approach have been followed:

(a) Developing types of question, and techniques for using them, that are primarily intended to teach, not to test.
(b) Developing other techniques for helping students to develop their own strategies for making sense of texts.

In this chapter we shall be considering the first of these: the kinds of question that can be considered attempts to teach, and how they can be used.

2 Can questions help readers?

Although we should try to find ways of improving on past performance, we ought not to make wholesale condemnation of well-tried methods. First, we ought to see whether traditional methods have anything to offer us. Probably you, like me, were trained by means of such methods, and have had this experience: you read a difficult text; you cannot understand it; you struggle to answer the questions on it; finally you read the whole text again, and you find that now you more or less understand it.

Between the first reading and the last, what happened? Is there a connection between answering questions and developing (not just demonstrating) understanding? If so, what kind of connection is it?

Perhaps the clue is in the word *struggle*. The questions that help you to understand are the ones that make you work at the text. They force you to contribute actively to the process of making sense of it, rather than expecting understanding just to happen. They make you realize which bits of the text you have not understood, so that you can concentrate on those bits.

If the key word is *struggle*, then not just the type of questions, but the way they are used, is crucial. Even a challenging question is useless to most of the class if the teacher simply accepts the first correct answer and moves on to the next question. It can only help understanding if every student actively tries to answer it. We have to make sure this happens.

This is one reason why multiple choice (MC) questions are often frowned on. It is so easy for an inexperienced teacher to accept the correct answer without even asking for the reasons why it is right, much less exploring the other answers to see why they are not appropriate.

Yet in the reading class, the answer to a question is not half so important as the *process* by which the student arrived at it. He may have given the right answer by accident: if so, it is valueless. Or he may give an answer you dismissed as wrong, but which he can defend, because he has interpreted the text validly, even though differently from you. Every teacher of reading has to be prepared for the occasion when a student interprets the text more effectively than the teacher: it may not happen often, but we have to acknowledge it and indeed welcome it when it does.

Because of this, it is essential to have a favourable classroom climate. Neither you nor the students must be afraid to be wrong. You must help them to see questions not as attempts to expose their ignorance, but as aids to the successful exploration of the text.

One key way in which you can help to achieve this is to *make sure that students always have their texts open* when they answer questions on them. The sort of questions we are interested in are not tests of memory. On the contrary, we want students to refer to the text when they reply. Some of our questions will be too difficult to answer from memory.

Finally, our attitude to wrong answers is important. A perfect answer teaches nothing, but each wrong answer is an opportunity for learning. It must be investigated to see why it was wrong, and how far: often it may be only partly incorrect.

We should praise the student for what he has understood correctly, and encourage him to look for the other clues that will lead him to a completely satisfactory interpretation. If you can develop this attitude in yourself and your class, you are already half-way to success.

3   Teaching through multiple choice

Oddly enough, MC questions in the hands of a skilled teacher are a highly effective instrument for training interpretive skills. We should not reject them just because they are sometimes badly used. Many teachers are obliged to use them, either because the textbook contains them, or to prepare for an examination that does. Hence a technique for using them effectively is important.

The approach we shall describe turns MC questions from shallow tests into the pointers we need for exploration. It is explained and exemplified in John Munby's book *Read and Think* (Longman, 1968). Briefly, the procedure is as follows:

(a) The students read the text silently and individually.

(b) The students attempt the questions (individually or in groups/pairs). Group work at this stage is preferred, because it produces instructive discussion and forces students to defend their choice of one option rather than another.

(c) When all the groups are ready, the teacher records their choices for the answer to question 1 and, without disclosing which is the best, promotes discussion between the groups about the reasons for their choices. Very often the students themselves will discover the correct answer by this process, even if they got it wrong at first.

The approach can be used with any multiple choice questions, but it is most successful when the distractors (i.e. the incorrect options) have been constructed to take account of possible misinterpretations of the text as in the sample from Munby's book in Appendix B, Text 5. The question setter, therefore, must be sensitive to the potential difficulties in the text. He must also be capable of devising plausible options that the student would choose if he had misunderstood in the predicted way. This is not easy.

4 Discussion is the key

The value of the approach, however, lies not so much in the questions themselves (though they have to be reasonably well constructed), but in the way they are used. Even if there is no group work in the second stage, the third stage essentially includes discussion of the alternative answers, and each will be defended or criticized by the students themselves. The teacher will do no more than keep the discussion on track, and ask occasional pointed questions if everyone has missed an important clue. He will also make sure that everyone is involved in the discussion.

This approach promotes the active struggle with the text that we have identified as a key ingredient in the development of interpretive skills. If group work is used, and the groups are kept small enough (five students is about the maximum), even the weaker students should be active and learning. The approach can be used at almost any level, and group discussion can be in the L1 if weaker students cannot manage it in the FL. It also produces a high level of motivation – not very common in the traditional comprehension lesson.

As we have said, skill in *using* the questions is critical. Even if you do not have MC questions, you can still make use of a modified version of the approach outlined, in which group work and active participation in discussion are the key factors.

5 The purpose of questioning

Poor questions may defeat even the ablest teacher, so you may need to devise some of your own to supplement or even replace the ones in the textbook. How do you set about devising questions?

First, get the purpose clear. Questioning in the reading class is not an attempt to test. The purpose is to make the student aware of the way language is used to convey meaning, and of the strategies he can use to recover the meaning from the text.

Let us recall what we said earlier about the aims of the reading class.

(a) It is not our aim just to investigate the language used in the text. It is not our aim to give practice in that language. One comes across questions on grammar or vocabulary which have little bearing on the meaning of the text. In the reading class it is never justified to ask a grammatical question and leave it at that. However, it may be necessary to draw attention to a grammatical feature if it plays a crucial part in the interpretation of the text; for example:

  (i) John lived here for ten years.
  (ii) John has lived here for ten years.

  Here the difference of tense is enough to tell us that in (i) John no longer lives here, while in (ii) he almost certainly still does. This point however needs to be related to other features of the text, the interpretation of other parts of it, and so on.

(b) It is not our aim just to investigate the content. One sometimes finds questions that are general knowledge questions rather than questions on the text. Some straightforward content questions need to be asked at the start of work on a text, but paradoxically it is only when there is a chance that students will give wrong answers (based on a misreading of the text, not on ignorance) that the real work of developing understanding can begin.

Having excluded these two kinds of question, we can identify the kinds of question that are relevant to our purpose, i.e. questions that help students to interpret what they read.

Broadly, questioning must support the approach outlined in earlier chapters. Some initial questions may result in scanning and skimming activities. Others may direct the reader's attention to diagrams or other non-text features that will help him to intepret the text. Some questions may promote the use of word-attack skills. But the focus of most questions will be the text-attack skills: all the other skills contribute to these, and these lead to the ultimate purpose: understanding the text as a whole.

All these are ways of helping students to understand. But they will only be successful if the students are aware when they do not understand. Recognizing that you do not understand, and identifying the source of the difficulty, are essential reading skills. You cannot deal with a difficulty if you are not aware of it.

For a question to be worth asking, it should contribute to this kind of awareness. We will look more closely at three aspects of questions to see how they relate to the purpose just outlined:

The **form** of the question.
The manner of **presentation**.
The **type** of the question.

6   Forms of question

Questions are often classified according to their form, and it is sometimes suggested that each form in turn should be used in questions on reading texts, as each is progressively more difficult to handle. We shall return to this suggestion shortly. However, the thing that makes a question form easier or more difficult is usually its answer rather than the question itself, as these examples will show:

1   **yes/no** questions
Is a trout a fish?   *Yes (it is).*
Did the man catch the trout?   *No (he didn't).*
2   Alternative questions
Is a trout a fish or a bird?   *It's a fish.*
Was the trout caught or did it escape?   *It escaped.*
3   **wh-** questions (*who, what, which, when, where*)
What is a trout?   *It's a fish.*
Where did the trout hide?   *Under a black stone.*
4   **how/why** questions
How did the trout escape?   *It managed to hide under a black stone.*
Why did the fisherman go away?   *He thought the trout had escaped.*

Answers to **yes/no** questions are very short and do not require the student to compose a sentence unless he wishes to. At the other extreme, **how/why** questions often require full sentence answers which are totally different in structure and content from the question.

This classification by form is useful mainly when you want to be sure that your students get graded language practice. This, however, is not our concern. We shall want to choose the form of question most suited to our reason for focusing on that particular aspect/section of the text.

We shall be interested in the student's reply, but not particularly interested in the form of it, provided it is comprehensible. In some circumstances, we might even be prepared to accept a reply in the L1; in that case the grammar of the FL would clearly be irrelevant.

We shall sometimes find a use for each form of question, but we shall from now on pay no further attention to this aspect of questioning.

7   Presentation of questions

7.1   Written or spoken?

Should you present questions in writing (in a book, on the blackboard or elsewhere) or should you do your questioning orally? There is something to be said for each.

Some kinds of question (notably multiple choice) are unsuitable for oral presentation, while other kinds are not very easy to write down in advance of the lesson, because they depend on responses that have been given to earlier questions.

Most reading lessons include some written questions, but it is usually necessary to ask a great many more orally. In fact the questions written down are never enough, and it would be very off-putting if they were, because there would be so many of them. Moreover, as we have said, many of the questions you ask depend on the way the class is responding: they may have difficulties that you did not predict, and you will then want to prompt them to help them to work out an answer, or probe to make sure that a correct answer was not given for the wrong reason.

Written questions may supply the skeleton of the reading lesson, but normally you will have to take care of what may be the most important part of the work by means of numerous oral questions. You certainly should not assume that your work is done when you have got through the questions in the textbook. However, if these are good questions, they can be used after most of the work on the text has been completed, as a way of summing up.

Written questions, of course, do not necessarily have to be answered in writing. Oral responses are often enough. It is the work of analysing and discussing the text that is important – the process of arriving at the answer as much as the answer itself; and this can only satisfactorily be dealt with orally.

7.2   Open-ended, Multiple Choice or True/False?

There is no reason to exclude any of these types of question. *Open-ended* questions (like those listed on p.128) are questions in which the student is free to compose any response that seems suitable to him (and the term is particularly often used of the **wh-** and **how/why** forms of question, since they offer the greatest scope). *Multiple choice* questions are those in which the student is offered a set of possible responses, of which he has to choose one, for example:

> What happened to the trout?
> A   It was caught.
> B   It escaped down the stream.
> C   The fisherman had it for supper.
> D   It hid under a black stone.

True/False questions present the student with a statement; he has to decide whether it is true or false in accordance with the text, for example:

> The trout was caught by the fisherman. T/F

Of these types, *the T/F question* is in some respects the most limited, but may be very useful and if skilfully formulated is not necessarily easy. T/F questions are useful in promoting discussion, rather like MC questions, and although more choices may make the discussion more interesting, T/F questions may be preferred when there is only one likely misinterpretation of the text. (In such cases, MC questions are often too contrived to be useful, as it is difficult to find convincing distractors.)

MC questions can be extremely successful if they are well-designed and used. They are, however, the most difficult of all to write successfully. The need to have at least three, preferably four, options often leads to very implausible items. But if they are not plausible, the number of genuine alternatives is reduced so that the choice is not really 'multiple' at all; in such cases, the T/F format is more satisfactory.

Guidance in composing MC questions can be found in a number of books, among them: Murphy (1969), Heaton (1975).

Open-ended questions may as we saw require very short answers, but typically they demand rather more than this and their disadvantages are therefore:

(a) *They cannot be marked objectively.*

This may be important when we wish to *test* reading ability, but not when we wish to *teach* people how to read effectively. As we have seen, the answer is not as important as the process by which the student arrives at it; and we can never mark this objectively, even if there were any point in doing so. This objection is therefore not important for most of our purposes.

(b) *They require students to produce responses in the FL.*

It is possible to understand FL texts without being able to express yourself adequately in the FL. However, if questions demand subtle or complicated responses, this is a problem: the student may be able to understand both the text and the questions, but unable to express the answer he would like to give.

One solution is to accept answers in the L1. This will be discussed below.

However, open-ended questions do have some advantages as well:

(a) *They are relatively easy to devise.*

Good comprehension questions always require skilful devising, but at least with open-ended ones you do not have to worry about supplying plausible distractors, as for MC, and you can go directly for the target – that is, the particular problem you want the question to focus on.

(b) *They can be used for virtually any purpose.*

So can MC questions, but it is sometimes clumsy to use them. If the point to be clarified by the question is a straightforward one, it may be uneconomical to use MC format. If it is very complex, or requires the collection of material from various parts of the text, the MC question may itself have to be very complex, so that to understand it becomes more of a task than to understand the text itself. In such cases, open-ended questions may be preferred.

(c) *They force the student to think things out for himself.*

Even the best devised MC questions have to include the correct answer as one of the options (unless you supply the option 'None of the above'). This can be an advantage: it provides guidance for the students and yet, if the distractors are well chosen, it makes them think. But with advanced students, you may not want to prompt them by expressing the correct answer at all, even in company with incorrect choices. You may want them to come to terms directly with the text itself, with no indication of your own view of it. In this case you will want to use open-ended questions in preference to MC or T/F.

7.3 The language of responses

We have already suggested that inability to express themselves in the FL needlessly limits the kinds of response students give, and the quality of the response too. It is quite possible that students who are permitted to use their L1 in responding will be able to explore the text more accurately and thoroughly than those who are restricted to responses in the FL.

Obviously, whether this is acceptable will depend upon the purposes for which your students are going to use the FL. The important point is that the idea is not dismissed today as it would have been a few years ago, when all use of the mother tongue in the FL class was frowned upon. Nowadays we accept that some students are learning the FL for purely receptive use; they may never need to express themselves in the language. Why should we not, in their case, accept responses in the language that will most clearly show us whether they have understood, or where their problems lie?

Some teachers, brought up in the earlier tradition, will find it unacceptable to permit the use of the L1; and you may well be uneasy about the amount of L1 that could result once you open the door to it. Perhaps a compromise is best: that when a student can make himself understood in the FL, you should urge him to do so, but that you should accept L1 responses when the FL is not being learnt for productive use, and when to insist on it would produce undue delay or result in poor quality answers.

7.4 The language of questions

This, like the language demanded by responses, is often a problem and one that is hard to solve if the text is at all difficult itself. Unfortunately you cannot always present a difficult text in a straightforward way. The use of MC or T/F questions certainly relieves the student from having to produce FL responses, but the language used in those questions may be unavoidably complex.

People sometimes maintain that reading the questions is part of the reading task, but this is only partly valid. It is certainly *a* reading task, but *the* reading task is making sense of the text itself, and we could argue that anything that distracts attention from this main task is unhelpful.

When you compose questions (especially written questions, where your voice and, if necessary, extra explanation, are not available), the language you use should be as clear and simple as you can make it. At the very least, it ought not to be more difficult than the language of the text itself.

If you find this impossible, there are two other solutions to explore. One is to phrase the questions in the L1. If the only alternative is to ask questions that you do not want to ask, simply because they are within the linguistic competence of your students, you should seriously consider this solution.

No doubt that suggestion will cause some raised eyebrows, and certainly the FL should be used whenever possible. But the L1 is already used for this purpose in many classrooms throughout the world, in classes where only the FL is supposed to be used. If its use is planned and open, instead of random and covert as it is at present, the result might be even a reduction in the amount of L1 being used, and could certainly be an improvement in the quality of questions asked. (At present, much of the L1 is translation of an intended FL question; if it were known that language would be no barrier, a better question might be devised.)

The other solution to the problem of difficult language in questions is to explore the possibility of a completely different approach which we shall look at in the next chapter.

8   Types of question

There have been a number of attempts to classify reading comprehension questions according to their content. The classification that follows is not particularly original. It is intended to be useful as a form of checklist; by classifying your questions against it you can find out whether you are omitting any important kinds of question and thus failing to give practice in some important skills.

8.1   Type 1   Questions of literal comprehension

These are questions whose answers are directly and explicitly available in the text. Questions of this kind could often be answered in the words of the text itself (though most teachers would not wish that to happen).

Such questions are essential preliminaries to serious work on a text, because until you are sure that the plain meaning of the text has been grasped, there is no point attempting more sophisticated exercises. Look at Appendix A Text 2. Some literal comprehension questions on this text might include the following:

(a) When did Rahman's wife have an accident?
(b) What was Yusof doing when the accident happened?
(c) Why didn't Yusof help his mother?

8.2   Type 2   Questions involving reorganization or reinterpretation

Slightly more difficult than Type 1 are questions which require the student to obtain literal information from various parts of the text and put it together, or to reinterpret information.

Such questions are valuable in making the student consider the text as a whole rather than thinking of each sentence on its own; or in making him assimilate fully the information he obtains; for example on Appendix A Test 2:

(a) How old was Yusof?   (Reinterpretation)
(b) How many children had Rahman?   (Reorganization)
(c) Was Yusof playing in the kitchen?   (Reinterpretation)

8.3   Type 3   Questions of inference

These are questions that oblige the student to 'read between the lines', to consider what is implied but not explicitly stated. Questions of this kind are considerably more difficult than either of the former types, because they require the student to understand the text well enough to work out its implications. The difficulty is intellectual rather than linguistic in most cases. Like Type 2, they often require the reader to put together in his mind pieces of information that are scattered in the text, so that their joint implications can be recognized.

Some examples of inferential questions on Appendix A Text 2 follow:

(a) Which people were in Rahman's house when the accident happened?
(b) Why was Rahman proud of his son?

Based on Appendix A Text 11:

(a) What differences would you find between trees in Dorset and trees near Birmingham?

(b) What hypothesis was confirmed by Dr Kettlewell's experiment in Dorset?

8.4 Type 4 Questions of evaluation

Evaluative questions involve the reader in making a considered judgment about the text in terms of what the writer is trying to do, and how far he has achieved it. The reader may be asked to judge, for example, the writer's honesty or bias (e.g. in newspaper reporting or advertising copy), the force of his argument (e.g. citing of evidence), or the effectiveness of his narrative power (e.g. in a novel).

Questions of this kind are the most sophisticated of all, since they ask the reader not merely to respond, but to analyse his response and discover the objective reasons for it, as well as measuring it against the presumed intention of the writer. We should include here questions of literary appreciation as the most sophisticated representatives of the type, since the central concern is to find out how the writer has produced his effects and how far he has succeeded in his aim.

This is an activity for advanced students, and many will never need to deal with questions of this kind.

8.5 Type 5 Questions of personal response

Of all the types of question, the answer to this type depends most on the reader and least on the writer. The reader is not asked to assess the techniques by means of which the writer influences him, but simply to record his reaction to the content of the text. This may range from 'I'm convinced' or 'I'm not interested' to 'I'm moved' or 'I'm horrified'.

If the text is suitable, into this category will fall such questions as 'What is your opinion of X's behaviour?' 'Would you like to live in Y?' 'How would you have felt if you had been Z?' Personal response is naturally most often invoked in relation to creative writing, but it is sometimes appropriate to other kinds of writing too, for example, 'What does this writer contribute to our understanding of the field?' 'Do you sympathize with the writer's arguments?' 'How far does your own experience agree with that described?'

Nevertheless, such responses cannot ignore the textual evidence; they do not rely only on the reader, but essentially involve him with the writer. So we need to ask the student to explain why the text makes him feel as he does, and we must make sure that his reponse is at least based on correct understanding of the text.

To divide questions into types like this is not particularly helpful in itself, except for evaluating the questions you find in textbooks, and for helping you to develop your own. You will find that many questions in textbooks fall into Type 1, with perhaps a few Types 2 and 5. Of course literal comprehension is an essential preliminary to any work on the text. But in fact it is Types 2, 3 and 4 that ought to concern us most, since it is questions of these types that force the reader to think about not just what the writer has written, but how he has written it. And unless our students think about that, they are not likely to become as competent as we would like in tackling difficult texts.

Questions of all these kinds, except perhaps Type 4, can be asked from the most elementary level, as the examples from Appendix A Text 2 show.

9 Questions concerned with how the writer says what he means

The types of question we have looked at so far all have as their main concern *what the writer says*, or in the case of Type 5, how the reader reacts. There is another kind of question much in use at present which has as its main concern *how the writer says* what he means. This kind of question is intended specifically to give students strategies for handling texts, rather than simply helping them to understand one particular text. It is aimed at making students aware of the word-attack and text-attack skills, i.e. making them conscious of what they do when they understand. You will find examples of questions like this in Appendix B Text 2 and Text 4.

10   Assessing questions

Here is a check-list you may find useful when you assess questions:

(a)   *Can the questions be answered without reading the text?*
      The answer should be **no**!
         It is quite surprising how often it turns out to be **yes**, especially when MC questions are concerned. Have a look at the examples below which are based on questions taken from actual textbooks. Why is it possible to answer them without even having seen the text?
(b)   *Are there several questions on every part of the text?*
      This is not a principle to be maintained at all costs, but it is unusual to find a part of a text that is not worth any attention. Some textbooks seem to have a ration of questions for each text and this may result in patchy coverage, if one part demands a lot of questions at the expense of others.
(c)   *Are there enough questions?*
      We have already pointed out that textbooks rarely supply anything like enough questions, but that many of the extra ones should be presented orally and geared to the difficulties that arise in class.
(d)   *Are the questions varied in type?*
      We are referring here to the types of questions described on pp. 132–133. Normally we should ask a lot of Type 1 questions first, followed by questions of Types 2 and 3 wherever possible, and finally 4 (for advanced students) and 5.
(e)   *Do some questions specifically try to make students aware of the strategies a reader needs?*
      We refer here to the kinds of question dealt with in section 9.
(f)   *Do the questions attempt to help students to understand?*
      Or have they been written simply as tests?
(g)   *Are they written in language that is more difficult than the text?*
      We hope for the answer **no**.
(h)   *Do the answers require language that is too difficult for the students to handle?*
      Again, we hope for **no**.

11   Unsatisfactory questions

Here are some examples of unsatisfactory questions, closely based (believe it or not) on examples from actual textbooks. Working out the right answer without the text may help you to avoid similar mistakes.

1   John's father considered him a model son, although
      (a)   he was not old enough to be interested in girls
      (b)   he was a very fine footballer
      (c)   his disobedience was extremely worrying
      (d)   at his age many sons are very troublesome

2   The murderer took the woman's corpse into the forest because
    (a) he did not want to hurt her any more
    (b) he wanted her to be comfortable
    (c) he did not want anyone to find her
    (d) he needed her car

3   Reattaching severed limbs by microsurgery is
    (a) never attempted
    (b) a very skilled task
    (c) always successful
    (d) simple

4   Housewives use mousetraps because
    (a) mice run about in the house
    (b) mice are very old
    (c) mice do a lot of damage
    (d) mice like cheese

5   World War II began in
    (a) 1945
    (b) 1940
    (c) 1914
    (d) 1939

6   The word *allege* in line 10 means
    (a) claim
    (b) agree
    (c) request
    (d) refuse

10 Other Forms of Exploitation

1   A more flexible approach

Different texts offer opportunities for different kinds of exploitation. Yet the passages in a traditional reading comprehension book have generally been exploited by means of questions of similar kinds for each text. This sometimes results from choosing texts of rather similar types, sometimes from the preference for having a fixed pattern for every lesson. Even when the compiler does respond to the variety of content or purpose, he seldom asks the reader to perform a task other than answering questions, writing essays or summarizing.

Recent books, however, adopt a more flexible approach; they respond to differences in the type of text by making use of different kinds of activities for exploiting them, and they devise many new activities to supplement (not to replace) questioning. Once you abandon the idea that all reading lessons should follow the same pattern, all sorts of interesting possibilities open up, and you can choose those that best suit the text you want to study. I have taken advantage throughout this book of the ideas produced by some of these recent textbook compilers (and it is interesting that most of them are teams of writers rather than individuals: devising varied and appropriate tasks is very demanding).

Unless your students need to be able to read only a limited range of texts, the wider the variety used for training purposes, the better. Your reading programme needs to reflect the fact that we read in different ways for different purposes, so texts should be capable of exploitation in a variety of useful and interesting ways.

2   Feedback: the process of understanding and the outcome

Since understanding is an invisible and private process, you need some way of making sure that it is taking place, in order to judge the success of your approach. It is the *process* of understanding, i.e. what the student does between starting to read a new text and eventually correctly answering questions on it, that interests us most, because it is during this period that learning takes place.

Information of this kind is extremely hard to get; you can never quite see the student's mind at work. The nearest you can get to it is in discussion. Discussion also gives weaker students a chance to see for themselves something of the process of making sense of a text, and will give all the students a chance to learn from one another.

However, you cannot listen to more than one person at a time, and that does not give you the spread of information you need about the class's progress. Since you cannot realistically hope to discuss a text with every individual student, some form of observable outcome is the only solution. We are really talking about a form of testing, of course, but this is testing to provide you with feedback: information about how the students are progressing and, perhaps, where their problems lie.

We are not talking about testing in the sense of providing marks for student records (although this can be a by-product) and we shall not be discussing formal testing of that kind in this book. Another book in the same series will deal with the topic. Our concern is with teaching, and therefore with the process of learning how to interpret; we want an observable outcome only because it provides evidence that the process has taken place.

3   The primary purpose of reading tasks: process, not outcome

In the case of questions, the responses automatically provide you with a means of checking progress. In other tasks, the outcome may be drawing a diagram, completing a table, making or doing something that does not involve paper and ink at all. However, it would be misleading to suggest that such tasks are to be used (or designed) primarily to give the teacher feedback. Their principal function is to make the student concentrate on the text and to give him a clear purpose for reading. We must devise tasks that force the reader to think through the implications of the text, its application, the uses to which its content can be put. In so doing we hope that he will establish the overall meaning of the text and recognize the contribution made to it by each part; and that he will acquire the ability to deal with texts in general.

4   Kinds of reading task

4.1   Outcomes mainly not requiring language

(a) Making, arranging, completing, checking or labelling non-verbal information, as described in Chapter 5.
(b) Constructing or labelling a text diagram, flow chart, classification diagram, etc., as described in Chapter 8.
(c) Doing something: if the text includes instructions for operating a machine, making a model, playing a game, the most effective outcome is to get the students to carry out the instructions. This is usually interesting in itself as well as good practice in functional comprehension.

4.2   Outcomes involving spoken language

(a) Dramatization and role play
Drama can be used to exploit suitable texts in ways that go far beyond the extemporizing of dialogue. As far as interpreting the texts goes, the value lies in the preparation rather than in the performance.

Understanding is deepened and made clearer when the student playing the role of X is obliged to decide – with the help of the others – what X is doing at any given point, what expression he is likely to have on his face, how he will behave towards Y (is he hostile or merely suspicious?), why he says this rather than that.

To find the answers to these questions involves close reading and full understanding. Preparation must involve frequent interruption and reference to the text to support one interpretation rather than another. The discussion involved can be both stimulating and fruitful. But you will need to be firm; otherwise most students will get away with a superficial reading and learn very little from the experience, though they will enjoy it. Properly conducted, the drama approach is not only enjoyable but very effective, although, like most good methods, it is time consuming.

While the use of drama is most obviously appropriate in the case of literary texts, its close relative, *role play*, can be used over a much wider range. Any topics that involve the analysis of people's actions, or the discussion of varying points of view that might be expressed orally at a meeting of some kind, can be brought alive by means of a simulation in which students represent either the original actors, or protagonists of the different viewpoints. (The nature of the discussion will depend on the text; it might be a meeting of school teachers discussing various approaches to education; economic advisers arguing the merits of alternative economic policies; farmers and agricultural extension workers putting forward their views about improved agricultural techniques; and so on.)

It is of course not implied that any such meeting is described in the text; the idea is that having identified various points of view in the text (arguments A, B, C, D for instance), each student is asked to adopt the role of a person holding one of these, to master the argument presented and be prepared to defend it against the others. How far you should let students go beyond the text, to produce their own additional arguments, depends on the text and on you, but if you do so, attention should at some point be drawn to the differences between the text and the class discussion.

When using drama or role play, it is not necessary that all the class should wait and watch while a few students act. For one thing, they should be actively involved in suggesting, discussing interpretations and so on: this is the justification of the method. Secondly, once the class is familiar with the method, group work can be used. All groups will work concurrently, with or without a presentation at the end. The process, not the product, is what matters.

(b) Debate and discussion

Much of what we said about role play applies also to *debates* based on the text; in fact, role play is often a form of debate made more lively by the simulation of real life. However, whereas role play is usually based on what the text says, debate may go far beyond it, using the text simply as the spark to set it going. Although the debate may not directly involve much reference to the text, it will often help students to interpret it, since we saw that what the student brings to the text (in terms of ideas, understanding, sympathy and so on) is crucial to his ability to interpret it: and debating is a good way of involving the student with the topic and exposing him to different points of view. In fact, some teachers have found that role play or debate can usefully *precede* reading: in that way the student is focused on the topic and will read more effectively.

It is not necessary to have a formal debate with proposer, seconder and so on. Informal class or group discussion is often far more effective. You may like to use the *buzz group* technique: groups discuss an issue for a given short time (five minutes or so; it depends on the complexity of the issue) and answer a specific question about it, or formulate their view in some other specific way. One of each group will then report to the class and whole class discussion will follow. Questions of Types 4 and 5 (p.133) are suitable for this treatment; give the groups a specific task (or tasks, for it is sometimes valuable for each group to discuss something different) in order to produce well focused discussion.

(c) Reading aloud

My instinct here is simply to repeat 'Don't'; we noted earlier (p. 22) that reading aloud is used far too much in FL classrooms, at the expense of silent reading for meaning. There is nothing easier for the teacher, and nothing drearier for the student, than reading aloud round the class. And there can be few commonly used methods of less value. You have only to look at the faces of the students who are not actually reading aloud to see that their minds are miles away; and nine times out of ten they are not even hearing a text read well. Moreover, as reading aloud is a great deal slower than silent reading, if your students are exposed to it frequently they will find it difficult to achieve good silent reading speeds.

So it is not surprising that most specialists condemn it unreservedly. Yet it is still a firm favourite in many classrooms and, as Alun Rees (1980) points out, the fact that an activity is open to abuse does not mean that it is bad of itself.

There are two ways in which it seems to me that reading aloud might be used with some justification:

(a) as the culmination of work on a text;
(b) as a method of helping elementary students to read in sense groups (which we noted in Chapter 4 is an important step in improving the reading competence of slow and inadequate readers).

We will deal with (a) first. There is no doubt that a good reading aloud shows some sort of understanding of the text. Yet it appears to be quite usual for people to read aloud fluently and yet be able to give only the sketchiest impression of what they have just read. Perhaps they are concentrating so much on pronunciation or expression that they have no time to assimilate the meaning as well. I cannot attempt to explain this paradox, but we need to remember that we want to produce people who can fully understand what they read, not people who can simply give a polished performance of the text. To read aloud really well, it is first necessary to study the text carefully and understand it fully; you can insist on this. An unsatisfactory first attempt can be repeated after the meaning has been discussed further, and reasons for disapproval explained and alternatives suggested.

However, this is an advanced skill, and reflects oral ability as well as understanding. The one who reads aloud does not learn much if anything about the meaning of the text from this activity; he shows what he has already learnt. (So it is a kind of test.)

The other reason, (b), for reading aloud is that described by Michael West (1960), who calls it the 'Read and look up' technique. Intended for use with students whose reading is at an elementary level, it can contribute to the development of some good reading habits. Briefly, West advocates this sequence:

(i) Break up the text into manageable sense units. (The length will depend on both reader and text; about five to ten words is likely to be the most anyone can recall easily.) Normally this is done by the teacher before reading aloud takes place. When a reader is able to do it for himself, during rather than before reading aloud, that is a sign that he is developing the skill of reading in sense groups for himself (which is our reason for using this technique). With students who need support, mark the sense groups by means of an oblique or other pencil marking in the text, for example:

John looked out of the window./ It was raining again/and the sky was very dark./ 'Why does it always rain on Saturdays?' he thought./

(ii) Once the text is marked, the student who is to read aloud silently assimilates the words in the first sense group.

(iii) Then he looks up from his text and looks at his audience.

(iv) Now he speaks the words without referring to the text, addressing them directly to the listeners and making every effort to convey the meaning.

(v) Then he continues with steps (ii) – (iv) with each subsequent sense group.

The advantage of this is that it forces the reader to take in a chunk of text, and to retain it in his mind long enough to look up and speak it. This gives him practice in reading in sense groups instead of word by word, and it thus prepares him to increase his reading speed and his comprehension.

There is another advantage: the pressure to look up while speaking forces the meaning of what was read to take precedence. You should not worry if the student departs slightly from the exact words of the original, provided he keeps the meaning; this is a good sign as it means he has correctly interpreted what he has read, and is not relying on parroting.

In conclusion: if you feel that you want to use reading aloud in spite of the almost universal criticism of it then:

> use it after you have worked on interpretation of the text, not before;
> use the read and look up technique;
> use it sparingly.

(d) Listening with the text

As long as students are tied to a text presented orally, they will not achieve rapid fluent reading. But we are obliged to recognize that some students are such slow and hesitant readers that a text read aloud by a good reader will be too fast for them, unless they follow the text with their eyes while they are listening.

This technique has been found extremely useful in helping slow readers to improve both their speed and their comprehension. The easiest way to organize it is to have texts read aloud and recorded on cassettes. The student then borrows both the text and the tape and listens as often as he likes while following the text with his eyes, if necessary using a card guide (see p. 39).

Many of the publishers who offer graded supplementary readers are now issuing cassette recordings of some titles. If you can afford them, these will provide an excellent source of material. Otherwise you and your colleagues should co-operate to build up a library of cassettes for joint use, read by yourselves. In fact, you should do this in any case, because you will need to have recordings of texts that are not available commercially, but which suit the needs of your students.

Many students now have access to cassette players at home, but you should obtain some for use in school as well. Luckily, for listening to speech it is not necessary to have an expensive machine; the cheap ones give quite adequate reproduction. If you can keep them in the classroom with a selection of tapes, they can be used whenever there is a spare moment. Using an earphone will prevent disturbance.

If you have a number of poor readers, you can more economically arrange for them to listen as a group, either to a cassette player or to you, reading aloud while the rest of the class gets on with other work.

The expectation is that after considerable exposure to taped texts, the reading fluency of the students will improve to the point where they no longer need this support but can continue to improve on their own. At that point they should be encouraged to think about increasing their reading speed in some of the ways suggested in Chapter 4.

4.3   Outcomes involving writing

It is current practice to distinguish between various language skills and teach only those for which students have an identifiable need. Many students who need to read the FL do not need to be able to write it, and the suggestions in this section may be considered inappropriate for them. This is a pity, because some of the most interesting ways of exploiting texts involve written outcomes.

(a) Reassembling and utilizing information

A good way of making sure that the reader gets to grips with the text is to give him a task that requires him to make use of what he has read. One alternative is to devise a writing task for this purpose.

The kind of task will depend on the text; it must not allow the student simply to quote chunks of the text, because he can do that without understanding very thoroughly. It may involve him in making use of information from the text, in order to do something comparatively unrelated to the text itself. Some examples might be:

(i) Plan a tourist brochure for a place described in the text.

(ii) Plan a shooting script of a documentary film sequence to illuminate the points made in the text (with or without actual commentary).

(iii) Write a memorandum from an appropriate official (health officer, social worker, forestry research worker etc.) proposing a course of action to deal with the problems outlined in the text.

(iv) Write a series of numbered rules for the (game) described in the text.

(v) Read these alternative accounts of an incident and note the points on which they differ. Now write a report for the (factory supervisor) attempting to explain what actually happened, and accounting for the different versions.

(vi) (For use with a text which has explained a classification system of some kind. Supply a selection of pictures/diagrams/descriptions of relevant objects.) Study these (pictures) and classify them according to the criteria explained in the text.

(vii) Write five statements that are supported by the information given in the text./ Write a hypothesis to explain the phenomena described in the text./ Suggest an experiment that would test the hypothesis made in the text. *etc.* (Be prepared to justify your answers in discussion.)

(viii) The story is told from (Jan's) point of view. Recount the incident as it must have appeared to (Lorna).

(ix) You are going to make a television programme on (a topic related to that discussed in the text) and (the writer of the text) is to appear in it. Prepare an outline design for the programme, going into some detail on the writer's part in it and how it will fit in with the contributions of others.

It must be emphasized that these are random examples. The possibilities are too wide to illustrate adequately; every text has its own potential and must be exploited in its own way.

Many tasks of this kind are suitable for group work, (i), (ii), (vi), (vii), (ix) would be particularly so, as they give scope for discussion and co-operative effort.

Further suggestions along similar lines will be found in White (1980) and Johnson (1981), together with many helpful ideas about the integration of reading and written work.

(b) Using diagrams

Diagrams are also an excellent basis for written work.

One way of using a diagram is to remove the text after it has been studied and leave the student with only the diagram. His job is then to recreate the text according to the diagram, but in his own words.

Another possibility is to present the student with a second diagram that is closely similar in structure to the one relating to the passage he has been studying, but which reflects different content. For example, the student has read a text about the production of coffee, and has completed a process diagram to illustrate it. He is now presented with a process diagram about the production of cocoa. The task is to write a description of the process as a coherent text, using the diagram and any other information that you consider necessary.

(c) Summarizing and note-taking

Tasks such as (*a*) (iv), p.141, could be used as a first step to the writing of a summary by the student himself. Or a gapped summary can be supplied (the omissions to be chosen carefully to pinpoint possible misinterpretations) which the student is asked to complete. Or an inaccurate one may be presented for the student to correct. It is a pity that summarizing has become rather an unfashionable exercise of late, because it is an extremely useful one, demanding full understanding of the text. It does, however, also require lucid and accurate expression which may be too much to expect of your students; this is why we do not suggest the writing of a full summary, at least to begin with.

If you are teaching students who can express themselves reasonably well, you could proceed to functional summary tasks after such introductory activities. By 'functional summary', we mean not the sort of task that instructs students to 'Summarize the passage in 150 words', etc., but a summary for a specified and plausible purpose, like the report for the supervisor in (*a*) (v) (p.141)

In order to devise tasks of this kind, you will need to consider what information in the text might be required in summary form, and for what purpose. Many tasks will involve selecting information as well as summarizing it; you need not ask for a summary of the whole text. Here are some samples:

(i) (On a text describing, among other things, the social and economic factors involved in constructing a road in an area which currently has none.)
Summarize for the director of the road works department the various social factors he will need to consider before deciding the course of the new road.

(ii) (On a text in which an account is given of an incident that took place in a school, for which several boys were to blame.)
Write notes for the headmaster on the part played by each boy, with a comment on the extent to which each was to blame.

(iii) (On a text discussing safety procedures in factories, in general terms.)
Various safety precautions are described in the text; extract these and produce a simple numbered list of safety rules to be posted on the factory notice-board.

(iv) (On a text in which something – for example, a place, a battle, an incident – is both described and discussed/assessed.)
Make a note of every *fact* stated about X, with its source when this is indicated (i.e. distinguish fact from comment).

Tasks of this kind also train the student in the sort of note-taking he may need when he goes on to study in a specific field. If it is relevant to your students' needs, it is also excellent practice to ask them to make notes for an essay on a topic that might reasonably follow from reading the text.

(d) Translation

Translation demands not only a literal understanding of the text but also a sensitive response and a high level of competence in both languages. It remains a supreme outcome of the interpretation of a text, but it is now recognized that translation is not needed by many students and is beyond the ability of most.

Often considered as a testing device rather than a way of teaching, it is undoubtedly a task which forces the students to get to grips with the text in the active way required for satisfactory comprehension.

Because of the difficulty of doing it satisfactorily, however, we do not commend translation for general use.

4.4 Cloze procedure as a teaching device

The use of the cloze technique for testing is by now well established (see p. 28). It can also be used for teaching. A cloze text is easy to prepare. Make sure that an introductory sentence without omissions is supplied to set the context:

> At last, the young hatch, chipping their way out of their shells with a small egg-tooth on the tip of the bill. Many of those that nest on . . . . .1. . . . . ground are covered with down when . . . . 2. . . . emerge and this gives them excellent . . . . 3. . . . They run away from their nest . . . . 4. . . . . as soon as they are dry . . . . 5. . . . . search for food under their mother's . . . . 6. . . . .
> (D. Attenborough, *Life on Earth*, (Collins/BBC 1979))

In this example, every seventh word is deleted; it is of course much shorter than any text you would be likely to use for teaching or even testing. Some people advocate a much longer ungapped lead-in – up to a paragraph.

The use of cloze to teach rather than test is similar in principle to the technique of using multiple choice questions for teaching, described on p. 126–127. In that technique,various options are given which reflect possible misunderstandings. In using cloze, this is not necessary (though it can be done by supplying options for each gap): the options are normally supplied by the students themselves, and thus mirror exactly their misunderstandings.

To use cloze for teaching the gapped text must first be prepared. For most of us, that means it must be put on stencil or prepared for the overhead projector; or it can be written out on a large sheet of newsprint and pinned up for all to see; or a roll-up or other spare blackboard can be used. It would of course take too long to write up a whole text in class time.

Once everyone can see the text, they should be given time to read through it; you cannot make a good choice until you have an idea of the general type of the text and its patterning.

When everyone is ready, call for suggestions to fill the first gap. This is where the learning begins. Not merely the correct choices but also the incorrect ones should be considered. (Write them up on the board if there are not too many.) The students themselves should choose the best and give their reasons; you should – as usual – do as little of the talking as possible. Reasons should be given for rejecting words; some will be not so much incorrect as, simply, not what the writer chose; in this case, the reasons for his choice may be explored with advanced students. Some may be wrong grammatically. Others – the most interesting for our purpose – will be wrong because they do not fit in with the meaning of the text as this becomes clear.

Choosing the right word may necessitate reading ahead, as well as bearing in mind what has been said already; and it may involve using inference as well as understanding of what is directly stated. To train these skills, you may find that the dogmatic deletion of words at regular intervals is not the best procedure. For example, the passage above might offer more interest if the deletions ran as follows:

> Many of those that nest on the . . . . .¹. . . . . are covered with down when they . . . . ². . . . and this gives them excellent . . . . ³. . . . They run away from their . . . . ⁴. . . . almost as soon as they are dry to . . . . ⁵. . . . for food . . . . ⁶. . . . their mother's supervision.

Here, gap 1 may be difficult to fill until you reach the words *run away* which provide a clue. The other gaps are more likely to be filled by choices that are not so much wrong as different from the writer's, but they will provide material for discussion and, for advanced students, for the beginnings of work on register or style.

Cloze can also be used to draw attention to specific features of text if the deletions are controlled. For example, in this text the deletions are of the cohesive devices such as reference words:

> Many of . . . . .¹. . . . . that nest on . . . . ². . . . . ground are covered with down when . . . . ³. . . . emerge and . . . . ⁴. . . . gives them excellent camouflage. . . . . ⁵. . . . run away from . . . . ⁶. . . . nest almost as soon as . . . .⁷. . . . are dry to search for food under . . . . ⁸. . . . mother's supervision.

Using a different text, deletions might draw attention to the use of superordinates (see pages 77–8):

> No sooner had he picked up the vase for this scrutiny than he dropped it. Priceless fragments of porcelain showered over his suede shoes. This . . . . .¹. . . . . he instantly felt would prove to be the beginning of a perfectly dreadful day. These . . . . ². . . . were realized all too quickly, for before he had properly embarked on clearing up the pieces, his aunt entered the room. This untoward . . . . ³. . . . shattered his nerves still further so that he fumbled and stuttered and put pieces of Ming into his pocket. Such . . . . ⁴. . . . did nothing to appease his aunt, who, with raised eyebrows and a voice like cold steel, asked what he imagined he was doing. This . . . . ⁵. . . . produced in him the liveliest terror and a complete inability to reply. The . . . . ⁶. . . . was not to be averted by the sudden ringing of the telephone, for sweeping from the room, his aunt merely uttered the single syllable 'Wait'. This, however, was an . . . .⁷. . . . . he had no intention of complying with.

4.5   Group work

(a) *Group sequencing*
Tasks that call for the ordering of sentences into a paragraph or paragraphs into a text (such as those recommended for training Text-Attack Skill 5, p. 110–111 ff.) work extremely well in groups.

(b) *Group prediction*
Tasks such as those described for training Text-Attack Skill 8 (p.120–122) are good for stimulating focused discussion with more advanced students.

(c) *Group cloze*
Using cloze as a teaching device depends on the discussion of the possible alternatives for filling each gap. This will be brisker and involve a greater number of students if it is done in groups.

Each group discusses and agrees on a choice for each gap; then the class comes together to discuss their findings under the guidance of the teacher.

The discussion can become quite sophisticated, and in the group phase it may well be in the L1; however, since the topic is the use of the FL, the FL is bound to play a considerable part, and we should not be too concerned if the quality of the discussion can only be maintained by conducting it in the L1.

The organisation of group work is further discussed in Chapter 11 p. 162 ff.

11 An Intensive Reading Lesson

1 Objectives of an intensive reading programme

It may be helpful to outline the main points that have been made which will be relevant to intensive reading. We can express these as a set of objectives.

After completing a reading course, the student will:

(a) Use skimming when appropriate to ensure that he reads only what is relevant, and to help subsequent comprehension.
(b) Make use of non-text information (especially diagrams etc.) to supplement the text and increase understanding.
(c) Read in different ways according to his purpose and the type of text.
(d) Not worry if he does not understand every word, except when complete accuracy is important.
(e) Recognize that a good writer chooses his words carefully and would have meant something different if he had chosen A rather than B. (An advanced student will also be able to explain the difference.)
(f) Make use of the reference system, discourse markers, etc., to help himself to unravel the meaning of difficult passages.
(g) Be aware that a sentence with the same signification may have a different value in different contexts; and be able to identify the value.
(h) Be able to make use of the rhetorical organization of the text to help him to interpret a complex message.
(i) Be aware that a writer does not express everything he means, and be able to make inferences as required.
(j) Be aware that his own expectations influence his interpretation and recognize those occasions when the writer's assumptions differ from his own.
(k) Be aware, when necessary, that he has not understood the text, and be able to locate the source of misunderstanding and tackle it.
(l) Respond fully to the text in whatever way is appropriate.

These objectives are not the only ones you will want to set, but they will serve to remind us of the many different things that we want to achieve in our reading programme.

2 Help from the teacher: how much and what kind?

Since we are now going to talk specifically about what might happen in the classroom during a reading lesson, we ought to remind ourselves first of the points made earlier about the amount and kind of help that a teacher should give.

2.1 Getting out of the way of the text

Broadly speaking, a teacher of reading should put a text in front of his students, assign tasks that will help the students to understand it (and may also enable the teacher to assess how far it has been understood) and then stand out of the way while the students get to grips with the text. This is not so easy to do. The text must be well chosen, the tasks suitable, and the students must have been trained to work on their own.

The most difficult part of all is to restrain yourself from getting in the way of the text. In most reading lessons, the teacher does too much of the work, not realizing that what he is doing devalues the text and undermines the student's role as reader. This may be easier to appreciate if we examine some of the activities that are often found in reading lessons.

2.2 The student's role as reader

The student's role as reader demands that he should make sense of the text for himself. In his reading lessons, he is supposed to learn how to do this: doing it for him will not teach him this. From the beginning, he must do for himself everything that he is capable of doing. This requires encouragement, especially the encouragement that comes from success; and success in turn comes from texts that are suitable and tasks that are well devised. These are things the teacher can influence, and hence ways in which he can help.

The most basic thing the reader has to do is associate the printed marks on the page with the spoken language he knows. If the teacher reads the text aloud before starting work on it, then this task is his, not the student's. He has already done one of the student's jobs for him.

The reader has to make sense of the text. So if the teacher begins by explaining or summarizing it, he is defeating the object of the lesson: he is telling the student something a reader ought to find out for himself. If, as the lesson proceeds, the student encounters problems and the teacher at once explains or translates, again this is the wrong kind of help: the student only has to understand his teacher, not the text.

All these activities are valid for some purposes and in some circumstances, but it is clear that they are not useful for training students in the independent skills of silent reading. Exposed to methods of this kind, the student will see the reader's role as a passive one, for he has had most of the work done for him. The teacher's well-meant help has undermined the purpose for which he is teaching.

2.3 The text and its effect on student performance

Methods of this kind are also harmful because they devalue the text itself. If the teacher reads the text aloud or gives a preliminary summary of it, then the process of getting meaning from the printed text is seen as merely subsidiary. In lessons like these, the printed text becomes almost redundant, since the meaning is obtained largely through the intervention of the teacher. Moreover, translation by the teacher into the L1 (which can be justified in some circumstances) is frequently used not just as an aid but as a substitute for understanding the text itself.

If you yourself regularly use the sort of activities just described, you will probably argue that without help of this kind, your students could not possibly understand the assigned texts. To this argument there are several responses.

First, you may be wrong. It is easy to underestimate students, and research shows that it commonly happens. Even if they cannot understand everything, they may be able to understand more than you are at present giving them a chance to attempt. You can only find out by trying.

2.4 Reasons why students fail

If you do try, and the students are not successful, again there may be more than one reason for their failure. Perhaps you expected them not to succeed: negative expectations are easily detected by students and are well known to have a very adverse influence on student performance.

Or perhaps the tasks you devised were at fault: study them again and if possible discuss them with colleagues. Or perhaps you were expecting too much too soon: students who are accustomed to a passive role must be gently eased into active participation, required only gradually to take responsibility for their reading, and given specific training in those skills that can be trained.

So it is essential for you to have a positive attitude – to expect your students to succeed in the end; to devise the right kind of tasks; and to be patient and tenacious, not expecting miracles overnight.

If, in spite of every effort, you find that you still cannot make progress without summarizing, explaining and translating most of the text, then the texts you are using must be unsuitable. You should consider with your colleagues whether it might be better to find something more appropriate to the level of your students. (And do not confuse the goal with the route by which it is reached: you may want students to be able to read texts of a certain kind by the end of the course, but it does not follow that they should be trained by working only on this same kind of text.)

2.5   The teacher's responsibilities

We have spent some time considering what not to do in reading lessons because the activities described, and the misconceptions that lead to them, are so widespread. Now we had better start to think more positively. As teachers, we must take responsibility for our students' progress: what kind of guidance can we give without undermining our whole purpose? How can we help them to become effective independent readers?

Our responsibilities include these:

(a) Finding out what our students can do and what they cannot, and working out a programme aimed at giving them the skills they need.

(b) Choosing suitable texts to work on.

(c) Choosing or devising tasks and activities to develop the required skills.

(d) Preparing the class to undertake the tasks.

(e) Making sure that everyone in the class works productively and extracting maximum effort and best results by encouraging the students; and by prompting and probing until they produce the answer, instead of telling them what it is.

(f) Making sure that everyone in the class improves steadily according to his own capabilities.

We have already dealt with (a) (b) and (c) and must now look at (d) (e) and (f). But first we should consider the general pattern of a reading lesson.

3   The need for a flexible programme

A point to be stressed at the outset is that many reading lessons will not conform to a pattern. Because different texts need different treatment, we cannot expect to handle them all within a single convenient framework. Moreover, not all our lessons will deal with only a single text. If we are interested in training a specific skill, such as the skill of prediction, we may design exercises to practise it which make use of several texts, none of them to be studied very thoroughly. Some skills may be practised by studying sentences, others by referring to whole books.

A major requirement of the reading programme is therefore that it should be flexible, so that you can respond to needs you did not foresee and move quickly over areas that give no trouble; and so that you can include all the different kinds of text and skill.

As we have seen, a number of distinct reading skills can be identified, and many of them can be trained by exercises specifically designed for the purpose. On the other hand, when we read a text we are seldom conscious of using these specific skills, and moreover, we have to make use of them together in a co-ordinated way. There is a limit to the usefulness of treating them separately.

In your reading programme, you will probably want to spend some time on specific skill training and some time working with texts which demand the use of all the skills together. Increasingly as the course progresses you are likely to do more work with texts so that the students have practice in co-ordinating all the skills.

We dealt with specific skills in earlier chapters, so here we shall be looking mainly at text-based lessons; but it is important to remember that they are not the only kind of reading lesson you will need to give.

4   Planning a text-based lesson

Planning a lesson begins, obviously enough, with the choice of text. We will assume that you have a text that satisfies the criteria laid down in Chapter 3, especially with regard to its readability. If it is too difficult for your students, you may be obliged to resort to the sort of methods we criticized earlier in this chapter, thus defeating your purpose.

Having chosen a good text, first study it yourself and see what potential it offers. Even if it is included in a set textbook with prepared questions, you should still do this, because few books ask anything like enough questions, and useful aspects of the text may be left untouched. You probably cannot cover every aspect in the time at your disposal, so pick the ones that will be most helpful to the class and devise extra questions or other tasks to cover them.

In any intensive reading lesson, you will want to include some of the following – perhaps even all of them occasionally:

(a) scanning, skimming, rapid reading practice (Chapter 4)

(b) tackling the interpretation of the text by means of
    (i)   utilizing non-text information (Chapter 5)
    (ii) word attack skills (Chapter 6)
    (iii) text attack skills (Chapters 7, 8)
    and making use of various kinds of question or other task (Chapters 9, 10)

(c) producing some sort of outcome based on the text as a whole (Chapter 10)

Whatever else we include, interpretation will be at the core of the intensive reading lesson. We want our students to be able, when they wish, to respond to a text in the way the writer intended, and this involves being able to interpret it accurately and fully. It is also important to give practice in flexibility of approach, in skipping difficulties when accuracy is not essential, and so on; we shall be looking at ways of doing this later. First, we need to consider what the relationship is between an understanding of the parts of a text, and an understanding of the whole.

4.1   Global or detailed study?

Understanding is the essence of reading; and usually our ultimate objective is for the students to achieve global understanding: that is, to understand the text as a whole and to be able to relate it to other texts, other sources of knowledge, personal experience and so on.

How far does global understanding depend on detailed understanding of every part of the text? This depends on the text itself, for instance on whether it is simply factual and direct, or whether it is subtle and slanted. It also depends on the reader's purpose; as we have already said, not all reading purposes require 100 per cent accuracy.

Which is to come first in class, global or detailed study? It may seem logically that we cannot understand the whole unless we have first understood its parts. But in fact comprehension does not work so tidily. Sometimes it is possible to interpret difficult parts of the text because we already have a fair understanding of the overall message. Global understanding enables us to dismiss various misinterpretations because they do not fit in with the overall message; and we may be able to conclude 'This part must mean something like X', and then use this prediction to help us disentangle the difficulty.

4.2   Reading as making hypotheses

The chief danger of this approach is that the reader may try to read into the text what he thinks ought to be there, rather than what the writer intended. To counteract this, students should be trained to treat interpretation as the making of a series of hypotheses, rather as in scientific method. If the first hypothesis ('I think this text means so-and-so') is correct, all the evidence in the text will support it. If it is incorrect, the reader will find it increasingly difficult to justify as he reads on and encounters contradictory evidence. A competent reader will then revise his hypothesis in accordance with the new evidence; this may involve going back to the beginning in order to reinterpret the text in the light of the new hypothesis. With very difficult texts, the whole process may have to be repeated several times. This is not a sign of incompetence, but the reverse; the competent reader is the one who notices contradictions and takes the trouble to sort them out.

A reader can often produce a reasonable hypothesis about a text after only a superficial reading. To do this, he must use resources such as common sense, general knowledge and experience, which he already has. Encouraging him to make use of them means that you can start work on a positive note ('What do we know about this text? So what do you think its message is likely to be?'). This is more encouraging than starting with the negative factors such as unfamiliar vocabulary. It is also good strategy, for students must learn to utilize all their resources in order to make sense of the text.

You can start by making hypotheses based on the title alone, if there is one, or the title of the book from which the text comes. Or you can ask your students to skim through the text and tell you very approximately what it is about. If there are several different views, subsequent closer reading can be focused on establishing which is the most accurate. If none of the views are appropriate, ask the class to try again when the detailed work has progressed far enough.

Active experience of forming predictions about a text (i.e. hypotheses), and confirming, rejecting or reformulating them, is as important for a reader as it is for a scientist. You need to be particularly on your guard when the text involves matters of opinion or emotion, because inexperienced readers often assume that the text will echo their own views; or, where that is clearly not the case, that the writer is hostile – which may be equally false.

4.3   Accuracy and overall message

Whether you begin with a global view of the text or not, you will normally end by considering its overall message. Sometimes this can be done without much detailed work on the text; it is important to give students practice in looking for the message and ignoring trivial causes of misunderstanding. To do this safely they must of course judge whether a difficulty is trivial or not, by determining how far it prevents them from understanding the overall message. This is not quite as circular as it sounds; for all good readers faced with a difficult text will move from global to detailed interpretation and back again many times during the course of their work on it, as each kind of interpretation supports the other.

Because the degree of detailed interpretation that is needed varies from text to text and purpose to purpose, students must be trained to approach a reading task flexibly, matching the approach to the needs. Nevertheless, most of our time is likely to be spent in making sure that our students learn to read accurately, for this is what the FL learner finds most difficult. Apart from anything else, it is easier to read for the main idea and ignore the details if the reader is confident that he can read with complete accuracy if he needs to. And the reader's response to a text is worthless if it is based on inaccurate understanding.

We shall therefore be concentrating in this chapter mainly on ways of approaching the training of accurate reading.

4.4   Assessing the learning potential of a text

At this point it seems a good idea to look at some texts and work out how we might use them in class. For this study, you will find it helpful to work with a group of colleagues. If you can do this, start by working on the text individually; in this way you will get more variety of insights and approaches than if you work together from the beginning. In subsequent discussion you will all benefit from this variety.

First, study texts 5, 6, 7, 8, 9 in Appendix A. Choose one of these that is about the right level for your own class if possible. Study the chosen text until you are satisfied that you understand what the writer expected you to get from it. Then go on to consider how you could help your students to understand it equally well. What sort of tasks would you want to set? What questions would you ask? How would you help them with the difficult parts? How would you tackle global understanding?

Sometimes ideas will come quickly; if there is a lot of physical description of a place in the text, it might be helpful to get the students to produce a map or diagram; if there are a lot of statistics, a chart or graph might be a suitable outcome. But not all texts offer such simple solutions and usually it will be necessary to devise a number of tasks or activities if you are to get at the core of the text.

In addition, any text will offer opportunities for training some of the reading skills we have discussed. The work done on a given text ought of course to contribute to an understanding of that particular text; but when you ask students to scan the text for a piece of information, or try to infer the meaning of an unknown word, or work out what the word *it* in line 6 refers to, you are not just helping them to understand the given text; you are also helping them to develop the particular skill involved. When you are looking at the potential of a text, both aspects need to be kept in mind.

When you have decided what you would want to get out of the text, and how you would do it, refer to Appendix B. There you will find the same text as it appears in a published reading course. Study the introductory notes, questions, tasks etc. supplied by the writer of the reading course. What does he want his students to get out of the text? If his objectives are different from yours, do you consider both to be equally valid and useful? What methods does he use to achieve his objectives? How do they differ from the ones you thought of ? Advantages and disadvantages?

I suggest you do this with several of the texts listed above, so that you begin to get a feel for the learning potential of a text. You will get the greatest benefit from this exercise if you do not look at Appendix B until after you have really worked on the text yourself.

When you have completed this introductory exercise, turn your attention to some of the texts you are actually going to use with your students and treat them in the same way. If they come from a comprehension book, ignore the questions supplied for the moment; they may well be excellent, but you need to free your mind of preconceptions and look straight at the text itself. What do you want your students to get from this text? How will you do it? Again, work with a group of colleagues if possible. Plan how you would use the text and what tasks and questions you would set, eventually incorporating any suitable ones supplied in the textbook.

Repeat this process with several texts, preferably of very different kinds, until you feel confident that there is little danger of your overlooking any significant learning potential in a text of any kind.

4.5   Guiding your students

Having chosen your text and worked out broadly what you want to do with it – what you hope the students will learn from it – how are you going to start tackling it in class? You can of course simply give the students the text and tell them to get on with it and then answer the questions; with the right class, this might even work. But with most, it will not. Most students need much more help than this if they are to grow into effective independent readers. But we have already dismissed as harmful several kinds of help that have traditionally been used. So what guidance can we give that will not devalue either the text, or the students' role as readers?

For convenience we can look at various suggestions in a roughly chronological way: guidance that can be given before reading; guidance to be given while reading is under way; and guidance that can follow when the reading is completed.

5   Guidance before reading

Before the students begin to read the text, we can do quite a lot to make their task more explicit and their way of tackling it more effective. We will consider these points:

1 Providing a reason for reading.
2 Introducing the text.
3 Breaking up the text.
4 Dealing with new language.
5 Asking signpost questions.

5.1 Providing a reason for reading

When you are deciding what to do with a text in class, you will have to face a central problem of lessons based on text extracts: why should anyone want to read this text? If you can choose texts that are geared to the actual needs and wants of your students, you are lucky. Unfortunately, many of us teach students with no really specific needs (other than to pass an examination), and many of us cannot choose the materials we use: the textbook is prescribed.

But in real life, we read for a purpose which influences the way we read. Consider, for example, Text 3 in Appendix A, *The Red Flag Canal*. You would read this in one way if your aim was to find out what sort of people the Chinese workers were, but in a very different way if you wanted to work out exactly the methods used so that you could employ them yourself on a similar project.

We need the framework of a reason for reading so that we can decide how detailed our understanding must be. So it is often helpful to give students an imaginary purpose for reading, to enable them to judge what they can skim over, what they must attend to in detail, according to its relevance to their purpose. Otherwise their reading lessons will simply strengthen their belief that if we do not understand the whole text completely, it is not possible to read it at all.

Naturally, since there are many purposes (understanding a legal document, for example) that do require us to understand every detail of a text, this too must be practised. So I am not suggesting that we abandon the pursuit of full and accurate interpretation. I am merely repeating what was said earlier: that other ways of reading are valid in certain circumstances, and that they require training. Our students usually need a lot of help in what we might loosely call 'reading for relevance'.

Suggesting an imaginary purpose is one way of supplying that help. You will not want to do this for every text, and not all texts lend themselves to this treatment. But when the text is suitable, let the students focus their reading for a specific purpose and ignore the rest of the text. You can always follow this with more detailed work if you wish. You will also find that to read the same text first for one purpose, then for another, generates interest as well as improving your students' flexibility of approach.

5.2 Introducing the text

Many teachers feel that they must introduce every text before allowing the students to start work on it. In fact it may not always be necessary, but an introduction can certainly be helpful.

However, the wrong kind of introduction is worse than none at all. In my experience, the commonest faults are these:

(a) The introduction is too long.
(b) The introduction gives away too much of the content of the text.
(c) The introduction is irrelevant (and thus may be actually confusing rather than helpful, since it sets up misleading expectations).
(d) The introduction is a monologue by the teacher, with no student involvement.

If you want to introduce the text first ask yourself why. It is seldom useful to give a potted biography of the writer, unless this has a direct bearing on the content. Nor are extensive background details often necessary; for example, you may not need to know much about Switzerland in order to understand a text on Alpine mountaineering. All we want the introduction to achieve is to point the students in the right direction, get them into the right mood for this particular text and, if possible, make them feel interested in reading it.

A lengthy introduction not only takes up valuable time but is likely (if it is not irrelevant) to give away too much of the content of the text. Have a look at the questions you are going to ask, or the other tasks you want the students to undertake. Will they be able to attempt any of them on the basis of your introduction alone? If so, change the introduction. It should not include anything that the student can find out from the text, either directly or by deduction. If it does, you are doing his work for him.

On the other hand, some texts are difficult to understand if you do not know the background, and it may not be possible to deduce enough information from the text itself. In such cases, of course it is sensible to make sure that the students have the necessary facts; but try to find out if they can give you the facts — someone almost always can, if you ask the right questions. The best introductions are the ones that come mostly from the class, with the teacher simply drawing them out. A monologue from you is not so likely to kindle curiosity as a discussion in which everyone is involved; some teachers have successfully used debate or role-playing as a way of getting the class into a receptive frame of mind for the text.

It is often easy to incorporate a signpost question (see p.158) into the introduction, or to deal with new language that will be needed for the text, which can often be introduced naturally at this point (see p.157). This is convenient; but above all try to arouse the students' interest in the text, and show them its relevance for themselves by asking questions like 'Have you ever . . .?' or 'What would you do if . . .?' or 'What's your opinion of . . .?'

(a) Practice in assessing an introduction

Suppose you wanted to use Text 1, *Archaeopteryx*, from Appendix A. Which of these introductions would you choose?

(i) I suppose you have all studied the geography of Europe and know where Bavaria is. It is a region of southwest Germany, bordering on Austria, over 27,000 square miles in size and with a population of over 10 million people. It is particularly well known for its beautiful mountains . . . (continue with further description of the region).

(ii) How many of you have heard of David Attenborough? I expect some of you have seen films with his brother Richard Attenborough in them. Well, David is interested in films, too; but he doesn't act in them, he makes them. If you have a TV, you've probably seen some of them. Can anyone tell me what kind of films they are? He made a famous series called 'Zoo Quest'. He studied zoology at Cambridge . . . (continue with information about David Attenborough).

(iii) This text comes from a book called *Life on Earth*. Have any of you read it or seen the TV series? What's it about, if you have? Well, what do you think it's likely to be about? Do these chapter titles give you any clues? 'The Infinite Variety' — 'Building Bodies' — 'The First Forests' — 'The Conquest of the Waters' — 'The Invasion of the Land'. Who has heard of Darwin? What theory did he put forward? Now, skim through the text and see who can be the first to tell me what this text has to do with the theory of evolution.

(iv) Have you ever heard of dinosaurs? Pterodactyls? When did they live? We are going to read about a creature that lived at about the same time, a sort of half bird, half reptile, called *archaeopteryx*. We know about it because its skeleton has been found embedded in limestone. I want you to read the text quickly and tell me where the limestone was found. I'll give you one minute.

(v) What sort of rock is sedimentary rock? Can you tell me the names of any sedimentary rocks? . . . Yes, limestone is one. Do you know what kind of sediment limestone is formed of? It was mainly calcareous, the remains of living organisms. What's the meaning of calcareous? The same sort of substance as chalk for instance. . . .Yes, it produces quicklime. Do you know what that is used for?

(b) *Comments on the introductions*

(i) Introduction (i) is off the point. Knowledge about Bavaria is of no importance to an understanding of the text.

(ii) This starts off promisingly but goes into too much biographical detail, not all of it even relevant to this text, and none of it very helpful.

(iii) I don't think this is particularly good, but it is the one I would choose if I couldn't think of something better, because it tries to help the student to see the significance of the text in relation to Attenborough's overall theme in the book from which it comes.

(iv) The initial questions might have led to an interesting introduction, but there is far too much information here which the student ought to extract from the text. And the skimming question focuses on a fact that is of no importance to the main theme of the text.

(v) While an understanding of how limestone is formed may help the student to interpret this text, the concentration on geological fact gives quite the wrong emphasis: the text is not about geology. This introduction also includes information that should be extracted from the text.

(c) *Qualities of a good introduction*

Several of the introductions above include questions; these often provide the most satisfactory way of preparing students to read, since the effort of trying to answer gets them actively involved and (provided they are the right questions) thinking along helpful lines. It is a good rule of thumb never to say anything yourself if a student could say it for you: most of the things that need saying can be elicited from the class.

To sum up, a good introduction will have these qualities:

(i) It is usually short.

(ii) It does not tell the student anything that he can find out himself by reading the text.

(iii) It makes the student want to read the text.

(iv) It helps the student to relate the text to his own experience, interests, aims.

(v) It involves the students actively, for example by means of questioning.

5.3 Breaking up the text

A long text, even if it is not difficult, may appear daunting to students whose reading is not very skilled or speedy. When you ask the class to read it silently, the slower students will feel even more inadequate, while the quicker ones will finish long before the time you have allowed. This is a nuisance and may be a problem if discipline is shaky, since it gives the better students time to create disturbances.

You cannot change the fact that some people read better than others (even in a streamed class) but you can reduce the effects of the differences by dealing with the text in several short sections instead of all at once. In this way, your quicker students may be kept waiting only a couple of minutes for each section, instead of a much longer time if the slower ones have to finish the whole text.

(a) Advantages of breaking up the text
Breaking up the text has other advantages besides improved discipline. It is easier to work in a thorough and organized way on a short section than on a complete long text. Locating words or sentences for comment is quicker; the new language can be dealt with a little at a time, section by section as it occurs, in digestible portions; and if you need to take more than one period to deal with a text, dividing it into sections gives you a simple way of dividing the work between the periods available.

A further advantage: it is easier to hold the students' interest if you handle a short section at a time. You can deal with one section fully and then move on to a fresh one. If you use reading aloud (even though it is not recommended), there is less chance of students becoming bored and restless when listening to a fellow student if he reads only a short section.

Moreover, you can vary your approach more easily, using silent reading as the main approach for some sections, practising scanning or skimming with others, reading aloud yourself if a section is particularly difficult, and so on.

Finally, handling a text in sections can lead to more effective learning. You can ensure more thorough understanding, so that when the first section has been dealt with, it helps the students to interpret the second, and so on. In this way interpretation becomes steadily easier as it builds on the understanding of the earlier sections. You can also train the important skills of anticipation and prediction by asking students what they think the writer is likely to say in the next section, what will happen next, etc.

(b) How to break up the text
If the text is not already divided into paragraphs of suitable length, you will have to decide where to split it. This is not usually difficult. If you cannot identify natural boundaries between parts of the text, split it arbitrarily: any break is better than none for your first work on a text. You can always combine sections for later work if you have had to split a part of the text that ought to be read as a whole.

If you are teaching elementary students, sections of 4 – 5 lines are long enough (50 words or so). Aim at sections of up to 20 lines (about 250 words) with fairly advanced students.

(c) Identifying learning points
Having decided where to break the text, you must next decide three more things:

(i) What is important in this part of the text?
Your answer to this will depend on your view of the text as a whole. How does this part contribute to the whole? What must be emphasized, what can be ignored?
(ii) What problems are the students likely to have in understanding this part of the text well enough to see what it contributes to the whole?
This involves predicting stumbling blocks and assessing their importance. We have already put the case for accepting less than 100 per cent comprehension in certain circumstances; if you think the stumbling blocks will not really interfere with adequate interpretation, try at least sometimes to persuade the students to ignore them. Otherwise, the next point comes into play:

(iii) How am I going to help the students to tackle the predicted problems and others that may appear?

This is the most difficult of the questions. We have made many suggestions already. Further ideas will be given later in this chapter.

(d) Working with the whole text

For some kinds of work the text cannot be handled in sections. You may want to do some skimming or scanning work related to the text as a whole: this would have to be done at the beginning, before the section by section work. On the other hand, work requiring a thorough understanding of the whole text (e.g. studying the development of the plot or argument, analysing the relationships between the paragraphs) is best tackled at the end, after all the sections have been dealt with in turn.

Perhaps two words of caution should be given. First, you will not always want to study each section closely. But even if you want to push your students to read fast and get just the gist, it is still easier to work with short sections to begin with.

Second, if you want the students to respond fully to the whole text, then they must have a secure understanding of all its parts. But working on sections of a text is like preparing the ingredients for a complex dish: it is a necessary preliminary, but it is not enough. It is easy to forget that our objective is an understanding of the whole text, especially if it is difficult and needs a lot of time.

Time must be allotted for dealing with the whole text, even if some of the sections have to be dealt with less thoroughly than you would like. (You can turn this necessity to advantage by showing the class that some parts of the text are more important than others.) Otherwise we shall be guilty of concentrating so much on the trees that the students never get a decent view of the forest.

5.4 Dealing with new language

This is a rather controversial issue. Many teachers like to teach all the new words and structures in the text before reading begins. I am not going to say that new language should never be taught this way, but I have often thought when watching reading classes that this is the dullest part of the lesson, and that the teaching would have been more effective if it had taken place actually during the process of reading.

It is difficult to make hard and fast rules, but you will frequently find that a new structure hardly needs explaining if it is taken in context; whether you want to teach it for active use is a matter beyond the scope of this book. For our purposes, if it can be understood without specific teaching, then it is not a barrier to the reader and to spend time on it would be pointless.

As we saw in Chapter 6, the same is true of vocabulary. You may feel the need to teach a few key words before the students begin to read, but other new words may be so unimportant that you do not want to draw attention to them, while others you will want to use for practising the skill of inferring meaning from context. If your list of key words to be taught is long, this is a warning that the text is too difficult.

Of course we are here facing the conflict between learning to read and learning the language. Your attitude will be determined partly by the kind of texts you use; if they are specifically intended to present new language, you cannot just ignore it. But the students have to learn to read as well; use supplementary texts for this if you can, but at least use the language teaching texts in such a way that they provide genuine reading tasks i.e. that students actually get practice in interpreting them. This will involve (among other things) not teaching all the new language beforehand; helping the students to use the context as a guide to interpreting some of the new language; and practising or drilling the new items after reading rather than before, in at least some cases.

Some of the problems will be alleviated by dealing with the text in short sections as suggested earlier. The new language from a single section will be more manageable than the new language from the whole text, so the dull preparatory work will be split up into short more acceptable bits.

Finally, when you introduce the text, you will often have opportunities for presenting key language items in the context of your introduction; this is more effective than presenting them as isolated items.

5.5   Signpost questions

A signpost stands at a crossroads to show travellers the way. Its function is to direct them along the right road, making the journey quicker and saving them from getting lost. A **signpost question** (SPQ) has a similar function: its purpose is not to test, but to guide the students when they read, directing their attention to the important points in the text, preventing them from going off along a false track.

Questions of this kind are particularly useful when your reading lesson is based mainly on silent reading. It is helpful to give the students a question or a task (it does not have to be an actual question) *before* they begin to read. This gives them a specific reason for reading, and they will read more purposefully in order to find the answer or complete the task. Look at Text 1 in Appendix B (*Airships*). What name do the compilers of that text give to SPQs?

An obvious danger is that the students will look only for the answer to the SPQ and will not read the rest of the text carefully. To avoid this:

1 Make sure the students know that you will always ask a lot more questions after they have finished reading. The main work on the text must of course follow the reading.
2 Make sure the SPQ cannot be answered until the whole (or most) of the section has been read.
3 Devise SPQs that do not require merely the location of information but involve more conscious consideration of the meaning of the text.

(a) Devising signpost questions

Writing good SPQs requires some skill, which you can acquire by practice coupled with constructive criticism from your colleagues. You may like to begin by criticizing somebody else's SPQs. Read the short text called *A Son to Be Proud of* (Text 2 in Appendix A) and decide which of the following would be the best SPQ for the whole text. If possible discuss your choice, and your reasons for rejecting the others, with your colleagues.

> Possible SPQs for *A Son to Be Proud of*
> 1 How old was Yusof when this story happened?
> 2 Why did Yusof run to the neighbour's house?
> 3 What did Rahman's wife tell him?
> 4 Why was Rahman proud of his son?
> 5 Who put out the fire?
> 6 Why did Yusof run to the kitchen?

Did you realise that the best SPQs relate either to the final part of the section, or to the section as a whole, so that they cannot be answered until the whole section has been read and understood? Did you also keep in mind the function of the SPQ? – not to test but to help the reader to understand by (a) directing his attention to things he might otherwise miss, particularly potential sources of misunderstanding; (b) focusing on the main point.

(b) Using signpost questions

Before silent reading, write the SPQ on the board or OHP. Then ask the students to read the text silently and find the answer. After the silent reading, check whether the class has been able to do this satisfactorily. If a fair number have not, turn to your other questions and tasks and return to the SPQ later, when the text has been studied thoroughly enough to make a satisfactory response likely. Avoid giving the answer yourself if you possibly can.

6   Guidance while reading is under way

The sort of guidance that can be provided while the reading process is actually going on will be largely determined by the sort of class organization you prefer. Of course there is no reason why you should not vary the way you organize your class, and thus vary the way guidance is provided.

6.1   Three kinds of class organization

We will consider three broad modes of class organization. First, there is the *individual mode*, where each student is working on his own for much of the time. Since the reading process is in essence private, this kind of class organization is particularly suitable for a reading lesson. Every reader must understand the text for himself; nobody else can do it for him. Hence it is often recommended that reading instruction should be made as individual as possible. Carried to its logical conclusion, this will entail providing a great variety of material to enable students with varying interests and varying levels of language ability to find texts that suit them. Every student might be working on a different text and responsible for his own progress, though in consultation with the teacher, who would be expected to keep a careful record of each student's work and progress, and to give help when necessary. The advantage is that every student can read material that suits him and can progress at his own pace; but naturally this demands careful organisation and a plentiful supply of materials.

At the opposite extreme is the familiar *teacher-centred class*. In this case, the class works with one text only, and the way the text is tackled is controlled largely by the teacher, who sets tasks, checks learning and – assuming that he is a capable teacher – does everything he can to ensure that every student participates actively in the process of making sense of the text. There are drawbacks to this approach: the whole class is obliged to work in roughly the same way and at roughly the same speed. The compensations are that the good teacher can keep his finger on the pulse most of the time, and will thus remain continually aware of problems and weaknesses; and that materials preparation and class organization are infinitely easier than in the individualized mode. This latter advantage must not be taken lightly, for if class organization is poor and the supply or design of materials is inadequate, an individualized approach can be disastrous.

The third mode that we shall consider is the use of *group work*; in this case, much of the guidance comes not from the teacher but from fellow-students. The effort to understand the text is made jointly – that is, the individual efforts are pooled and discussed in the hope of arriving together at the best interpretation. While this mode suffers from some of the disadvantages of individualization (some people may not be working; some may be wasting time pursuing the wrong idea, etc.) and of class-centred work (the pace and approach will not suit everyone), nevertheless both teachers and students who have used group work are usually very enthusiastic about it. Its principal virtues are that motivation is generally high, especially if the group tasks are challenging and promote discussion, and that individuals make more effort to participate when they are working as a group, since it is more obvious that everyone's contribution counts.

Finally, it should be clear that these three approaches do not have to be mutually exclusive; they can readily be combined during the sequence of a reading lesson, which might for example begin with individual reading, move on to group work and end with a teacher-centred phase. This sort of combination is ruled out only when a fully individualized programme is operating, with every student reading different material; but even in this case, you do not have to operate the programme every period, but can alternate periods of individualized reading with periods of group or teacher-centred work.

6.2   Guidance from the text: the individualized approach

If the student is expected to work individually, the first necessity is that the text itself should contain all the guidance he needs; or more accurately, that the text should be accompanied by all the necessary guidance in printed form.

If the system is to be completely individualized, you will need to have a wide range of texts each with its own guidance material. These might be books (we shall deal with extensive reading programmes in the next chapter) but are more commonly shorter texts for intensive work, often in the form of stencilled sheets, or mounted on card. Commercially produced materials of this kind are available (e.g. the SRA Reading Laboratories), usually in the form of a large set of reading cards. (See Chapter 12, p.188.)

Most currently available reading card systems offer less true guidance than we might wish; they generally consist of text and questions, with answers available so that the student can check his own progress. However, cards of this kind are successful in motivating the student to read. There is an obvious satisfaction in completing a card and getting another, in seeing your total mounting and your comprehension score perhaps improving steadily. And since it is accepted that the best way to improve your reading is to read, we must also accept that reading cards can play a valuable part in a reading programme.

To say that most published reading cards (in fact all, to the best of my knowledge) do not supply real guidance is therefore not necessarily to criticize them, if they work well without it. But throughout this book we have taken the view that questioning is not the only way of dealing with a text, and is not always the way that gives most help to the reader. If other approaches are more helpful, it would be desirable to incorporate them in material to be used by students working on their own.

However, there is a major problem of presentation to be solved. A text is a unit, not just a collection of fragments; also it is linear: that is, it is sequenced in a certain way on the page. But the reading process is not linear; as we read, our minds dart ahead to anticipate what comes next, or return to previous parts to correct an interpretation that has proved to be mistaken, and so on. Moreover, although reading is ideally a unitary process, for the FL reader this ideal is only reached after a period of struggle with some of the difficult fragments that make up the whole text.

The question is: how do we present the text to a reader who will be studying it on his own? Do we print tasks before it, after it, or both? How do we indicate the most helpful ways of studying the text? Do we print a set of instructions which the student must follow in sequence, with the text printed separately? Or, if we want the student to concentrate first on lines 1– 4 of the text, for example, do we print just those lines together with the tasks or questions on them?

The ideal solution to the problem has yet to be found; if we were to ask all the questions and set all the tasks that might be needed, the text itself would be lost among them. For self-study, a sequenced set of instructions (incorporating tasks and questions as well as instructions about what part to read next and so on) might be put on a separate sheet; the students would have to be trained to follow the sequence recommended on this sheet, rather than reading the text in their own way.

A number of books have appeared recently which have tackled this problem in various ways. Examples from some of them appear in Appendix B. Most of them interrupt the text on the printed page by notes or questions. In some cases, the notes and questions are placed in wide margins and printed in different type. In the original version of *Reading and Thinking in English*, a different colour is used for the texts themselves so that they stand out from the study aids that accompany them.

It is important to recognize that the questions asked in these books are not intended to test but to teach: to draw the reader's attention to possible pitfalls, make him stop and think and, it is hoped, avoid them. Testing questions may also be asked (if so they usually follow the text) but the questions that are interpolated in the text itself are meant to guide the reader in much the same way (as we shall see below) as a good teacher would try to guide his students. A feature of *English in Focus* is that the book offers not only the correct answers to the questions, but also a brief explanation of why one answer is right, another wrong. It is thus moving towards being a self-contained self-teaching text, which is what an individualized reading programme requires (since the teacher cannot give individual tuition to every student in his class).

If you want to use a partially individualized approach, you can put similar texts on to an OHP or distribute stencilled copies of a text prepared in this way. The students can then work independently of you, at any rate to begin with; but unless they can work on different texts the effort of preparing the material is hardly worthwhile. If you are using what is basically a class text, it is more economical to use the next method.

6.3   Guidance from the teacher: the whole class approach

The questions and comments incorporated in the texts described above resemble the questions that would be used by a teacher interacting with a class. This is a teacher-centred approach which some people will criticize, but it has some decided advantages.

In the first place, it is possible to ask a great many more questions orally than in writing; if we tried to write them all down, the page would get so cluttered with questions that the text would be lost. Asking more questions is only an advantage if there are a great many useful questions to be asked, but this is usually the case, at any rate with texts that offer any degree of challenge.

Secondly, and more importantly, the questions you ask and the tasks you set in face-to-face interaction will respond more sensitively to the needs of the students than is possible if they have to be written down beforehand. If you are sensitive to your students you will detect areas of difficulty which need more attention; you can probe to find out why a wrong answer was given or whether a correct one was given for the right reasons; you can prompt students who are hesitant, draw attention to clues that have been missed and, in short, thoroughly involve yourself with the struggle for understanding. Your perception of the students' needs will dominate what you do.

A lesson of this kind is certainly very much under the control of the teacher, with everyone of necessity working at the same rate and in the same way. You may well not wish to use this approach for every text, or every section of a text. Nevertheless, it provides such valuable insights about the way students read, and the things they find difficult, that you ought to use it sometimes. Usually it will come best after the students have made a first attempt on the text silently (and hence individually). You can follow up the silent reading with some initial questioning and then, if the response justifies it, work through the text again from the beginning, in as much detail as you consider suitable.

6.4   Guidance from fellow students: the group approach

By dividing the class into groups you make it possible for students to help one another, and in successful groups, the interaction that takes place achieves far more than the individuals can working on their own. Working together can produce excellent motivation, and a slight sense of competition between groups does no harm if it is not allowed to get out of hand. (Too much stress on competition may lead groups to take short cuts to get results, instead of making sure that every member is playing a full part in discussion.)

(a) Organizing groups

It is important that the groups should not be large; if they contain more than five students, it is too easy for some individuals to opt out and let the others do the work. If you have students with these tendencies, try grouping them together; it may make them participate, and at any rate they will not be disturbing the others.

The students should sit as a proper group, i.e. in a closed circle or square, not in a line. Physical proximity helps to create group solidarity, and it is more difficult for people to be left out if they are facing each other rather than seated at the end of a line. For reading work, a group table is not essential but if you prefer, desks can be pushed together and the group can sit round them.

Whether you choose mixed ability groups or streamed groups is a matter for you to decide. In mixed groups, the weaker students may benefit from the help of the others, but they may also be too conscious of their weakness to make a proper attempt to participate. If you use streamed groups, you can help the slower groups yourself and you may find that the weaker students take more part in the activity if they are working together.

You can also, of course, assign different tasks or different texts to different groups, according to their ability. This is worth doing if there is a wide range in your class, even though it will make your class organization more complex. Occasionally it is interesting to get each group to do a different task, but all related to the same text; the various aspects that are revealed, and the variety of responses, make for interesting discussion.

While the groups are working, your job is mainly to be available for consultation; this should mean not solving their problems for them, but rather showing them how to solve the problems themselves. You will also want to listen to what is going on in several groups (without disturbing them) in case any matters crop up which ought to be dealt with in class in a later period. Of course, if you assign different texts to different groups, you will have to spend some time with each, since you will not be able to hold any report-back session with the whole class together.

(b) Planning group tasks

For most of the time, the groups will be working independently of you, since you cannot be with them all at once. This means that the tasks you give them must be very explicit so that there is no doubt about what they have to do. Less explicit tasks such as 'Discuss the text' are generally unsuccessful.

If you have a comprehension textbook, you may find that some of the questions in it are suitable for group work, or you may be able to supply extra tasks for this purpose. To be useful for group work, a task needs to be explicit, to engage each member of the group, and to promote vigorous discussion. Suitable tasks have been described in earlier chapters (e.g. pp. 126, 144), and there are many other possibilities.

You might like to look again at the questions and tasks set on the texts in Appendix B, and decide which would be suitable for group work. Can you modify the format of some of them to make them more suitable, while not changing the basic nature of the task?

If you are planning to use group work, you must work out how you want to sequence the activity, because this may affect the way you prepare your materials. For instance, if you want to include work on predicting what will come next, you will have to arrange that the students have access only to part of the text, for you cannot reasonably expect them not to look ahead if they have the whole text. If you want to use the cloze technique, a gapped text will have to be prepared.

Of course there is no best way of structuring the activity. One way would be to get the groups to tackle the text section by section (as described earlier in this chapter), with a class report-back discussion after each section is completed. This would probably follow a few minutes of introductory work with the whole class, and perhaps individual work on skimming or silent reading. It would certainly be followed by work on the text as a whole, either in groups, as individuals or as a class. Many variations are possible.

(c) Worksheets and answer sheets

A useful way of controlling group activity is to supply worksheets setting out the tasks. You might have one worksheet containing all the work to be done on one text; on the other hand, you might have several worksheets for a single text, to be worked through in sequence. The groups would be encouraged to work at their own speeds, but would have to complete one worksheet satisfactorily before being given the next. This gives you the opportunity to check the rate of progress and make sure that the work has been done properly. Some of the tasks set on the texts in Appendix B would be suitable for use in a sequence of worksheets.

You may feel that it is pointless extra work to prepare worksheets, but if you try it I think you will agree that it is worth the effort. I have already pointed out that group work produces excellent motivation, and to make group work successful you will almost certainly have to prepare some extra activities beyond those given in the textbook. From there it is an easy step to assemble all the activities in a single worksheet; and from there again, the extra work involved in making a sequenced series of worksheets is minimal. Using worksheets gives you an effective and simple method of controlling what goes on, and a chance to make the group tasks very clear and explicit. Moreover, completing one worksheet and collecting a fresh one is motivating in itself.

If you have a large class and cannot pay enough attention to every group, you can prepare answer sheets to match the worksheets. When a group has completed its worksheet, the answer sheet can be issued if you cannot check the answers yourself. The group are expected to check their own answers and discuss them. Some explanation of the reasons for accepting or rejecting answers should be included on the sheet so that there is no need to refer to you every time they make a mistake they do not understand. (For one possible form for such explanations, see the 'Solutions' section of Text 3, Appendix B.) Use the L1 for this purpose if the explanation cannot be expressed simply enough in the FL.

Worksheets and answer sheets can be issued as stencilled copies which the students can keep, but this is not essential. An alternative is to prepare enough copies for each group to have one; mount them on thin card; and get your colleagues in the library to cover them with the transparent plastic used to protect library books. With this protection your cards will last for years. But try them out before going to all that trouble, so that you can change any questions or tasks that do not work well.

7   Guidance when reading has been completed

When the detailed work is over, global understanding must be attended to, and the text as a whole evaluated and responded to.

Even if you chose to do some global work before studying the text in detail, there is always much more to be done afterwards. Now is the time to reconsider the hypotheses that the students made about the text in the early stages. Their opinions about the writer's aims, about the main message of the text, etc., can be substantiated and refined, or if necessary rejected and replaced.

Now is the time to put questions of *evaluation* and *personal response* and to help the students to relate the text to the world in which it is placed. If the text belongs to a particular field of study, now is the time to judge it in relation to the rest of the field. (Does it put forward accepted or controversial ideas? What research could be done to substantiate or refute them? What practical applications might result from them?) If it is primarily argumentative, now is the time to evaluate the arguments, react to them personally and, for advanced students, assess the effectiveness with which they are presented. If it is taken from a book which the class is reading, now is the time to consider the place of this passage in the development of the overall plot, theme, argument, etc.

Each kind of text, and each individual text, requires different treatment. The work to be done at this stage may include some of the following:

(a)   eliciting a personal response from the reader (agree/disagree; like/dislike, etc.)

(b)   linking the content with the reader's own experience/knowledge

(c)   considering the significance of the text in the book from which it was taken

(d)   establishing the connection between the content and other work in the same field

(e)   suggesting practical applications of theories or principles

(f)   working out the implications for research/policy/theory, etc., of the ideas/ facts in the text

(g)   drawing comparisons/contrasts between facts etc. in this text and others

(h)   recognizing relationships of cause and effect

(i)   ascertaining chronological sequence (e.g. where a narrative shifts from one time to another or uses flashbacks)

(j)   tracing the development of thought/argument

(k)   distinguishing fact from opinion

(l)   weighing evidence

(m) recognizing bias

(n)   discussing/evaluating characters, incidents, ideas, arguments

(o)   speculating about what had happened before/would happen afterwards; or about motives, reasons, feelings, etc. where these are unexpressed.

This list is not intended to be exhaustive, but merely to suggest the kind of work to be undertaken at this stage.

Most of the work discussed so far will be best done orally; it could culminate in written work. Some of the more specific tasks could be undertaken in groups before whole class discussion. One specific task which can be done in groups at this stage is choosing a title. If you are using this as a group task, it is best to give four or five alternative titles rather than allowing a free choice. Make sure that one of the titles is too broad, another too narrow, a third wrong in emphasis and so on. This task, though often thought of as dreary, can produce heated argument if done as group work, and is an excellent way of summing up the accumulated understanding of the text.

Finally, it is at this stage that most of the outcomes described in Chapter 10, section 4.2 will be introduced: you are asked to refer back to that chapter for the details.

8   Footnote: a possible sequence of teaching

To summarize the suggestions outlined in this chapter, they are tabulated below to show a possible sequence of teaching.

Intensive reading

Possible sequence for lessons in class and group modes

Step 1   Set overall purpose for reading this text.
Step 2   Introduce the text.
Step 3   Skimming/scanning exercise on whole text.
Step 4   Tackle the text section by section.

> Procedure for each section:

> (a)   Deal with essential language points for section (if any).
> (b)   Assign SPQ for the section.
> (c)   Silent reading of the section by whole class.
> (d)   Check answer to SPQ and assign other questions for the section.

Class mode	*Group mode*
(e) Individuals reread text and do tasks/prepare answers to questions.	(e) Group reread, discuss tasks/questions and prepare answers.
(f) Class, with teacher's guidance, works through section orally, discussing questions/tasks and ensuring thorough understanding of all important elements. (If you must include reading aloud, it will come best at the end of this step.)	(f) Report back session: answers of different groups compared and discussed by class.
(g) Return to SPQ if necessary and then assess the section as a whole; predict what will follow (unless it is the last section); relate it to what has gone before (unless it is the first); predict or discuss its function in/contribution to the whole text.	(g) As for (f) in class mode if necessary; or proceed to (h). (h) As for (g) in class mode, but doing some of the work by means of further group assignments followed by class discussion of various group answers.

Step 5   After completing section by section study, assign tasks (group or individual) requiring assessment of the text as a whole, drawing together information obtained from the detailed study and including the contribution of each part to the total message.
Step 6   Groups or individuals attempt tasks.
Step 7   Report-back session and final discussion/evaluation.

Note: Depending on the text, these steps might be spread over several lesson periods and homework assignments.

12 An Extensive Reading Programme

In this chapter we are moving away from the classroom and into the private world of reading for our own interest. So far this book has been occupied mainly with the sort of help the teacher can give to inexpert or reluctant readers. Here we are mainly concerned with what the student can do for himself. But the teacher still has a part to play: he has to make sure that books are available, and that as many students as possible obey the slogan

Get hooked on books!

1 The cycle of frustration and the cycle of growth

If you have read up to this point, there is presumably no need to convince you of the importance of reading to the individual and society. So we will take that for granted. Why is it that many people fail to make much progress in such a valuable skill?

Many of us teach students who are trapped in the vicious circle shown in Figure 25.

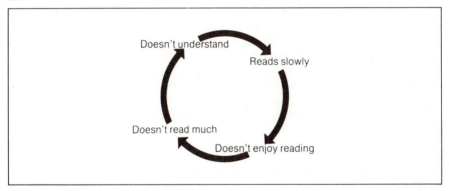

Fig. 25   The vicious circle of the weak reader

It doesn't matter where you enter the circle, because any of the factors that make it up will produce any of the others. A slow reader is seldom able to develop much interest in what he reads, let alone enjoyment. Since he gets no pleasure from it, he reads as little as possible. Deprived of practice, he continues to find it difficult to understand what he reads, so his reading rate does not increase. He remains a slow reader: and so on.

Somehow or other we must help him to get out of this cycle of frustration and enter instead the cycle of growth represented in Figure 26.

As we have seen in earlier chapters, speed, enjoyment and comprehension are closely linked with one another and with the amount of practice a reader gets. Any of the factors could provide the key that will get us out of the vicious circle and into the virtuous one; but the most hopeful, I think, is *enjoyment*, closely followed by *quantity*.

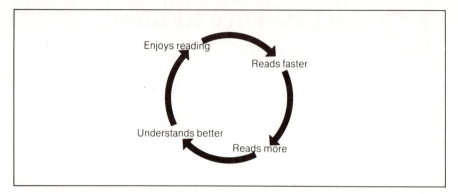

Fig. 26   The virtuous circle of the good reader

2   Why encourage extensive reading?

At the heart of this chapter is the slogan

> We learn to read by reading.

This is so unoriginal that I do not know who said it first; and it is perfectly accurate. However, we learn something else by reading too, and this provides another useful slogan:

> The best way to improve your knowledge of a foreign language is to go and live among its speakers. The next best way is to read extensively in it.

You may find this useful when prevailing upon headmasters to give you funds to buy books, or convincing parents that reading is not a waste of time, or persuading students that it will actually help them to pass their examinations. Students who read a lot will not become fluent overnight, and it may take a year or two before you notice a marked improvement in their productive skills; but then it often comes as a breakthrough that results in their progressing at increasing speed and far outstripping their classmates who have not developed the reading habit.

3   Reading more and reading better

We want our students to be able to read *better*: fast and with full understanding. To do this they need to read *more*. And there seem to be two ways of getting them to read more: requiring them to do so and tempting them to do so. The latter leads us straight back to the factor of enjoyment, which we shall be considering at length; but first let us consider the former.

4   Requiring them to read

4.1   Reading in the classroom

Recent studies (see Lunzer and Gardner, 1979, ch.5) have shown that in British classrooms at least there is surprisingly little reading done, right across the curriculum. It occupied not more than fifteen per cent of lesson time overall, and much of the reading observed was fragmentary rather than continuous. Even reading comprehension work was found to involve more writing than reading. We cannot assume that the position is the same in every country, but both probability and observation suggest that in many it is not very different.

Of course this is unintentional and it has taken people a long time to realize what is happening. But since so little use is made of reading, students may be starting to feel that it is a redundant art.

Teachers may have good reasons for not using more reading in class; they may feel that it is better programmed for out-of-school work, so that class time can be used for things that can be done nowhere else. This is fine as long as out-of-school reading assignments are in fact given. If they are not, we should not be surprised if reading standards are low. If nobody gives assignments that require them to read, some students will never feel the need to read at all and thus will never acquire the habit or the skill.

4.2   Second language reading across the curriculum

Find out from your colleagues teaching other subjects the amount of reading they require students to do. If the language you teach is a FL, the reading assignments will presumably not be in that language; even so, the reading habit created in the L1 may be of help.

If, however, you teach a second language (SL), and especially if it is the medium of instruction for other subjects, then reading tasks assigned by other teachers will make a direct contribution to your own efforts. In this case it is important to get the other teachers on your side and to support one another's work.

If the other teachers are prepared to co-operate with you, you can give them help in these ways:

(a) *Selecting texts*: Have a look at the SL textbooks in other subjects that the students are expected to read. You will often find that they are far beyond the linguistic level of the students. Talk this over with the subject teacher and show him the problems: if he is aware of them he may be able to moderate them. If it is not possible to choose another book, he may be able to give more specific guidance, as described in the next paragraph.

(b) *Guiding study reading*: Even a textbook at the right level (whether in L1 or SL) will be studied more effectively if the student has been given a specific purpose for reading. This means that he is not told merely to read the chapter and make notes, but is asked to find certain information, trace an argument, explain the evidence for the writer's conclusions, etc. If your colleagues do not use such methods already, they should be introduced to them. Those who are really interested might perhaps read Chapter 11 for themselves; many of the ideas suggested there can be usefully applied to study reading. The use of group work for this purpose is particularly rewarding, provided the tasks are well defined.

(c) *The SQ3R technique*: Work in other subjects (in any language) will benefit if you introduce this study reading technique to the students. It is essentially a strategy for private study (first described in Robinson, (1964)) and consists of five steps: Survey (S), Question (Q), Read (R), Recite (R), Review (R). Some of these labels are a little misleading, so read the notes below or go back to the original source.

   (i) *Survey*: Go through the text rapidly (skim) to make sure it is relevant and to get an overview of its main points.
   (ii) *Question*: Pause to ask yourself the questions you want the text to answer; beginners could usefully write them down. Note that it is the

reader who must supply the questions; this is part of the study process, intended to make you think about your purpose in reading – what you want to get out of the text. It also involves some attempt at prediction: what help is the text expected to supply?

(iii) *Read*: Now read carefully, looking for the answers to your questions and also making sure you have not overlooked anything else that is relevant.

(iv) *Recite*: This is not reciting the text, but the answers to your questions. Speaking the answers aloud to yourself is recommended because the effort involved will help to fix them in your mind; writing them down would also be effective. The essential thing is to reprocess in some way the salient points gained from the text.

(v) *Review*: Remind yourself again of what you have learned, but this time organize the information in your mind, consider its implications for other things you know, assess its importance and so on. At this stage your aim is to process the information in a useful form and to integrate it with your previous knowledge or experience. This stage may with advantage take place some time later, rather than immediately after stage (iv), to provide reinforcement and revision.

You will realize that this study technique is particularly useful if the teacher has not provided guidance; step (ii) in effect makes the student responsible for providing his own guidance. With able students, this produces purposeful and active involvement. But even weaker (and younger) students have improved their study reading by using this kind of approach.

The above are just some of the ways in which you can co-operate with teachers of other subjects. It is also helpful to take some texts for reading lessons from the SL textbooks used in other subjects; the students will then see the immediate relevance of what they are doing.

If you can offer help of this kind, your colleagues may be more willing to set reading assignments, thus supporting your own efforts by increasing the overall amount of reading required in the school.

4.3   Reading in FL and L1

If you are teaching a FL, most of the previous section will be inapplicable (though SQ3R is valid in any language of course).

But it is not a good idea for you to work in isolation from the work being done on reading in the L1 classes. If you and your L1 colleagues can agree on common approaches, each person's work will complement the others'. As you must have realized, most of the approaches suggested in this book will apply to reading in any language, including the mother tongue. Reading skills can be transferred from one language to another, so the work done in the FL and the L1 classes will be mutually beneficial if similar approaches are used.

You may, however, be teaching in a society where L1 reading is not encouraged, or where L1 reading materials are few and unattractive. In these circumstances you will not get much support from your L1 teacher colleagues. On the other hand, if little suitable L1 material is available, a variety of FL supplementary readers, particularly fiction, will supply food for the students' minds and imagination, so that promoting the desire to read the FL is not very difficult.

However, reading skills are better developed in the L1 before the FL, so it will be in everybody's best interests (most of all the students') to have a strong successful L1 reading programme on which your FL programme may be built.

5 Making them want to read

If your colleagues agree to increase the number of reading assignments given, you have got one prong of a two-pronged approach to increasing the amount of reading done: you have made sure that the students are *required* to read. The second prong is to make them *want* to read, and this involves mainly the factor of enjoyment. *Needing* to read books, for study or other purposes, is also an incentive for some students; but wanting to read books because you enjoy them is an incentive for everybody.

5.1 Promoting the reading habit

Provided the books are well chosen, it is not as difficult as you might think to establish the reading habit. In any class there are a few students who respond slowly or not at all to the attractions of reading, but there are always many others who quickly develop a real appetite for books. It may even become difficult to supply enough books to satisfy the demand; but this is a difficulty any teacher would be proud to have.

In schools where there is active promotion of the reading habit, and where plenty of enjoyable easy books are available, it is not at all unusual to find students reading a book a week, and many read more than this. A great deal depends on the difficulty of the books available. To develop fluent reading it is far more useful to read a lot of easy books than a few difficult ones. You ought therefore to aim at a class library with at least twice as many books as students; four times is the ideal. And think twice before buying two copies of the same book in preference to two different titles.

Active promotion of reading is needed, though, if you are to get results like this. There was a school in Africa where, as part of the reading programme, the uniforms were designed with pockets big enough to hold a book, and it was an offence to be caught without one. We shall consider other devices too; so if, at present, you find it hard to push your students through even one book a term, do not despair yet, but read on.

5.2 Choosing books

When I said that creating the reading habit was not very difficult, I made a proviso: that the books offered must be enjoyable. This is more powerful than any other motivation. We shall be concerned with how to organize a reading programme focused principally on making reading enjoyable.

In Chapter 3 we considered the criteria for selecting texts. When we are choosing books for extensive reading, the criteria of readability (i.e. suiting the linguistic level of the reader) and suitability of content are even more important than when we are choosing a class text, because we are expecting the student to read the books on his own.

To summarize, extensive reading materials should be:

(a) *Appealing*: They must appeal to the intended readers, supplying what they really want (not just what they say they want). The appeal is greater if the book is attractive in appearance, well printed and with good coloured illustrations — more illustrations and bigger print for more elementary students. The books should look like the books we buy from choice: i.e. they should not smell of the schoolroom; notes and questions are better omitted.

(b) *Easy*: The language must be easier than that found in the current FL coursebook. We cannot expect students to read from choice, or to read fluently, if the language is a struggle. Reading improvement comes from reading a lot of easy material.

(c) *Short*: The length of the book must not be intimidating; elementary students need short books that they can finish quickly without a sense of strain and without getting bored.

(d) *Varied*: There must be a wide choice suiting the various needs of the readers in terms of content, language and intellectual maturity.

There is no excuse nowadays, at any rate in the field of English as a foreign language (EFL) for not having a plentiful and varied collection of books. The major EFL publishers have had a good range of supplementary readers for years, and others are now following suit. (See the list in Appendix C.) An excellent guide to the whole range is published by the British Council (Brumfit, 1979), grouping the books according to the intended level of difficulty (vocabulary of 300 words, 800 words, etc.).

5.3   Acquiring books

If you teach English, your problem is more likely to be how to obtain the books than how to choose them. One very widespread difficulty is getting enough money. Teachers have found some ingenious solutions to this; for example:

(a) Persuading the headmaster to allocate school funds to buy books. Do your homework first: find out the cost of the books, together with anything else you need to buy (storage, transparent plastic for covering books, etc.). Your ultimate target should be a collection of four books per head; but at least one book per head with ten or twenty extra to give some room for choice and varying reading speeds. Work out the procedures you will use for lending the books and so on, so that you can answer all the questions the headmaster will want to ask. And of course be ready with a persuasive explanation of the advantages to be expected, as outlined earlier in this chapter.

(b) Getting each student to buy or, better, contribute money for one book. Provided you buy different titles, not duplicates, a class of 30 students will have 30 different books to read; a good foundation, but needing additional titles from other resources to provide for differing tastes etc.

(c) Organizing fund raising events with the help of the class. The students will appreciate the books more if they themselves have made some effort to obtain the purchase money. Students can perhaps get their family and friends to sponsor them for some activity such as a race or other form of achievement (i.e. they will offer to pay a certain amount of money if the student succeeds, or for every mile run, etc.). Figure 27 shows how one class increased the size of its library by taking part in a sponsored spelling test!

(d) Appealing to local donors: individuals, firms, organizations are all likely sources of funds. Request money rather than books, since donations of books from people who do not know your students are likely to include some very unsuitable titles. (It is not true that any books are better than none: see below p. 179.)

(e) Making arrangements for multiple loans from a library. Sometimes libraries are prepared to organize book boxes, on loan for about a term and then

Fig. 27   Results of a sponsored spelling test (*Times Educational Supplement,* 24 April 1981)

replaced by a new selection. Try to help in selecting the books, however, or you may get unsuitable ones.

Sometimes a local bookseller can be made to take an interest in your activities: help him to select suitable titles which he can bring along to the school for sale (perhaps during a parent/teacher meeting when students are also present). A display of colourful new books is a persuasive means of getting students to buy. Persuade them to donate the books to the class library after reading them; or organize a second-hand book exchange scheme by means of which students swap books regularly.

In some countries, schemes involving money provoke distrust; a cautious and tactful approach, and meticulous accounts and organization, may still win the day. The headmaster's approval is essential. If there is a parent/teacher organization, seek their support by making sure they understand your aims and the details of your programme; involve them as far as you can, so that they feel proud of their contribution instead of mistrusting the scheme. Secure the co-operation of your fellow teachers if possible. Other teachers of the same language should be involved with the scheme from the start and should be building up collections for their own classes, so that planning, fund raising etc. can be done jointly.

Once the books have been acquired and are ready for borrowing, invite parents and teachers and donors to inspect the books, handle them and admire them, so that everyone can see that the funds have been used to good effect.

Note: For EFL books, if local book suppliers cannot get the books you want, write to your local office of The British Council or to the publishers whose addresses are given in Appendix C.

6   Organizing a library

The first decision to take is whether you and your colleagues, working together, should organize a FL supplementary readers collection in the school library; or whether you will build up a class library in each of the classes you teach.

6.1   A class library

There is a lot to be said for having a class library if you can. It means you can choose books that are particularly suited to the age, proficiency and interests of the students; and this in turn means that they will not waste time and get discouraged by looking through books that are inappropriate.

The fact that the books are kept in the classroom is also important. If the students have helped to buy them, they will naturally prefer the books to be kept in their own room, where they will be a normal and essential part of classroom life, picked up in spare moments, referred to for information, easily available without making a special journey to the library or waiting for a special time of opening. And you can keep a much closer eye on the books, and who reads what, if they are there in your own territory.

6.2   The school library

If funds are very limited, your school may feel that any books have to be put in a common collection, since there is sure to be more duplication of titles if you have a class library system, where several classes may all need copies of the same book. In a central library, you could manage with fewer copies and you could afford to cater for minority interests; there may be a dozen railway enthusiasts in the school but only one in any one class. So a good central collection has to be the first priority, but class libraries should also be developed if you can possibly afford them.

The school library may not be under your control, but if your FL books are stored there, do everything you can to make sure that it is open frequently for students to both browse and borrow books; the minimum should be once a day, at a time when all students are able to go. You should also be there with the students frequently, so that you can help them to find their way round the collection, and to choose books sensibly.

6.3   Running the library

It is important to keep the library looking tidy and attractive, and of course to have an efficient system of control to prevent too many losses. Even with young children, much of the work can be delegated to students. I remember a library full of old papers and dusty books piled in dark cupboards and populated by frogs. Not surprisingly, nobody went there. A year later it had been repaired and redecorated, the frogs had decamped, shelves had replaced the deep cupboards, the rubbish had been cleared out and new books bought. It was thereafter kept that way for as long as I knew it by an efficient student librarian and his assistants, who ran it so well that, while many books were borrowed, hardly any were lost.

Of course there must be no question of not allowing the books to be borrowed; the whole point about an extensive reading scheme is that it should operate almost entirely out of class time. There is, for one thing, nothing like enough time in class for the necessary amount of reading to be completed; and for another, we want to remove, if we can, the association of books with the drudgery of the classroom. So work out a system that enables students to borrow at least one book and keep it at home for long enough to read it. Preferably, have a card in each book that can be removed each time it is borrowed, and stored until it is returned. If the card has spaces to record the names of the borrowers, it will provide useful information about individual students' tastes, and about the popularity of the book.

6.4   Storing supplementary readers

You may well have to keep your class library in a lockable container such as a cupboard or box. As this is not an attractive way of storing books, you should avoid it if possible (for instance, if the classroom itself can be locked). In any case the library monitor should take the books out of the container and put them on display each day while the room is in use.

The best way to display books is to have a book corner or, perhaps even better, shelves running round the room. Given the right classroom atmosphere, it is surprising how few books are lost from such collections.

One of the problems of storing the usual kind of EFL supplementary reader is that it has no spine, or only a very narrow one, so that the title is not visible when the book is placed on the shelf in the usual way. A shelf of readers stored in this way looks untempting, and it is difficult to locate specific books.

If you can find the space, therefore, arrange to store at least some of your readers so that the front cover (often attractively illustrated) is showing. Below are a number of ways of doing this.

(a) A free-standing book rack, similar to the ones sometimes found holding paperbacks in bookshops. This is ideal if you have the space. (See Figure 28.)

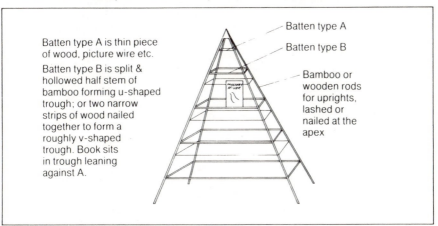

Batten type A is thin piece of wood, picture wire etc.

Batten type B is split & hollowed half stem of bamboo forming u-shaped trough; or two narrow strips of wood nailed together to form a roughly v-shaped trough. Book sits in trough leaning against A.

Batten type A

Batten type B

Bamboo or wooden rods for uprights, lashed or nailed at the apex

Fig. 28   Free standing book rack
This can have either three or four legs and be from about a metre to a metre and a half in height, depending on the space available. Check the sizes of your books before finalizing your design: the distances between the battens can be adjusted to take varying heights. The B type battens (in which the books stand) will need to be on average about 22 cm apart from one another, while an A type batten, against which the books rest, will be about 10–15 cm above each B type.

(b) A sloping shelf running round the classroom walls (under the windows, for example, unless rain would be a problem). (See Figure 29.)

(c) A folding and lockable library corner as shown in Figure 30. This is very practical but is heavy and takes up a good deal of space.

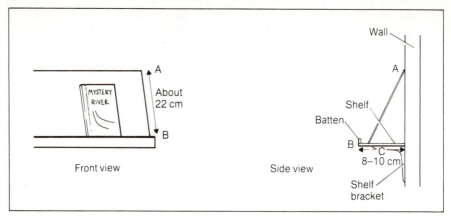

Fig. 29   Sloping shelf round classroom wall
The sloping shelf should be made of light stiff material such as plywood, hardboard or stiff cardboard. It is supported by a little shelf attached to the wall by a bracket; the shelf need be only 8–10 cm deep. Along the front of the shelf and at the foot of the slope runs a short vertical batten preventing books from sliding off.

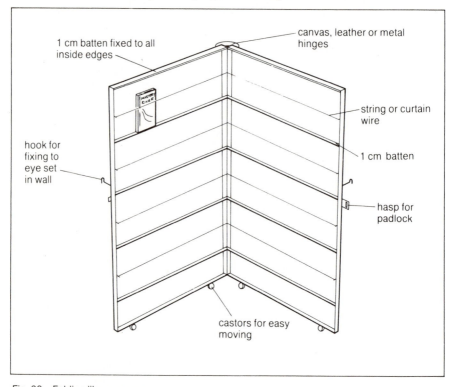

Fig. 30   Folding library corner
The two screens are of hardboard, plywood, etc., each 1–1½ metres high and 60–75 cm wide. Join down one side by means of hinges. Fit a hasp which can be secured by a padlock when the two open sides are brought together so that the library is closed. The books can remain in position, standing on narrow battens and kept upright by tight curtain wires stretched across in front of them, about 10–15 cm above each batten. If the screen can be placed in the corner of the room, it can be kept steady while open by fixing two hooks into eyes set in the walls.

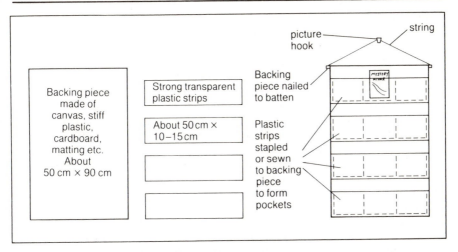

Fig. 31   Hanging wall pockets for storing readers
The plastic strips need to be divided into 3 or 4 pockets, about 18–20 cm wide,
according to the size of the books and the width of the backing piece.

(d) Hanging wall pockets with a backing of strong cloth or plastic, and preferably transparent plastic front so that deep pockets can be made without hiding the front covers of the books. (See Figure 31.) Several of these will be needed, as they do not hold many books. The pockets are easy to store (either leave them on the wall, empty, or roll them up and put them in the cupboard with the books).

You do not need to display all your readers at once, but get your librarians to choose different ones each day or week.

6.5   Classifying the class library

In your class library, it is possible to classify books either according to their content (fiction/non-fiction, with further subclassification into different subjects, different kinds of stories etc.) or according to their linguistic level. Which is more useful?

For reading to become a pleasurable habit, as we have seen, both content and language must be suited to the reader. For an individual student with a particular book, we cannot say which will be more important: will he read it because, though not particularly interesting, it is written in language he can understand? Or will he read it because it enthrals him, even though the language is difficult?

If your class library does not need to cater for widely differing linguistic levels, it should be classified according to content, because once the language level is left out of account, it is naturally the content that determines the student's choice. But if you have to supply books for students of very different levels of proficiency, it is more helpful for the primary classification to be in terms of linguistic level, so that students do not waste time or get discouraged trying to find suitable books.

6.6   Coding linguistic levels

It will be helpful to have a coding system for linguistic levels that can operate throughout the school, so that when students move from one class to another they do not have to learn a new system each time. For example, you can use readability indexes as described on pp. 26 – 28. If you have a full range of proficiency in the school, from beginners to advanced, you will require quite a lot of levels; while if your students are all at, say, roughly the intermediate stage, you maybe able to manage with fewer levels, or you may prefer to make your grading more sensitive, i.e. to increase the number of levels by defining each level more narrowly. Hence in one school level 3 might be books of 1000 – 1500 words, in another another level 3 might be 1000 – 1250 and level 4 1250 – 1500.

You and your colleagues will have to make these decisions according to your own circumstances. If you are not very experienced, set up a system that you can modify later if it does not work as well as it should. You will find Brumfit (1979) very helpful in allocating books to levels.

Different EFL publishers grade their books according to different criteria, so that it is not possible to match exactly the books produced by any two of them. Appendix D gives a rough indication of comparative levels. An approximate match is enough for our purposes, since our students will not be at exactly matched levels either. Some EFL publishers (see Appendix C) supply guides or leaflets about their grading systems, which are worth asking for.

The publishers' grading systems are not foolproof, and there is some variation even within a single level from a single publisher, so be prepared to change the level of a book if it turns out to be easier or more difficult than its grading indicates. Get your students to tell you when a grading seems mistaken.

If your collection includes books (e.g. Ladybird readers; Macdonald Starters; some of Blackwell's simple information books) that are not graded with FL readers in mind, you can assess them according to one of the methods outlined in Chapter 3. Use the same method to assess a few samples from each of your graded levels so that the ungraded books can be slotted in appropriately. Or use cloze extracts from the books with students whose linguistic level you already know.

When you have worked out the best system for your own collection, you may find yourself with, say, twelve levels as follows:

Level 1	Up to 500 words vocabulary	Red
Level 2	500 – 750	Yellow
Level 3	750 – 1000	Dark green
Level 4	1000 – 1250	Purple
Level 5	1250 – 1500	Light blue
Level 6	1500 – 1750	Brown
Level 7	1750 – 2000	Light green
Level 8	2000 – 2250	Orange
Level 9	2250 – 2500	Pink
Level 10	2500 – 2750	Dark blue
Level 11	2750 – 3000	Turquoise
Level 12	3000 – 3500	Black

The colour coding shown on the right makes shelving and choosing books easier; buy adhesive coloured paper spots (i.e. small circular patches about 1 cm diameter), or make your own using felt pens or paints. Stick these on the spines of the books so that the level can be identified at a glance. If you cannot find enough colours, you can combine different colours with different numbers of spots to give the required number of symbols. If the books are shelved according to level, the shelf labels can carry the same colour code.

If you use a colour coding system, it is quite practicable to classify your library by subject; the reader looks for books on his desired subject and the colour directs him to those which are suitable for his own linguistic level.

6.7   Classifying supplementary readers in the school library

Most school libraries will be classified according to subject (e.g. by the Dewey system). Graded readers can, of course, also be classified in that way; but in that case they will be dispersed throughout the library. This means that one major advantage of grading is lost: the books cannot be grouped together according to linguistic level, to help students to choose suitable books easily.

The school librarian may feel uneasy about any departures from his usual system (especially if it involves him in extra work). But the function of a library classification is to make it as simple as possible for the right reader and the right book to come together. There is therefore little doubt that books specially written for foreign learners should be classed separately from the main collection: it is the controlled language rather than the subject that is their primary feature.

Try to persuade the librarian to shelve the graded readers separately from the main collection. If this is done, you can classify them in accordance with the suggestions for classifying class library books. If the library users come from a wide age range, it may be necessary to subdivide at least the lower levels according to whether the books are intended for children or adults. (Either use extra colours for the extra subdivisions, or use an additional label – e.g. a red star – for the books at each level intended for children.) Shelve the children's books separately if possible.

If the librarian is not prepared to operate a system of this kind, try to persuade him to shelve at least the graded fiction readers separately – at the end of the main fiction section, for example, instead of scattered throughout according to the alphabetical order of the authors' names. Since most graded readers are fiction, this concession would be a great help.

Whatever the shelving/cataloguing problems, you should be able to persuade the librarian to make use of a colour coding system for linguistic levels, provided you do not expect him to do the coding himself. This is arguably a job better done by a professional language teacher anyway, so you and your colleagues should be prepared to undertake it.

6.8   Discarding books

If you have inherited a library, skim through each book to assess whether it should be there at all. There is a surprising amount of junk to be found in libraries that are not regularly weeded. This is particularly likely if the medium of instruction has changed during the last ten years or so; you may find that many of the books are no longer suitable linguistically for the students now in your class.

Be ruthless and throw out all books that are beyond your students' language level, unless they are so attractively produced that the students enjoy them in spite of their difficulty. In any case, shelve them apart from the graded collection.

Be equally ruthless with graded readers if they are too old-fashioned or foreign in content to appeal to your students, or if they are tattered or dirty. Interpret this advice with common sense: a really popular book may well become shabby, but should not be discarded if it is still readable and if it cannot be replaced. Similarly, let the students decide which books are appealing and which are not; many stories are likely to have a foreign background, but they are not automatically disqualified on that account. (Student preferences are best assessed by noting which books are often borrowed.)

Many people have been put off reading for life by being faced with shelves full of unsuitable books, among which the suitable ones are hardly visible. Don't let this happen in your library. Shelves of suitable books, cared for and attractively displayed, are hard to resist and help to create the reading habit. It is better to have a few that are suitable than a lot that are mostly not.

6.9   Losses and damage

Some librarians are excessively worried about losing books, even going so far as to keep them safely locked up rather than run the risk of anyone borrowing them. But of course the only justification for spending money on books is to enable people to read them. The more people read them the more justified the expenditure.

If you work in a place where life is dominated by inventories, this can be a problem. However, it is generally possible to negotiate with the authorities if you employ patience, good humour and logic. The first thing to do is to establish the principle that library books cannot be expected to survive indefinitely, as tables and chairs can. A paperback in frequent use will last only four to five years. Even tables and chairs get written off eventually; get the authorities to agree that up to a certain proportion of your books may be written off each year. About ten per cent is considered acceptable by public libraries; you should be able to do better than this. If you write off fewer than seven per cent a year, your headmaster should congratulate you.

Books may need to be written off for several reasons: they may be lost, they may be too badly damaged to read, or they may be discarded as unsuitable. Obviously we must see to it that all of these factors are kept to a minimum.

The best way to reduce loss and damage is to educate the students in valuing and caring for books. Your own attitude is more important than anything else, and your example is necessary if your students come from homes where books are not much used. When books are given out in your class, are they thrown or handed to the recipient? Do you ever read to the class from a book that is folded back on itself? Have you ever been seen turning down the corner of a page to mark your place? Set the example, but also draw attention explicitly to good reading manners. Help your students to see that, if we are privileged to read new, clean, attractive books, we are also under an obligation to keep them that way.

Build on this attitude by giving the students a lot of the responsibility for taking care of their books and organizing the system, as described earlier. From responsibility comes pride in a well-run library and consequent reduction of losses and damage. (Moreover, students often know who has borrowed a 'missing' book and can recover it more easily than you could.)

In addition, take all sensible precautions to protect the books from both loss and damage. Cover them with Vistafoil or similar transparent plastic; check them regularly for damage that can be repaired and encourage the students to report such damage or repair it themselves. Set up proper systems for borrowing books, and make sure that they are kept to. But take every step you can think of to ensure that nobody is discouraged from borrowing, otherwise there is no point in having a library at all.

6.10   Recurrent budget

Even if your library is now about the right size (e.g. for a school library, about eight times as many books as readers; for a class FL library, about four times), you will need to continue spending on it. This is sometimes overlooked by those who control the funds, so it is important to get the principle accepted.

Recurrent funds are needed because, as we have seen, about ten per cent of your book stock will have to be written off each year. But they are also needed because new books are being published all the time and must be added to the library to keep it attractive and up to date.

Find out the average cost of a supplementary reader at the time when you have to submit your budget. Add ten per cent for probable inflation (or more according to local conditions), and budget for replacement or purchase of a number of readers equivalent to about fifteen per cent of your book stock. Add whatever is needed for ancillary purchases (labels, plastic, etc.) and repairs. Your calculations might look like Figure 32.

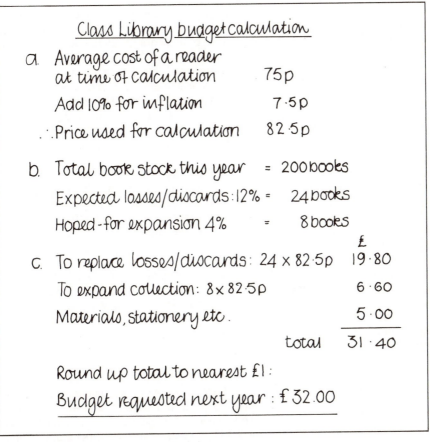

Fig. 32   Sample class library budget calculation

6.11   Training library skills

Having assembled a good collection of books, classified them helpfully and shelved them attractively, you cannot just sit down and expect them to be well used (unless your students are already hooked on books). You have to motivate the students to read, and this we shall return to shortly. Another task is to train them to use the library.

Proper use of a library is a study skill rather than a reading skill, so it will not be fully discussed here; but since it gives access to books and enables students to choose books effectively, it is an important ancillary skill to a reading programme.

The school librarian is the best person to undertake this training, and both he and the students should have provision for it in their timetables. (A librarian cannot operate effectively if he is not allocated time to do this job.)

Library skills cannot be trained in just one lesson, either, but need continual exercise and development. Ideally this should begin early, when the students first enter the school, to equip them with a broad understanding of how the library is organized, what it contains and how to make use of it. This will require a series of lessons fairly close together. Training should continue at intervals and become more sophisticated as the students' needs change and they assume more responsibility for researching their assignments.

If you have to give library training yourself, take care to make it practical. Students will learn most if you set them tasks that make them use the information you have given about where various kinds of book are located, how the catalogue is organized, and so on. A team race to see which group can be the first to produce answers to a list of (say) 50 questions testing basic library skills will be enjoyable as well as instructive for first-year students. (I don't, of course, mean theoretical questions, but questions that require the students to run around the library and use the catalogue, such as: How many books by S. T. Anderson are there in the library? How many of them are on the shelf at present? What does the classification number 401 mean and how many books with this classification does the library hold?)

Later, subject specialists should collaborate with the librarian by setting assignments that require the use of references, so that the librarian can show students how to find information on specific topics; and how to select suitable sources and reject unsuitable ones for a given purpose. This will involve using bibliographies and encyclopaedias, as well as making use of titles, contents pages, indexes and so on as described in Chapter 5.

All these skills need training primarily in the L1, if that is the medium of instruction. You, as the FL teacher, have a special responsibility to help students to find their way round the FL collection – both that in the main library and that in the classroom, if there is one. To do this, you need to be familiar yourself with the entire range of books available, and to have at least some knowledge of the contents of most of them. Students prefer to seek help from a person rather than from inanimate reference tools such as catalogues. For the FL collection, you must be the person.

This means that when students are choosing books, you should be available – suggesting, describing, checking that they have not chosen a book that is too far beyond them linguistically, encouraging them. If a student is at a loss, choose several books that might suit him and then let him make the final selection himself. Find out about their preferences so that you can order more books of the kinds they like. Chat to them about the books they have just finished, so that you can assess without formal testing how far they have understood them. Make sure the books are treated with respect and the borrowing system is working properly. Notice the ones who read little and give them special help and encouragement. In short, be a help and show an interest.

7   Organizing a reading programme

7.1   Co-operation

If possible, get together with your colleagues and plan a reading programme for the school, in which you all co-operate. If this does not work, you can still plan for your own classes, but a continuing programme will be much more effective. By the time you have succeeded in making your students want to read, they may be about to leave you to join someone else's class. This doesn't matter if all teachers are working in a similar way; but if they are not, your efforts may have less success than they deserve.

7.2 Assessing linguistic levels

When you get a new class, one of the first things you will want to know is their level of reading ability. If you have a school reading programme, and this is not a first-year class, you should be able to get the information you need from the previous teacher. ('Homer is still reading books in level 4, but has also read and enjoyed a few from level 5. Keen on mysteries and travel books'.) Comments by teachers are more informative than test results; there is no point testing unless you really need to. So organize reading records that are passed on from one class teacher to the next. A loose-leaf form is best, to allow for students transferring to different classes.

However, if you are teaching first-year students, or if you have no record system, it is desirable to find out their ability by means of a test, because to wait for experience to supply the information would take too long. If you are teaching complete beginners, testing them would be pointless; but I am assuming that your class is entering the school after having had some instruction in the FL elsewhere.

There are, of course, a lot of commercially produced reading tests; over 90 are said to exist for English. But these are not suitable for learners of English as a foreign language, because of assumptions about the structures and (particularly) vocabulary that will be familiar, as well as because of possible cultural bias. It is likely then that you will have to devise your own test.

If you are going to have a reading programme for the whole school, you may have to include provision for testing if you have to provide evidence of progress. For your own internal purposes, the evidence you need is provided by your own records (see p. 187) of each student's developing ability, shown by his moving up from one reading level to the next. This you know without testing; so on the whole it seems best to test only in the first year, to provide baseline data; and at later stages only when there is external pressure for evidence of progress.

I would strongly recommend that the extensive reading programme should not be expected to produce marks for the end-of-year assessments, because that defeats the aim of encouraging reading for pleasure. It also encourages students to cheat, which is not difficult with a programme of this kind; we want a programme of personal reading development, in which the student is in a position to cheat nobody except himself.

7.3 A graded cloze test

Probably the easiest and most effective way of assessing reading level is to administer a graded cloze test. Such a test is, for example, in use in Malaysia in connection with a reading programme used in secondary schools. The principle is to have a test consisting of a series of brief texts of steadily increasing difficulty, related in level to the linguistic grading used in classifying your FL supplementary readers. The student's performance in the test will enable you to assess which level he is capable of starting at; or, if you have weak students, it will warn you not to start the extensive reading programme too early, but to spend time on remedial or preparatory work first.

A test of this kind is not difficult to prepare; you can take the texts from library books of the various levels. Choose passages of 50 – 100 words that are typical of that level and change any proper names that occur, and other details if necessary, so that the extract is not readily identifiable. This is important if you wish to re-use the test year after year. Include several texts, from different books, at each level.

Since these test scores are not intended to be competitive, but simply to provide you with information, there is no need to release them to the students, so keeping the test secure from year to year should not be much of a problem. The same test can be used to monitor student progress, if necessary; but do not use it too frequently or students will begin to recognize it. If you need to monitor more than once every two years or so, construct parallel versions of the test and alternate them. I cannot go into statistical details here, but since no two tests will be exactly parallel, you will first need to test the tests and adjust the scores to make them comparable. Get help from your mathematical colleagues.

Interpreting the test scores is more difficult than constructing the test. Ideally you should try out the test on a full range of students, from the most elementary to the most advanced, whose levels you already know from direct experience or from reports of other teachers. Check the scores to make sure that there are no obvious flaws in the test; students whose work you know to be similar should have similar scores, better students should have higher scores than weaker ones, and so on. If there are flaws find out where the fault lies, alter the test and try it again.

When you are satisfied that it is reasonably valid, work out how the scores should be interpreted by comparing the scores and the known reading levels of all the students who took the test. Unless there are further unsuspected flaws in the test, or unless your previous assessment of the students' reading levels is astray, you should find that students who are reading at the same level have roughly similar scores in the test. If, for instance, students who have been reading comfortably at level 4 all score somewhere between 35 and 45, then you would predict that any unknown student who scored similarly would also be able to read at level 4.

Note: Test construction and the interpretation of test statistics are large and complex subjects. Consult J. P. B. Allen and A. Davies (eds), *The Edinburgh Course in Applied Linguistics, vol. 4, Testing and Experimental Methods (OUP, 1977)*.

7.4   Rough and ready assessment by cloze testing

If you lack the resources to develop a cloze test of the kind described, or if you require a test to help you assess only your own class (and you have reason to think the range of ability is not very wide), you can still make use of the cloze procedure. Prepare a test on the principles already described, i.e. a series of cloze texts taken from typical readers at each of the levels. You may not need to use the full range of levels for a test for a single class; but start with the level below what you think will be the lowest, and end with a text from the level above what you expect to be the highest. (Two levels below and above the first time you administer the test.)

You do not need to obtain scores if you simply want a rough and ready estimate of your students' reading levels. All you need to do is inspect the test paper of each individual student and observe at which level of texts he begins to have difficulty in supplying the right words. Provided that you chose texts that really were representative of each level, you can assume that the level where the student begins to have problems is the level beyond his comfortable reading level. Make sure that he begins his extensive reading with books at least one level below. Your results will be more reliable if you include several texts from each level, taken from different books.

Unless you are going to develop a school reading programme with carefully monitored progress, it is not necessary to devise the more elaborately controlled and scored cloze test described first; the rough and ready method is quite adequate for day-to-day purposes. In any case, it is the way you interpret the test results that is important, and this will only be perfected after you have had some experience. Even the best test may produce results that do not correspond with a student's true ability, so you need to keep an eye on all your students to make sure that they are not being expected – or trying – to read books that are too difficult.

If you are in any doubt, encourage the student to begin with books that are at a lower rather than a higher level; you can always adjust upward when you have got a clearer idea of his true level, but it is damaging to his self-esteem to ask him to go back to a lower level. Nevertheless, you should recommend him to read at a lower level if he is clearly having difficulty. *Reading skills will develop much better if he reads a lot of books that are too easy rather than a few that are too difficult.*

7.5 Remedial reading

If you are going to measure student reading ability, in however rough and ready a way, you must be prepared for some surprises. Some of them may be pleasant; if students turn out to read unexpectedly well, your only problem will be to supply them with enough books at a suitable level.

The main problem will be the students who turn out to read very badly. How you deal with the problem depends on the level at which you are teaching, and the nature of the deficiency. If the student simply reads too slowly, it may be enough to supply him with a lot of very easy material on which he can practise improving his speed without much help from you, though he will need a lot of encouragement. But if he has more severe problems, he will need special attention.

In some school systems, there are remedial classes for those who need help, but in many there are none. In that case, it is your responsibility to do what you can for those whose reading is weak. If you teach a language that is also the medium of instruction, it is obviously essential that you take pains with remedial work, whether the school officially recognizes the need or not.

It is not possible here to go into the question of remedial reading adequately. You will find many ideas that can be adapted to remedial teaching in earlier chapters of this book. A successful 'language experience' approach is described in Walker (1974), chapter 8, and in Mackay *et al.* (1970) and is readily adaptable to FL learning needs. Many ideas and bibliographical references will be found in Melnik *et al.* (1972a and b).

The most important ingredients in a remedial programme, however, seem to be time and caring. You can perhaps make time by using group work as suggested in Chapter 11, though this will not be enough. Extra time of a kind can be gained by using worksheets that the student can work through on his own, though they are difficult to devise for the lowest levels. Other activities that can be done without a teacher include listening to taped readings while following the text in the book as described in Chapter 10; this is very helpful and is enjoyed.

Concern about what happens to those with difficulties is even more important, but this book cannot tell you how to acquire it.

7.6   Creating interest in reading

Once you know the levels at which your students should be reading, you can take positive steps to interest them in books at these levels. Here are some suggestions for doing this.

(a) Read aloud to the class from one of the books, stopping the story at a suitably tantalizing point. Help the students to speculate about what might happen next and encourage them to read on by themselves. (For activities of this kind, have the class sitting round you in a group – on the floor if appropriate – and keep the atmosphere friendly and informal.)

(b) Get a student who has enjoyed a particular book to talk about it or write a brief note for display on the notice board or wall newspaper. (Without giving away the end!)

(c) Show new books to the class and talk a little about each one – enough to whet the appetite but not to give away the whole plot.

(d) Buy cassette recordings of some of the readers for loan with the books. Play parts of them in class. Or play a whole cassette in instalments of about five minutes at the end of each lesson. (If you or a friend read well, make your own cassettes if the published ones are beyond your pocket.)

(e) Encourage students to make or do things arising out of their reading. Producing illustrations for display or taping a dramatized version of the story, or part of it, are examples. More advanced students may enjoy preparing materials of this kind to interest their friends in lower classes, with benefit to both.

(f) Promote discussion of the practical or ethical problems faced by characters in the books. This can either take place after a fair number of students have read the book (the others may then be tempted to do the same), or can follow an outline of the problem given by a student who has read it.

7.7   Incentives to read

Students will read more willingly if they have visible signs of their own progress.

Moving from one reading level to the next is the most obvious sign, but of course does not happen very often. Finishing a book is itself one of the best incentives: this is why it is important to start students off with short easy books, so that they quickly experience the satisfaction of this achievement. The feeling of success will motivate them to start another book, and success will build on success, provided you make sure that they don't move to more difficult books until they are ready.

But you can provide other incentives apart from this basic satisfaction. Some teachers like to display a chart showing the number of books each student has read; for children, this may be in the form of a ladder, each step representing a book, with students' names moving up the ladder according to the number of books they have read.

However, charts of this kind may be counterproductive as far as weak students are concerned. It's nice to see your name climbing steadily upwards, but depressing to stay on the bottom step for weeks. A less competitive form of display may be better: for example, a graph showing how many books the whole class finishes each week, so that collective rather than individual progress is emphasized.

As it is the individual's own progress that matters, however, it may be more useful for each student to keep a personal chart or graph showing how much he has read each week (in terms of the number of pages, for instance), or showing how many books he has finished. He should also keep a record of the titles and, if he chooses, a few comments about the book – but this must not be made into just another classroom chore or it will take away from the pleasure of the achievement.

All your students, but particularly the weaker ones, will find your own interest and encouragement an incentive to read, so give as much individual attention as you can.

7.8   Checking extensive reading

Should you check how well a student has understood an extensive reading book? This is a controversial issue.

One school of thought believes that a student should always answer a few questions, however brief and straightforward, to show that he has really read the book. It is sometimes claimed that students themselves prefer this, as they get satisfaction from being able to answer the questions.

The opposite view is that since extensive reading is essentially a private activity and intended to be above all enjoyable, any attempt to make it seem like school work is likely to be a deterrent.

You are free to adhere to either view or, indeed, both, since it seems likely that different students may respond well to each. When I was a student, I hated having my leisure reading interfered with by teachers' questions (but I liked them to take a friendly interest – very different) and I would not want to inhibit any students who felt the same way. Equally, I would be happy to offer questions to students who wanted them.

Partly this issue depends on whether you have to assign marks for external reading. As I have already said, I very much hope that you don't, because as soon as marks come in, enjoyment tends to go out and reading for pleasure becomes reading for credit.

If you do decide to supply questions, write them on a card and keep the card either in a pocket stuck inside the book cover, or in a file in your own desk. In the latter case, the student comes to you for the card when he is ready; you can please yourself whether to make this optional or obligatory.

However, you can find out by chatting to the student at least as much as you can by getting him to answer written questions, and it is a less intrusive method of finding out what progress he is making and what help he needs.

For your own information you should keep a record of what each student reads, and any special problems he has. The easiest way is to have a book with a page for every student; loose-leaf is best, in case some students read so much that they have to have a second page. You can get the information from the system you use for recording loans, or you can ask students to see you each time they finish a book. The record will have many uses: it helps you to keep an eye on students who are not making progress, it provides information about each student's tastes, and it will be of great help to the teacher of the next class into which the student moves, who should be given a copy or at least a summary.

One word of warning: if your record shows that a student has kept a book for several weeks, or if you can see that he is struggling with it, find out what is wrong and, unless there are good reasons why he should continue, encourage him to return the book without finishing it and pick something else. The whole point about the extensive reading programme is that choice is free; students may be encouraged or even urged to read, but should not be forced to. When the choice is free, there is no virtue in finishing a book if you find you do not like it.

7.9   Reading cards and reading laboratories

In addition to graded readers, reading cards and their more elaborate relatives, reading laboratories, can be used as part of your extensive reading programme.

A reading card consists of a text with questions or other tasks on it, printed or pasted on a card which can be stored with others in a box file, filing cabinet, etc. A reading laboratory consists of a large collection of reading cards, graded in level and intended to be used systematically. The best known laboratories in English are those produced by Science Research Associates (SRA), two of which (*Multiread A, Multiread 2*) are said to be suitable for learners of English as a FL. Longman (*Reading Routes*) and Ward Lock Educational (*Reading Workshops*) publish similar materials, not intended for use by EFL students. A series of cards designed for secondary school EFL learners in Europe is produced by the Centre for British Teachers (*Reading Box*). CUP publishes *Reading Choices*, a set of cards graded from elementary to upper intermediate levels.

Reading cards are used independently of the teacher and can, for instance, be taken home to read. Nevertheless, they do not serve the same purpose as supplementary readers and are less suitable for encouraging reading for pleasure. They are mentioned here for two reasons.

First, they are popular with students. For some students, even a short and easy book may seem out of reach. If you can persuade them to try reading a short and easy card, they will be encouraged by their success and progress to other cards. Keep up a supply of simple cards so that further progress is rapid, and motivation will be high. You can then gradually increase the length until confidence is sufficient to persuade the student to try reading a book. (His first book should be easier than his last card if possible.)

The second reason is that the cards can be tied in with your collection of supplementary readers, if you make your own. Extracts from the readers can be used as the texts on the cards; in this way, interest in the book may be created and some of the students who have worked through the card will move on to read the book.

If you make your own cards, plan a series of cards at the various reading levels of the students in your class. The cards should be colour coded using the same system as you use for library books. Students should achieve consistently high scores at one level before they move on to the next.

Texts for reading cards can be obtained from many sources besides the class library books. Sometimes old books (even old textbooks) contain a few suitable stories; you can cut up the book and throw away the unwanted parts (which will probably include the exercises). Even quite dull material has been successful when transformed into a set of reading cards. Of course the texts should not come from textbooks that the student has used; the material must be new to him. If you enjoy writing your own material, you can find stories in newspapers or magazines like *Reader's Digest* which you can simplify to the level required. Keep the texts very short: ten lines is ample to begin with. Include pictures if possible (e.g. cut from magazines).

The questions and other tasks on the card can follow the patterns suggested earlier and answer cards should be supplied if you cannot cope with a heavy marking load. For out of class use, however, you may prefer to have cards with fewer and simpler questions, just enough to give the student a feeling of achievement, and to give him a purpose in reading.

The main snag about reading cards is that you need a great many of them, since you must cater for students at various levels. Co-operating with your colleagues can help: one set of cards may be used with several classes, especially if copies can be made by Xerox. Be careful to provide plenty of cards at the lowest levels, so that the cards can be used for remedial work. Since they are intended to be worked through independently of the teacher, they are ideal for use by any student who is far above or below the level of the rest of the class.

7.10   Using a class reader

Most of this chapter is about ways of getting students to want to read; this part is about one way of requiring students to read, by using some language classes for studying a class reader. This should also increase the students' interest in reading, but lessons on a class reader can also be very dreary and not at all likely to tempt people to read more; so a few guidelines may be useful.

First, as usual, is the choice of book. If it doesn't appeal to most of the students, no amount of effort is likely to make it enjoyable. Use the criteria in Chapter 3. Reading level is bound to be a problem: pitch it lower rather than higher, but if it has to be so low that you can't find any books of interest to the majority of the students, do not use this approach.

The second crucial element is the way you deal with the book. Readers take a long time to finish, if they are handled by reading them aloud for perhaps one lesson a week. It is difficult to create and maintain any enthusiasm for a story under these circumstances (unless it is exceptionally gripping: perhaps we ought to take hints from serial stories in magazines). Students who are interested usually read on by themselves and are consequently bored during subsequent periods. (Issuing a book a chapter at a time, like a serial, in duplicated form, gets round the last difficulty but is seldom feasible.)

A more satisfactory approach is not to read the book in class, but to assign most of it for home reading. In this way, you can get through a book quite quickly; the aim should be to take only four or five weeks over the average reader of 80 pages or so.

Of course if the students are to read on their own you will see the importance of choosing a book that is not difficult: it should be a good deal easier than your current textbook, so that you can push them to read it quickly without feeling that you are being unrealistic. In this way it is possible to read six or seven books a year, if that number of suitable class sets is available; and the additional practice will pay dividends at examination time.

Cost, however, is a factor: supplying the required number of class sets, even assuming that each set is used by several different classes each year, is an expensive undertaking. Useful though class readers are, they should not be bought at the expense of the class library; for 30 readers in a class set means only one book to be read by any individual student, while 30 titles for the class library means that he can read all of them. If you cannot afford enough class sets to supply your needs for a whole year, use what you can, but do not spin out the reading to cover a longer time; instead get through them quickly to maintain motivation.

When using the method recommended here, you will use your class periods mainly not for reading but for discussion, so choose books that are worth discussing and thinking about. A typical programme for a book might look like this:

Lesson 1   Introductory. (Setting the scene, creating anticipation. etc.)
            Teacher reads aloud from opening chapter, or plays tape of it, or sets
            guided silent reading.
            Set first reading task (to be done outside class hours): chapters 1–5,
            with SPQs (see p.158).
Lesson 2   Discuss answers to SPQs and go on to wider discussion of chapters
            1–5; deal with any problems.
            Set reading task: chapters 6–10 with SPQs.
Lesson 3   As for lesson 2, but dealing with chapters 6–10.
            Set reading task: chapters 11–17 (last chapter) with SPQs.
Lesson 4   As for lesson 2, but dealing with chapters 11–17.
            Set final task: overall assessment.
Lesson 5   Discuss overall assessment of book.
            Follow-up activity.

Obviously the details can be varied; the only essential features of the approach
are the fact that almost all the reading is done outside school hours, and the fact
that the book is dealt with fairly rapidly. The general approach will be similar to that
recommended in Chapter 11, with the major difference that there will be no time
for detailed study of the whole text of the reader. But the suggestions made in
Chapter 11 about introducing a text, making reading tasks purposeful and asking
signpost questions (SPQs) apply to books as well as short texts. Our aim in
studying a class reader will be to get students to understand the writer's message
without paying too much attention to details of language, so the SPQs are more
likely to focus on interpretation of the action rather than on interpretation of the
language.

7.11   Key passages

However, there is one approach which combines the methods of intensive
reading with the broader approach needed when studying a whole book. A
passage is chosen which illuminates some aspect of the book that you consider
important: perhaps someone's character, or some critical point in the plot, or
some central problem. The passage may be as little as ten lines long, or as long as
a page or two.

You can set a study of the passage as part of the home reading task, together
with questions designed to draw attention to the features that make the passage
significant in the book. Occasionally you may prefer the study to be done in the
classroom, in the intensive reading lesson. This enables you to relate the passage
to its wider context in a way that is impossible when you use intensive reading
texts that are divorced from the book from which they are taken.

After the students have attempted the questions on their own (and handed in
their answers if you want them), class discussion can focus on the passage and its
place in the text. It should be possible to make the students themselves draw
most of the conclusions you consider necessary, since the questions you
originally set will have ensured that a lot of thinking along the right lines has
already been done.

7.12   Overall assessment and follow-up activity

The last piece of work on a class reader should help the student to see the book
as a whole. A number of the activities suggested in Chapter 10 may be

appropriate, or questions of personal response (see Chapter 9) can be discussed by the class.

At this stage, the aim should be to help the student to understand and evaluate the events in the book, not just to check whether he can recall them. He should be made to use his powers of reasoning and imagination, and to explore his feelings about what happens in the story. Work out specific questions about the book to achieve this purpose.

This approach brings us to the edge of literature (which cannot be discussed in this book). The questions will explore the motives of characters, the way one event in the plot leads to another, whether an action is right or wrong in the writer's view and in the view of the class, and so on. Here are a few skeleton questions that may give you some ideas about how to exploit the book:

(a) Was X responsible for (a key event)?

(b) Why did X . . .? (Not worth asking unless the motives or causes were complex.)

(c) Was X right to . . .? What would you have done?

(d) Did X deserve what happened to him?

(e) Was X a good (father)?

(f) Would you have wanted X for your (father)?

(g) Who was most (unlucky), X or Y?

(h) Why was (a key event) so important?

(i) What would have happened if . . .?

(j) What do you think will happen to the characters after the end of the story?

We have assumed that the class reader will be a narrative, rather than a non-fiction book, because stories are more commonly enjoyed by the whole class, and our aim is for everyone to enjoy the experience so that they are encouraged to read more on their own.

Conclusion: The Teacher as Reader

In this final section we are going to consider what you as a person have to contribute to make your reading programme a success.

The rest of this book has made it clear that *hard work* is one necessity. Another is your *concern* for your students' progress. Your *professional skill* is needed to plan work so that every student is successful more often than not, because success builds on success. So is the *positive approach* that leads you to comment on what the reader has got right, and helps him to build on it, rather than simply pointing out what he has got wrong.

1 Readers are made by readers

All these qualities are self evident, or have become apparent in the course of the book. But there is one factor that has not been mentioned so far and that is of central importance: your own *interest in reading*. To demonstrate its relevance, here are two more slogans:

Readers are made by readers. (*Readers* refers to people in both cases.)

Reading is like an infectious disease: it is caught not taught. (And you can't catch it from someone who hasn't got it himself.)

Perhaps your students read a great deal already (at least in their L1) and do not need to catch reading from you; but some at least are likely to come from homes where little reading takes place. Some of these may not even recognize that reading is useful, let alone that it can be enjoyable; and this may be true of reading in the L1 as well as in the FL.

Now you have these students with you for a year or so: not much in the context of a lifetime, but enough to set the habit of a lifetime if the opportunity is used well. For disadvantaged students, you may be the only reader they meet – the only person from whom they can 'catch' reading. This is why they must be able to see that you are a reader, both in your L1 and (if it is not your L1) in the FL.

Showing that you are a reader means carrying books around with you, referring to books as you teach, reading out brief passages that may interest students, talking about what you are reading at the moment, and handling books as if you loved them. *Being* a reader means reading.

2 How much do you read?

At this point we come to a question that will be no problem at all for many teachers, but may be the most serious problem of all for others: how much reading do you do yourself?

We will consider three possible answers:

(a) I read a lot, both in the FL and (if it is different) in my L1.
(b) I read a lot in my L1, but not much in the FL.
(c) I don't read much in any language.

If your answer is (a), there is no problem for you. You just need to make sure that the students see that you care about books. This book has told you all it can and your own interest will make you a successful teacher of reading.

If your answer is (b) or (c), however, there is a problem. The last few paragraphs of the book are directed to you, in the hope that you may be able to solve it.

3 If you read very little in any language

Let us take answer (c) first. If you don't read much in any language, start by asking yourself why. Perhaps you have never been lucky enough to catch the reading habit from anyone, perhaps the people you live among consider reading a waste of time, perhaps you have been discouraged by finding that reading is difficult and takes a long time, or perhaps you have never really considered the things you might do if you could read more effectively.

These are matters that only you can decide; but the fact that you have read the book up to this point means that you do have some interest in reading. This can be developed to your own advantage, as well as to the advantage of your students.

No matter what the problems are that cause you to read so little, the first thing to recognize is that if you want to, you can train yourself to read effectively. This means that you will be able to read much faster and hence that you will be able to read a great deal more than you do now, even if you do not spend more time on reading. You will, however, need to spend some time on the initial training.

If this prospect attracts you, motivate yourself by thinking of things you will be able to do once you can read fast; set yourself goals and offer yourself rewards. Start by improving your reading efficiency in the language which will be most use to you; this may be your L1 rather than the FL, but similar techniques can be used. Read Chapter 4 again, or get a book about reading efficiency and follow its suggestions. Once you have improved your reading in the L1, you can go on to improve your FL reading as suggested below.

4 If you don't read much in the FL

If you read a lot in your L1, the problem is not likely to be too serious. However, you will teach with more confidence and conviction if you can organize your day so that you do more FL reading than at present.

Why do you read so little in the FL? Perhaps it is because you have no real need to, or perhaps your FL reading speed is rather slow, so that you get little pleasure from FL reading. In either case, you must motivate yourself by choosing more suitable books. Use the same criteria that you use when choosing books for your class: choosing books that are easy to read and of interest to the reader is as important for yourself as for your students. If you do not actually need to read the FL much, the only way you will persuade yourself to read it is to read it for enjoyment and interest.

This may not have been the reason why you have read the FL in the past. You may have been accustomed to read in the FL only books that relate to your studies, and many of these were probably linguistically difficult. Perhaps you feel that a teacher should not read light fiction or anything written in simplified language. Probably you studied mainly FL classics at school and university: the classics seldom make compelling reading and are often difficult even for L1 readers. Even if you appreciated them, you probably had to read slowly. In fact it is likely that you are not a very fluent reader in the FL.

You can find this out by testing your own reading speed as described in Chapter 4. If it is less than 350 w.p.m. on straightforward material, you can easily improve it.

5   Reading the class library

A good way to start will kill two birds with one stone. Read all the FL readers available in the school or class library, starting with the easiest levels and reading them as fast as you can. Gradually work upwards, reading every book you can find at each level before you go on to the next. Continue to read as fast as possible, not stopping to look up new vocabulary (if any) or puzzle over difficulties. Use skimming for books that don't interest you much.

By the end of this exercise, you will be familiar with the whole range of available readers, which we said was necessary anyway. Jot down the author and title of each book with two or three lines of comment, in a notebook or card index you can continue for this purpose. You can then refer to it when the students want advice on what to choose, or when you want to check that they have read the book successfully.

6   Improving your own reading

When you have completed this assignment, plan a programme for yourself to develop your own reading efficiency. You can make use of one of the reading efficiency handbooks if you like, but the most important part of the programme is the substantial increase in the quantity of reading done.

For this purpose, choose books that are easy enough for you to read quickly and that you will find enjoyable. Don't choose classics or serious works that deserve to be read with care. If you wish, use simplified or abridged editions: it isn't cheating to choose short books, it's common sense. Leave the long ones for later.

Set yourself targets and force yourself to read fast. Read without too much attention to detail, skip difficulties and ignore unfamiliar vocabulary. (Don't use the dictionary if you can possibly manage without it.) In fact, use all the strategies that you will be helping your students to develop. You can learn a lot from this experience that will be useful to you in your teaching.

Do some FL reading every day and try to finish one FL book at least every week. You are no doubt busy, with little spare time, and this may sound unrealistic. But if you read in the way described, it is perfectly possible. The key is to be honest with yourself about what you really enjoy: thrillers, women's magazines, newspapers – it really doesn't matter what you read as long as it genuinely interests you, because that is the only certain way to motivate yourself to read. It is not possible to reach good speeds by practising on material that is difficult or dull.

If you pursue this programme for only a few months, you should achieve a very marked increase in your reading efficiency. What you do with your FL reading skill when you have developed it is up to you: you may want to go back to the classics or use it to study for a further qualification. The point is that in order to develop the skill, a great deal of practice on easy interesting material is essential. If you can prove this to yourself by developing your own reading skill by this method, your teaching will carry the conviction that comes only from experience.

In addition, I hope that in the course of the programme you will develop a love of reading that will not only help you to be an excellent reading teacher, but will also give you a source of profit and enjoyment that will last throughout your life.

Appendix A: Texts

1 Archaeopteryx

Almost all the characteristics that distinguish birds from other animals can be traced one way or another to the benefits brought by feathers. Indeed, the very possession of a feather is enough to define a creature as a bird.

When, in 1860, in Solnhofen in Bavaria, the delicate and unmistakable outline of a single isolated feather, seven centimetres long, was found impressed in a slab of limestone, it caused a sensation. It lay on the rock, as eloquent as a Red Indian sign, proclaiming that a bird had been there. Yet these limestones dated from the days of the dinosaurs, long before birds were thought to exist.

The sediments from which they are formed were deposited on the bottom of a shallow tropical lagoon enclosed by a reef of sponges and lime-depositing algae. The water was tepid and poor in oxygen. Cut off from the open sea, there were few if any currents. Lime, partly from the disintegrating reef and partly produced by bacteria, was deposited as ooze on the bottom. Such conditions suited few animals. Those that did stray there and died, fell to the bottom and lay undisturbed in the still water as they were covered by the slowly accumulating ooze.

The Solnhofen limestones have been quarried for centuries because their fine even grain makes them excellent for building and ideal for use in lithographic printing. They are also immaculate blanks for nature to impress with the fine detail of the evidence of evolution. The stone, if it is thoroughly weathered, splits along the bedding planes so that a block can be opened into leaves, like a book. When you visit one of the quarries, it is almost impossible to resist the temptation to turn the pages of every boulder that you see, knowing that no one has ever looked at them before and that whatever they contain will not have been exposed to daylight for a hundred and forty million years. Most, of course, are blank, but every now and then, the quarrymen find fossils of a near-miraculous perfection — fish with every bone and shining scale in place, horseshoe crabs lying just where they died at the end of their last furrow through the silt, lobsters with even their finest antennae intact, small dinosaurs, ichthyosaurs and pterodactyls, lying with the bony scaffolds of their wings crumpled but unbroken and the shadow of their leathery flight membranes plain to see. But in 1860, that beautiful and enigmatic feather was the first indication that birds had been living in such company.

To what kind of bird had it belonged? Science, on the strength of the feather alone, called it Archaeopteryx, 'ancient bird'. A year later, in a quarry close by the first, searchers discovered an almost complete skeleton of a feathered creature the size of a pigeon. It lay sprawling on the rock, its wings outstretched, one long leg disarticulated, the other still connected with four clawed toes, and all around it, dramatically and indisputably, the clear impress of its feathers. It was certainly apt to call it an 'ancient bird' but it differed substantially from any known living bird. The long feathered tail that flared out behind it was supported by a bony extension of its spine; and it had claws, not only on its feet but on the three digits of its feathered fore-limbs. It was almost as much a reptile as a bird and its discovery within two years of the publication of *The Origin of Species* was a providentially timed confirmation of Darwin's proposition that one group of animals developed into another by way of intermediate forms. Indeed, Huxley, Darwin's champion, had predicted that just such a creature must have existed, and had prophetically described its details. Even today, there is no more convincing example of such a link.

(From *Life on Earth* by D. Attenborough, (Collins/BBC))

2   A Son to be proud of

Last week, Rahman's wife had an accident. Rahman's youngest child, Yusof, was at home when it happened. He was playing with his new toy car. Rahman had given it to him the week before, for his third birthday.

Suddenly Yusof heard his mother calling 'Help! Help!' He ran to the kitchen. His mother had burnt herself with some hot cooking oil. She was crying with pain and the pan was on fire.

Rahman had gone to his office. Both the other children had gone to school. Yusof was too small to help his mother, and she was too frightened to speak sensibly to him. But he ran to the neighbour's house and asked her to come and help his mother. She soon put out the fire and took Yusof's mother to the clinic.

When Rahman came home, his wife told him what had happened. He was very proud of his son. 'When you are a man, you will be just like your father,' he said.

3   The Red Flag Canal

Explaining why he had headed the group in charge of explosives, Lu Yin replied: 'For three generations my family have been quarry workers. At county and commune level, they asked me to work on the canal. I wanted nothing better. We quarry workers put our heads together and discussed all the problems. We are not technicians, but the advice of the older people is respected and we learned from each other. We were used to handling explosives in the straightforward way you do in quarrying, and we had to work out new techniques for cutting a canal out of the rock face and especially for tunnelling. But we managed because everyone was determined to solve the water problem once and for all.'

The tunnelling was a major problem. The further the tunnellers progressed, the longer it took for the fumes from the black powder explosives to clear away. Without any ventilation or mechanical smoke evacuation equipment, it took longer and longer between charges before the workmen could get in to clear out the fallen rock. As tunnels up to 4,000 yards long had to be driven through, the problem seemed insoluble, until Wang She-tung got the idea of blasting out a series of 'chimneys' down to the canal-bed level, wide enough for workers to be lowered to set the explosives, and then working out in both directions until the bases of the 'chimneys' were linked up. The fumes would thus be evacuated by natural draught and the 'chimneys' filled in later. For the 4,000 yard tunnel, thirty-four such 'chimneys' were blasted out, with Wang She-tung in the vanguard lowered down, level by level, to set their first explosives, hauled up before the fuses set off the charges, until he got to the levels calculated by Lu Yin with his wash-basin 'theodolites'. Five feet in diameter and almost 200 feet deep in the centre of the tunnel, the vertical shafts were blasted out and the dynamiters and those who cleared the debris lowered and hauled up by improvised winches until bedrock level was reached and the shafts had all been linked up to permit the horizontal clearing and stone-facing work to continue. Wang She-tung looked older than his forty-three years at the time we met him, with his cropped hair and sun-tanned, lean face which lit up into wrinkled smiles when he touched on a particularly hair-raising incident – a hitch in the winch with the fuse sputtering away below him! What had motivated him?

(Adapted from *China: The Quality of Life* by W. Burchett and R. Alley, (Penguin))

4   The House on the Hill

It was a beautiful summer evening. Paul was happy. No more exams. College was finished. Now he needed a job. He wanted to be a writer and work for a newspaper. But first he needed a rest.

It was hot in the house. There was no wind.

'I'll go for a walk,' said Paul to himself. 'I'll go down to the river.'

Paul lived in a small town and he was soon outside in the country. He walked near the river and watched the water birds.

Suddenly, he saw the girl. She was standing alone, looking into the water. She was young, and very beautiful. She had long, dark hair, and she was wearing a pretty white dress.

Paul went up to her.

'Hello,' he said. 'What's your name?'

'I'm Maria,' she said, and she smiled at him.

Paul and Maria talked for a long time. The sun went down. It was nearly dark.

'I must go home,' said Maria.

'Where do you live?' asked Paul.

'In the big white house on the hill,' said Maria. 'Where do you live?'.

'In the little brown house near the market,' said Paul.

They laughed. But Paul was sad. The house on the hill was big and important. Maria was rich, and he was poor. And Paul was in love.

(From *The House on the Hill* by Elizabeth Laird, (Heinemann Educational Books))

5   Airships

In the age of supersonic airliners it is difficult to realize that at the beginning of the twentieth century no one had ever flown in an aeroplane. However, people were flying in balloons and airships. The airship was based on the principle of the semi-rigid structure. In 1900 Ferdinand von Zeppelin fitted a petrol engine to a rigid balloon. This craft was the first really successful steerable airship. In 1919 an airship first carried passengers across the Atlantic, and in 1929 one travelled round the world. During this time the design of airships was constantly being improved and up to 1937 they carried thousands of passengers on regular transatlantic services for millions of miles.

However, airships had many defects. They were very large and could not fly well in bad weather. Above all, they suffered many accidents because of the inflammability of the hydrogen used to inflate them. In 1937 the Hindenburg airship exploded in New Jersey and 35 out of 100 passengers were killed.

Today airships cannot compete with jet aircraft. However, they have been greatly improved. They can be filled with helium, and advances in meteorology make it possible to choose calm routes. They can remain static in the air and are being used in the American navy for observation of icebergs in the Arctic. It is possible that they will be used for other purposes in the future.

(From *Reading and Thinking in English: Exploring Functions*, (OUP))

6   Ecology

No living creature, plant or animal, can exist in complete isolation. An animal is bound to depend on other living creatures, ultimately plants, for its food supply; it must also depend upon the activities of plants for a continued oxygen supply for its respiration. Apart from these two basic relationships it may be affected directly or indirectly in countless different ways by other plants and animals around it. Other animals prey on it or compete with it for the same food; plants may provide shelter, concealment or nesting material, and so on. Similarly, the animal will produce its own effect on the surrounding plants and animals: some it may eat or destroy, for others it will provide food; and through its contribution of manure it may influence the texture and fertility of the soil.

This dependence on other living things is not confined to animals. Though plants manufacture their own food by photosynthesis, they are dependent on animal respiration for at least a part of the carbon dioxide which they use as raw material in this process. Supplies of mineral salts which they use to build up their substance can only be maintained through the activities of fungi and bacteria breaking down the organic matter left in the soil by other living creatures. Again, many plants are entirely dependent on animals for pollination or for the dispersal of their seeds. Moreover, despite the apparently peaceful relationships in plant communities, there is intense competition going on for water, nutrient salts, and above all, for light.

We see, then, that other plants and animals, through their effects both direct and indirect, form an integral part of the environment of every living organism. In a well-defined community, such as exists in a wood, or a pond, the population of plants and animals is influenced not only by physical factors like light, tempera-ture, or humidity, but also by the complex interrelationships between the living creatures themselves. As a result, the population of different competing species exists in a state of delicate balance easily swayed by the slightest change in any factor.

Ecology thus seeks to explain these interrelationships between all the different members of a community as a whole. To the ecologist the reactions and behaviour of any plant or animal are like a piece of a jigsaw puzzle: he must find out how it fits into the picture of the whole community. Man is seen in perspective as just another piece in this grand jigsaw, and his activities in terms of the effects, good or bad, that they are likely to produce on the communities and soils from which he derives his food.

The whole complex of the plants and animals forming a community, together with all the interacting physical factors of the environment, really forms a single unit, which has been called an ecosystem. It will be seen that the final aim of ecology – the complete understanding of ecosystems – is an ideal one can scarcely hope to attain. It is nevertheless an ideal well worth pursuing and valuable progress has been made towards it.

(Adapted from *Plant Ecology* by Maurice Ashby, (Macmillan Company of Canada Ltd 1963) (From *Reading and Thinking in English: Discovering Discourse* (OUP))

7 Acids

An acid is a compound containing hydrogen which can be replaced, directly or indirectly, by a metal. Its solution in water turns blue litmus red.

Acids can be classified into two groups. Acids which always contain the element carbon are called organic acids and they often come from growing things, like fruit. Citric acid, which is found in lemons and oranges and other citrus fruits, and acetic acid, which is found in vinegar, are organic acids. Acids which do not contain the element carbon are known as inorganic acids. They are usually prepared from non-living matter. Inorganic acids consist only of hydrogen and an acid radical.

Hydrochloric acid consists of hydrogen and the chloride radical, and sulphuric acid consists of hydrogen and the sulphate radical. They are inorganic acids.

The hydrogen in an acid is replaceable by a metal. Acids can be divided into classes according to the number of atoms in each molecule which a metal can replace. Those which have only one replaceable hydrogen atom in each molecule are known as monobasic acids. Other acids may contain either two or three such replaceable hydrogen atoms in each molecule and these are known as dibasic and tribasic acids respectively. All the atoms of hydrogen in the molecule of inorganic acids are replaceable by a metal. Sulphuric acid is an inorganic acid which is dibasic. Hydrochloric acid is an example of an inorganic acid which is monobasic. Orthophosphoric acid, whose molecules contain three atoms of hydrogen, is tribasic. Acetic acid molecules each contain four hydrogen atoms but only one of these can be replaced by a metal. Acetic acid is monobasic.

(From *English in Focus: English in Physical Science* by J. P. B. Allen and H. G. Widdowson, (OUP))

8   Malnutrition

The struggle against malnutrition and hunger is as old as man himself, and never across the face of our planet has the outcome been more in doubt. Malnourishment afflicts an estimated 400 million to 1.5 billion of the world's poor. Even in the affluent U.S., poverty means undernourishment for an estimated ten to twenty million. Hardest hit are children, whose growing bodies demand two and a half times more protein, pound for pound, than those of adults. Nutrition experts estimate that 70 per cent of the children in low-income countries are affected.

Misshapen bodies tell the tragic story of malnutrition. Medical science identifies two major types of malnutrition which usually occur in combination. The first, kwashiorkor, is typified by the bloated look, the opposite of what we associate with starvation. Accumulated fluids pushing against wasted muscles account for the plumpness of hands, feet, belly, and face. Emaciated shoulders reveal striking thinness. Caused by an acute lack of protein, kwashiorkor (a West African word) can bring brain damage, anemia, diarrhea, irritability, apathy, and loss of appetite.

On the other hand, stick limbs, a bloated belly, wide eyes, and the stretched-skin face of an old person mark victims of marasmus, a word taken from the Greek 'to waste away'. Lacking calories as well as protein, sufferers may weigh only half as much as normal. With fat gone, the skin hangs in wrinkles or draws tight over bones. With marasmus comes anemia, diarrhea, dehydration, and a ravenous appetite. Children, whose growing bodies require large amounts of protein, are afflicted in greatest numbers, but perhaps only three per cent of all child victims suffer the extreme stages described.

Scientists are working feverishly to develop new weapons against malnutrition and starvation. But two thirds of the human population of 3.9 billion live in the poorest countries which also have the highest birth rates. Thus, of the 74 million people added to the population each year, four out of five will be born in a have-not country – a country unable to supply its people's nutritional needs.

(From *Foundation Reading II, vol 3* by the Chulalongkorn University Language Institute)

9   Schoolboy Tyranny

I still remember – my hands and my finger-tips still remember! – what used to lie in store for us on our return to school from the holidays. The guava trees in the school yard would be in full leaf again, and the old leaves would be lying around in scattered heaps. In places there were even more than just heaps of them: it would be like a muddy sea of leaves.

'Get that all swept up!' the headmaster would tell us. 'I want the whole place cleaned up, at once!'

'At once!' There was enough work there, very hard work, too, to last for over a week. Especially since the only tools with which we were provided were our hands, our fingers, our nails.

'Now see that it's done properly, and be quick about it,' the headmaster would say to the older pupils, 'or you'll have to answer for it!'

So at an order from the older boys we would all line up like peasants about to cut and gather in crops, and we would set to work like members of a chain-gang.

If the work was not going as quickly as the headmaster expected, the big boys, instead of giving us a helping hand, used to find it simpler to whip us with branches pulled from the trees.

In order to avoid these blows, we used to bribe our tyrants with the juicy cakes of Indian corn, the couscous made of meat or fish which we used to bring for our midday meal. And if we happened to have any money on us the coins changed hands at once. If we did not do this, if we were afraid of going home with an empty stomach or an empty purse, the blows were re-doubled. They hit us so violently and often, and with such devilish enjoyment, that even a deaf and dumb person would have realised that we were being flogged not so much to make us work harder, but rather to beat us into a state of obedience in which we would be only too glad to give up our food and money.

Occasionally, one of us, worn out by such calculated cruelty, would have the courage to complain to the headmaster. He would of course be very angry, but the punishment he inflicted on the older boys was always very small – nothing compared to what they had done to us. And the fact is that however much we complained, our situation did not improve in the slightest. Perhaps we should have let our parents know what was going on, but somehow we never dreamed of doing so; I don't know whether it was loyalty or pride that kept us silent, but I can see now that we were foolish to keep quiet about it, for such beatings were completely foreign to our nature.

(Adapted from 'The African Child' by Camara Laye in *Read and Think* by J. Munby,
(Longman))

10   Pollution

Pollution spoils our environment in many ways. The air we breathe, for instance, is constantly polluted by smoke and by chemicals such as carbon monoxide in the exhaust fumes of cars and other kinds of motor vehicles.

For wild life, however, there are even greater dangers in the pollution of water – of rivers, for example, or lakes and seas. A good illustration of this is the oil released from tankers at sea. It kills all kinds of sea animals, including birds, whose feathers become covered with oil so they cannot fly, as well as fish and other forms of marine life. Other causes of water pollution include power stations, which release warm water into rivers. This kills the fish and plants which live there. These are only a few examples; there are many more.

(From *Skills for Learning: Reading for Academic Study* by the Language Centre,
University of Malaya, (University of Malaya Press/Nelson))

11 Survival of the Fittest

On each tree there is a moth. They are both quite clearly visible. Any predator would see his prey very clearly. But suppose the light moth was sitting on the light tree and vice versa. A dark moth on a dark tree would be less visible and have a better chance of survival from the attacks of predators. This is known as camouflage. Some animals, like the chameleon, for instance, are able to change colour according to their background. This kind of change is not evolutionary change (though of course the chameleon has evolved this ability to make the change). However, a change in colour is evolutionary if the new creature is able to reproduce itself so that its young also have the new colour.

The example of the moth is a real one and was investigated in England in the 1950's by a scientist called Dr Kettlewell. It is a very well-known example of evolutionary change.

The species of moth is the Peppered Moth. It was typically light brown in colour and settled on the trunks of trees which were a similar colour and camouflaged it. Then came a change in the environment. Industry began to grow up in parts of England with the result that smoke and other forms of pollution began to fill the atmosphere.

The pollution from the factories covered the bark on the tree trunks with soot and grime so the light brown Peppered Moths became very visible to their predators and were eaten. Then gradually they began to change colour. The darker ones were more likely to survive, so their colour gradually became darker. How did they become darker? This is one of the mysteries of science, but it has been called 'natural selection' since Charles Darwin published his famous book *The Origin of Species* in 1859. Natural selection does not make anything happen. You cannot force a moth to change colour, for instance, nor can a moth decide to change. The point is that every creature has a genetic structure consisting of genes and chromosomes. This structure can change naturally, by accident. Perhaps this change does not matter. Perhaps, on the other hand, it produces a 'deformed' individual which the others reject or even kill because it is different. These things happen all the time. But if the change (or 'mutation') happens to fit the new environment, then the new creature, instead of being rejected or killed by the others, will survive.

This is natural selection. A mutation (which is always possible) happens to suit a new environment, and the 'odd' creature survives because it is better fitted. Then it reproduces and a new type of creature evolves. Meanwhile the others have become unsuited to the changed environment. They must either change their behaviour or become extinct.

Dr Kettlewell wanted to discover whether the dark Peppered Moths were in fact a new type of Peppered Moth which had adapted to its environment. In the first experiment, he released light and dark moths into the woods near Birmingham (a large industrial city in England). In the second he released his moths into the woods in a country district called Dorset in the south of England. Finally, he placed examples of each kind of moth on trees of the opposite colour and watched what happened.

Here are the results from his experiment in Birmingham.

	light	dark
Number of moths released	201	601
Number of moths recaptured	34	205
Percentage of moths recaptured	16%	34.1%

Dr Kettlewell's technique was to release moths which were specially marked, then recapture as many as possible after a time.

Later, to find additional support for his hypothesis, Dr Kettlewell repeated the same experiment in Dorset. The result proved he was right:

	light	dark
Number of moths released	496	473
Number of moths recaptured	63	30
Percentage of moths recaptured	12.5%	6.3%

Finally, he placed an equal number of moths of each colour on trees and watched what happened. He quickly discovered that several species of birds searched the tree trunk for moths and other insects and that these birds more readily found the one that contrasted with its background than the one that blended with the bark:

	Moths eaten by birds	
	light	dark
Unpolluted woods	26	164
Polluted woods	43	15

(From: Robert E. Ricklefs *Ecology*, (Thomas Nelson, 1973) in *Skills for Learning: Reading for Academic Study* by The Language Centre, University of Malaya)

Appendix B: Extracts from Reading Courses

1 Airships

Part 4
Development

Study this part in the same way as Part 4 of Unit 3.

Introduction
Airships were equipped with a balloon filled with gas.
They were developed during the nineteenth century.
In the first part of the twentieth century, they carried passengers across the Atlantic Ocean.
They had many accidents.
They have been replaced by aeroplanes.
They are not now being used for passenger transport.

Purpose question

Which of these statements is the opinion of the writer?

a Airships are of no use today.
b Airships should replace jet aircraft.
c There is a possibility of using airships in the future.
d Airships have not been used since 1947.

THE HISTORY OF THE AIRSHIP

Supersonic airliners are very common today ∴ we forget that there were no aeroplanes in 1900.

In an age of supersonic airliners it is difficult to realize that at the beginning of the twentieth century no one had ever flown in an aeroplane. However, people were flying in balloons and airships.[1] The airship was based on the principle of the semi-rigid structure. In 1900 Ferdinand von Zeppelin fitted a petrol engine to a rigid balloon. This craft was the first really successful steerable airship. In 1919 an airship first carried passengers across the Atlantic, and in 1929 one travelled round the world.[2] During this time the design of airships was constantly being improved[3] and up to 1937 they carried thousands of passengers on regular transatlantic services for millions of miles.

steerable = can be steered

to improve = make better

[1] When were people flying in airships and balloons?

[2] Did airships carry passengers across the Atlantic before 1919?

[3] When was the design being improved?

1 What was the achievement of von Zeppelin?
2 What were airships used for?

THIS PARAGRAPH LISTS SOME DISADVANTAGES OF AIRSHIPS

above all introduces the most important point

However, airships had many defects. They were very large and could not fly well in bad weather. Above all, they suffered many accidents[4] because of the inflammability of the hydrogen used to inflate them.[5] In 1937 the Hindenburg airship exploded in New Jersey and 35 out of 100 passengers were killed.

[4] What was their main defect?

[5] What caused the accidents?

3 Why did they not continue to be the main form of air transport?

THIS PARAGRAPH IS ABOUT AIRSHIPS TODAY

Sentence 1 means that airships are not able to do what jet aircraft can do.

static = not moving

Today airships cannot compete with jet aircraft. However, they have been greatly improved. They can be filled with helium,[6] and advances in meteorology make it possible to choose calm routes. They can remain static in the air and are being used by the American navy for observation of icebergs in the Arctic.[7] It is possible that they will be used for other purposes in the future.

[6] Helium can be used instead of ......

[7] Why are they appropriate for this purpose?

4   Use information from the whole passage to complete this table. The table summarizes the development of the airship.

Date	Event
	The first successful airship was built.
1919	
1919 ⏐ 1937	Designs were being improved.
1937	
1937	
	Airships in use for observation of icebergs.

5   Now use information from the whole passage to complete this table. The table shows how airships have been improved.

Defects of airships in the past	Modern improvements
size	
	can be inflated with helium

(From *Reading and Thinking in English: Exploring Functions* (OUP))

2   Ecology

Part 5
Application of reading strategies

The following passage contains different levels of generalizations. First, look at this diagram which presents information from the passage visually. Then use the diagram to answer the questions which follow it.

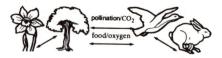

1   What do plants obtain from animals?
2   How do plants depend on animals?
3   Can you think of examples of relations between animals?
4   Can you think of examples of relations between plants?

The answers to the questions will provide you with a prediction of the main content of the passage.

Now choose one item from the following list and read the passage rapidly in order to obtain the relevant information.

1   The purpose of ecology.
2   The way in which ecologists consider man.
3   Ways in which animals affect each other.
4   The effects plants have on other plants.

Now read the passage again paragraph by paragraph in order to answer the comprehension questions. If you have difficulty in understanding the passage, the language study questions in the margins may help you. However, you do not need to answer all the language study questions yet.

THE SCOPE OF ECOLOGY

No living creature, plant or animal, can exist in complete isolation. An animal[1] is bound to depend on other living creatures, ultimately plants, for its food supply; it must also depend upon the activities of plants for a continued oxygen supply for its respiration.[2] Apart from these two basic relationships[3] it may be affected directly or indirectly in countless different ways by other plants and animals around it. Other animals prey on it or compete with it for the same food; plants may provide shelter, concealment or nesting material, and so on. Similarly, the animal will produce its own effects on the surrounding plants and animals: some it may eat or destroy, for others it will provide food;[4] and through its contribution of manure it may influence the texture and fertility of the soil.

[1] Does this refer to animals in general or to a particular animal?

[2] There are two examples of *its* and one example of *it* in this sentence. Do they refer to the same thing?

[3] Which two basic relationships have just been mentioned?

[4] What do *some* and *others* refer to?

1   Complete the following table to show the levels of generality expressed in the paragraph.

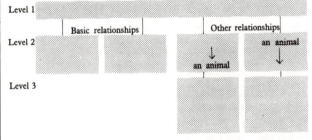

Level 1

| Basic relationships | | Other relationships | |

Level 2

an animal

Level 3

an animal

This dependence on other living things is not confined to animals.[5] Though plants manufacture their own food by photosynthesis, they are dependent on animal respiration for at least a part of the carbon dioxide which they use as raw material in this process.[6] Supplies of mineral salts which they use to build up their substance can only be maintained through the activities of fungi and bacteria breaking down the organic matter left in the soil by other living creatures.[7] Again,[8] many plants are entirely dependent on animals for pollination or for the dispersal of their seeds. Moreover,[9] despite the apparently peaceful relationships in plant communities, there is intense competition going on for water, nutrient salts, and above all, for light.

[5] Does *this dependence* refer to all the relationships mentioned in paragraph 1 or some of them?

[6] Which process?

[7] What maintains supplies of mineral salts?

[8-9] Which of the following relationships do *again* and *moreover* express?
a   consequence
b   contrast
c   addition

2   Suggest a title for the paragraph.
3   List the processes for which plants need other living things.
4   The final sentence in the paragraph concerns:
    a   relations between plants
    b   dependence of plants on animals
    c   peaceful relationships in plant communities.

We see, then, that other plants and animals, through their effects both direct and indirect, form an integral part of the environment of every living organism.[10] In a well-defined community, such as exists in a wood, or a pond,[11] the population of plants and animals is influenced not only by physical factors like light, temperature, or humidity, but also by the complex interrelationships between the living creatures themselves. As a result, the population of different competing species exists in a state of delicate balance easily swayed[12] by the slightest change in any factor.

[10] This sentence
a   follows the previous paragraph, chronologically.
b   is in contrast to the previous paragraphs.
c   summarizes the previous paragraphs.

[11] What are *a wood* and *a pond* examples of?

[12] Species exist in a state of balance or equilibrium. If there is a change in one of the factors which influence the species, the state of balance may be swayed ∴ what can we deduce as the meaning of *swayed*?

5   What kinds of factors influence a community?
6   What is the consequence of these influences?

Ecology thus seeks to explain these interrelationships between all the different members of a community as a whole. To the ecologist the reactions and behaviour of any plant or animal are like a piece of jigsaw puzzle:[13] he must find out how it[14] fits into the picture of the whole community. Man is seen in perspective as just another piece in this grand jigsaw, and his activities in terms of the effects, good or bad, that they are likely to produce on the communities and soils from which he derives his food.[15]

[14] What must the ecologist fit into the picture of the whole community?

[13] This is a jigsaw puzzle. For the ecologist what forms the pieces? What is the whole puzzle?

7   In what ways are living things like pieces of a jigsaw puzzle?

The whole complex of the plants and animals forming a community, together with all the interacting physical factors of the environment, really forms a single unit, which has been called an ecosystem.[16] It will be seen that the final aim of ecology—the complete understanding of ecosystems—is an ideal one can scarcely hope to attain.[17] It is nevertheless an ideal well worth pursuing and valuable progress has been made towards it.
Adapted from: Maurice Ashby *Plant Ecology* (Macmillan Company of Canada Ltd 1963) by permission of Macmillans, London and Basingstoke

[15] Complete these statements:
Man is seen as a . . . .
His activities . . . . . . in terms of their effects.
(Notice that the verb *is seen* is not repeated in the passage.)

[16] What does an ecosystem consist of?

[17] What is the final aim of ecology?

8   According to this paragraph, the aim of ecology is:
    a   realistic and valuable
    b   idealistic and a waste of time
    c   idealistic but valuable.

WRITING A SUMMARY
Order the following statements from the passage according to their level of generality.

a   Plants need animal respiration for the manufacture of food.
b   Animals depend on plants and other animals in many ways.

c	Living creatures cannot exist in complete isolation.
d	Plants depend on other plants and on animals.
e	Other plants and animals form part of the environment of every living organism.
f	Animals depend on plants for their food supply.

Now write the statements in the form of a paragraph beginning with the most general. Use each of the following connectors once: *in addition, for example, similarly.*

(From *Reading and Thinking in English: Discovering Discourse* (OUP))

3 Acids

The text that follows is interrupted by a number of statements (a) to (i). The student is required to study them carefully and decide whether each is true or not true, according to the information expressed above them. The answers are given in the section 'Solutions' following the passage.

I READING AND COMPREHENSION

[1]An acid is a compound containing hydrogen which can be replaced, directly or indirectly, by a metal. [2]Its solution in water turns blue litmus red.

[3]Acids can be classified into two groups. [4]Acids which always contain the element carbon are called organic acids and they often come from growing things, like fruit. [5]Citric acid, which is found in lemons and oranges and other citrus fruits, and acetic acid, which is found in vinegar, are organic acids. [6]Acids which do not contain the element carbon are known as inorganic acids. [7]They are usually prepared from non-living matter. [8]Inorganic acids consist only of hydrogen and an acid radical. [9]Hydrochloric acid consists of hydrogen and the chloride radical, and sulphuric acid consists of hydrogen and the sulphate radical. [10]They are inorganic acids.

(a) All acids contain hydrogen.
(b) Inorganic acids contain the chloride radical.
(c) Organic acids always come from growing things.
(d) Lemons and oranges are not citrus fruits.

[11]The hydrogen in an acid is replaceable by a metal. [12]Acids can be divided into classes according to the number of atoms in each molecule which a metal can replace. [13]Those which have only one replaceable hydrogen atom in each molecule are known as monobasic acids. [14]Other acids may contain either two or three such replaceable hydrogen atoms in each molecule and these are known as dibasic and tribasic acids respectively. [15]All the atoms of hydrogen in the molecules of inorganic acids are replaceable by a metal. [16]Sulphuric acid is an inorganic acid which is dibasic. [17]Hydrochloric acid is an example of an inorganic acid which is monobasic. [18]Orthophosphoric acid, whose molecules contain three atoms of hydrogen, is tribasic. [19]Acetic acid molecules each contain four hydrogen atoms but only one of these can be replaced by a metal. [20]Acetic acid is monobasic.

(e) A molecule of hydrochloric acid contains one atom of hydrogen.
(f) Inorganic acids are monobasic.
(g) Hydrochloric acid is the only monobasic acid.
(h) A molecule of sulphuric acid contains three atoms of hydrogen.
(i) Orthophosphoric acid is an inorganic acid.

Solutions

(a) An acid is a compound containing hydrogen which can be replaced by a metal. (1)
∴ An acid contains hydrogen.
= *All acids contain hydrogen.*

(b) Sulphuric and hydrochloric acids are inorganic acids. (9, 10)
Inorganic acids consist only of hydrogen and an acid radical. (8)
i.e. Inorganic acids contain AN acid radical.
Hydrochloric acid consists of hydrogen and the chloride radical, and sulphuric acid consists of hydrogen and the sulphate radical. (9)
i.e. HYDROCHLORIC acid contains the CHLORIDE radical.
SULPHURIC acid contains the SULPHATE radical.
∴ It is NOT TRUE that all inorganic acids contain the chloride radical.

(c) Organic acids OFTEN (not always) come from growing things. (4)
i.e. Organic acids DO NOT ALWAYS come from growing things.

(d) lemons and oranges and OTHER CITRUS FRUITS (5)
i.e. Lemons and oranges ARE citrus fruits.

(e) Hydrochloric acid is an example of an inorganic acid which is mono-basic. (17)
i.e. Hydrochloric acid is BOTH inorganic and monobasic.
Acids which have only one replaceable hydrogen atom in each molecule are known as monobasic acids. (13)
i.e. Monobasic acids have ONLY ONE REPLACEABLE hydrogen atom in each molecule.
but ALL the atoms of hydrogen in the molecules of inorganic acids are replaceable by a metal. (15)
∴ Hydrochloric acid has ONLY ONE hydrogen atom in each molecule.
= *A molecule of hydrochloric acid contains one atom of hydrogen.*

(f) Inorganic acids are monobasic.
= ALL inorganic acids are monobasic.
but Sulphuric acid is an inorganic acid which is also a dibasic acid. (16)
∴ It is NOT TRUE that inorganic acids (= all inorganic acids) are mono-basic.

(g) Hydrochloric acid is AN EXAMPLE of an inorganic acid which is mono-basic. (17)
i.e. There are other monobasic acids.
∴ It is NOT TRUE that hydrochloric acid is the only monobasic acid.

(h) Other acids may contain either two or three replaceable hydrogen atoms in each molecule and these are known as dibasic and tribasic acids respectively. (14)

i.e. An acid which contains two replaceable atoms of hydrogen in each molecule is known as a dibasic acid.

An acid which contains three replaceable atoms of hydrogen in each molecule is known as a tribasic acid.

Sulphuric acid is a dibasic acid. (16)

∴ A molecule of sulphuric acid contains TWO atoms of hydrogen.

(i) An acid which contains three replaceable atoms of hydrogen in each molecule is known as a tribasic acid. (14)

Orthophosphoric acid, whose molecules contain three atoms of hydrogen, is tribasic. (18)

= Orthophosphoric acid contains three atoms of hydrogen in each molecule AND it is tribasic.

i.e. ALL the atoms of hydrogen are replaceable.

ALL the atoms of hydrogen in the molecules of inorganic acids are replaceable by a metal. (15)

∴ *Orthophosphoric acid is an inorganic acid.*

EXERCISE A *Contextual reference*

1. In sentence 2, *its* refers to:
   (a) Acid
   (b) Hydrogen
   (c) Metal
2. In sentence 4, *they* refers to:
   (a) Acids
   (b) Organic acids
3. In sentence 10, *They* refers to:
   (a) Hydrogen and the chloride radical
   (b) Hydrogen and the sulphate radical
   (c) Hydrochloric acid and sulphuric acid
4. In sentence 13, *Those* refers to:
   (a) Classes
   (b) Acids
   (c) Atoms
5. In sentence 19, *these* refers to:
   (a) Acetic acid molecules
   (b) The four hydrogen atoms

EXERCISE B *Rephrasing*

Rewrite the following sentences replacing the words printed in italics with expressions from the text which have the same meaning. (Refer to Exercise B in Unit 1.)

1. All the *atoms of hydrogen* in the molecules of inorganic acids *are replaceable* by a metal.
2. Acids which do not contain the element carbon are *known as* inorganic acids.

3. Acids can be *divided into classes* according to the number of atoms in each molecule which *a metal can replace.*
4. Sulphuric acid *has two replaceable hydrogen atoms in each molecule.*
5. Orthophosphoric acid *contains* three atoms of hydrogen in each molecule.
6. Orthophosphoric acid, *whose molecules contain three atoms of hydrogen,* is tribasic.

EXERCISE C *Relationships between statements*

Place the following expressions in the sentences indicated. Replace and re-order the words in the sentence where necessary. (Refer to Exercise C in Unit 1.)

(a) can be defined as (1)   (e) however (15)
(b) are classified as (5)   (f) whereas (16+17)
(c) for example (9)   (g) although (19)
(d) therefore (10)   (h) therefore (20)

EXERCISE D *Statements based on diagrams: definitions*

Draw the following diagram and complete it by reference to the reading passage. Then use it to write out:

1. *definitions* of the different kinds of acid mentioned in the text as follows: (a) → (b) → (c)

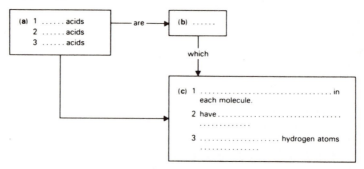

EXAMPLE
Monobasic acids are acids which have one replaceable hydrogen atom in each molecule.
2. *generalizations* about the different acids mentioned in the text as follows: (a) → (c)

EXAMPLE
Monobasic acids have one replaceable hydrogen atom in each molecule.

Now do the same with this diagram.

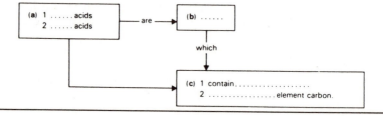

EXERCISE E *Statements based on diagrams: classifications*

1. Draw the following diagram and complete it by reference to the text, giving examples of the different classes of acid.

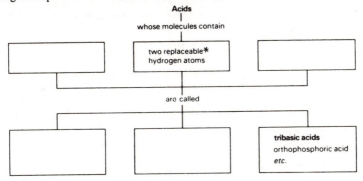

*i.e. replaceable by a metal

Use your completed diagram to make statements of the form:

Acids whose molecules contain . . . replaceable hydrogen atoms are called . . . acids. . . . acid, for example, is a . . . acid.

2. Draw the following table and complete it by reference to the text. Give examples of the two classes of acid other than those mentioned in the reading passage.

Acids	
+ carbon	
acetic	

(From *English in Focus: English in Physical Science* by J. P. B. Allen and H. G. Widdowson (OUP))

4 Malnutrition

SECTION A: READING FOR COMPREHENSION

1. Do you know what malnutrition is? It is a condition which people suffer from when they are undernourished, that is, when they do not get enough food (or enough of the right kind of food) to eat. As the following text shows, it is a serious problem for huge numbers of people in the world today. Answer the questions in the text and in the margin as you are reading.

Malnutrition

I   The struggle against malnutrition and hunger is as old as man himself, and never across the face of our planet has the outcome been more in doubt.[1] Malnourishment afflicts an estimated 400 million to 1.5 billion of the world's poor. Even in the affluent U.S., poverty means undernourishment for an estimated ten to twenty million. Hardest hit are children,[2] whose growing bodies demand two and a half times more protein, pound for pound, than those of adults. Nutrition experts estimate that 70 percent of the children in low-income countries are affected.[3]

[1]*Malnutrition is:*

a. *not as serious now as before.*
b. *as serious now as at an time before.*
c. *likely to become less serious.*

INTRODUCTION: TEXT
MAIN IDEA & SUPPORTING
FACTS

[2]*Children suffer more/less than adults.*

[3]*Two other words used for malnutrition are:*

II   Misshapen bodies tell the tragic story of
malnutrition. Medical science identifies
two major types of malnutrition which usually occur in combination. The first, kwashiorkor, is typified by the bloated[5] look, the
opposite of what we associate with starvation.
Accumulated fluids pushing against wasted
muscles account for the plumpness of hands,
feet, belly, and face. Emaciated[6] shoulders
reveal striking thinness. Caused by an acute lack
of protein, kwashiorkor (a West African word) can
bring brain damage, anemia, diarrhea, irritability,
apathy, and loss of appetite.

a. _____
b. _____

[4]*What do you expect to read about next?*
_____

[5]*means* _____

DEVELOPMENT BY ANALYSIS:
a. CLASSIFIES: TWO TYPES
b. IDENTIFIES PHYSICAL
FEATURES, EXPLAINS
CAUSES/EFFECTS OF ONE
TYPE

[6]*means* _____

7. *What do you expect the next paragraph to be about?* _____
_____

[III]   On the other hand, stick[8] limbs, a bloated
belly, wide eyes, and the stretched-skin
face of an old person mark victims of marasmus, a word taken from the Greek 'to waste
away.'[9] Lacking calories as well as protein,
sufferers may weigh only half as much as
normal. With fat gone, the skin hangs in
wrinkles or draws tight over bones. With
marasmus comes anemia, diarrhea, dehydration, and a ravenous appetite. Children,
whose growing bodies require large amounts of protein, are afflicted in greatest numbers, but perhaps
only three percent of all child victims suffer the
extreme stages described.

[8]*Very thick/thin.*

[9]*The appearance of a marasmus victim and of a kwashiorkor victim is compared/contrasted.*

DEVELOPMENT BY ANALYSIS:
CONTRAST PHYSICAL FEA-
TURES, CAUSES AND EFFECTS
OF SECOND TYPE

IV   Scientists are working feverishly[10] to develop
new weapons against malnutrition and starvation.
But two thirds of the human population of 3.9 billion live in the poorest countries which also have
the highest birth rates. Thus, of the 74 million
people added to the population each year, four out
of five will be born in a have-not country[11] – a country
unable to supply its people's nutritional needs.

[10]*working while ill/slowly with care/hard at great speed.*

CONCLUSION

[11]*The 'have-not' countries are the* _____

12. *The writer concludes that the struggle against malnutrition is likely/unlikely to succeed.*

2.   Now answer Question 13 - 18 below.

TEXT COMPREHENSION QUESTIONS:

Paragraph I:

3.   Complete the following summary of Paragraph I.

a. _____ has been and still is a serious global problem. Even in wealthy
b. _____, like the c. _____, being poor often means being d. _____.
e. _____ suffer most because they need more f. _____ than g. _____.

Paragraph II-III:

14. Using information from these two paragraphs, complete the following diagram, which
    illustrates the effects of malnutrition on appearance.

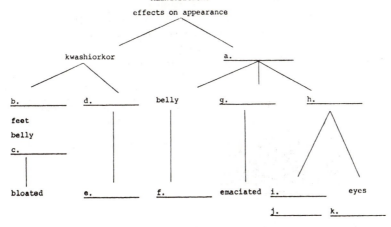

Malnutrition:
effects on appearance

kwashiorkor   a. _____

b. _____   d. _____   belly   g. _____   h. _____
feet
belly
c. _____

bloated   e. _____   f. _____   emaciated   i. _____   eyes

j. _____   k. _____

15. Complete the following statement which explains why kwashiorkor victims look
    the way they do.

    a. _____ which b. _____ in the body c. _____ against
    d. _____ which have e. _____ away; this causes the
    f. _____ to look g. _____ .

16. Select the appropriate word from each pair given to complete the following
    statement.

    The text suggests that a person who eats only rice, potatoes, and
    bread could eventually suffer from a. kwashiorkor/marasmus, even
    though he had plenty to eat, because these foods lack b. protein/
    calories. He would not suffer from c. kwashiorkor/marasmus because
    the foods contain a lot of d. protein/calories.

17. Look at the following table. It summarizes the effects of kwashiorkor and
    marasmus.
    a. Complete the 'Effects' column by writing in the blanks words or phrases
       from the text which have the same meaning as the phrases in parentheses.
    b. Put ticks in the appropriate places in the 'Causes' columns to show
       whether the effects are caused by kwashiorkor or marasmus. Be careful;
       some of the effects are caused by both illnesses.

Effects		Causes	
		Kwashiorkor	Marasmus
1. _____	(easily made angry)	_____	_____
2. _____	(extreme hunger)	_____	_____
3. _____	(loss of water from body tissues)	_____	_____
4. _____	(lack of healthy blood)	_____	_____
5. _____	(too frequent discharge from bowels)	_____	_____
6. _____	(lack of interest/concern)	_____	_____
7. _____	(some loss of brain activity)	_____	_____
8. _____	(having no desire to eat)	_____	_____

Paragraph IV:

18. Complete the following summary of the writer's conclusion.

The a._____ population is increasing by about 74 million

b._____ each c._____. Most of this d._____

is in the e._____ countries which already have 67% of the

world's f._____. These countries will not be able to

provide enough g._____ for all of their people. Therefore

the problem of h._____ will probably become i._____

rather than smaller.

Check your answers on pages 123-124.

| Possible number right = 59 |
| Number right = |
| Percent right = |

SECTION B: ORGANIZING INFORMATION IN A TEXT

Look at the organization of the whole passage in SECTION A.

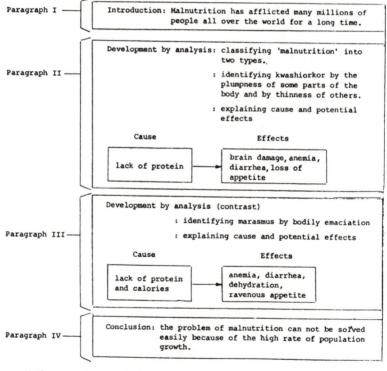

Paragraph I —— Introduction: Malnutrition has afflicted many millions of people all over the world for a long time.

Paragraph II —— Development by analysis: classifying 'malnutrition' into two types.
: identifying kwashiorkor by the plumpness of some parts of the body and by thinness of others.
: explaining cause and potential effects

Cause | Effects
lack of protein → brain damage, anemia, diarrhea, loss of appetite

Paragraph III —— Development by analysis (contrast)
: identifying marasmus by bodily emaciation
: explaining cause and potential effects

Cause | Effects
lack of protein and calories → anemia, diarrhea, dehydration, ravenous appetite

Paragraph IV —— Conclusion: the problem of malnutrition can not be solved easily because of the high rate of population growth.

So there are three parts in the passage:

1. the introduction;

2. development (by analysis: classifying the two types, then contrasting them by explaining the cause and effect of each);

3. the conclusion.

EXERCISE B

Using information from the text and the first part of the section, complete the following summary of the text.

1. _____

Men has struggled against 7. _____ for a long time; still the result is in doubt. It 8. _____ up to about 9. _____ of the poor all over the world. 10. _____ are hardest hit because their bodies need more protein than those of adults.

5. _____

Malnutrition can be divided into 11. _____ types: 12. _____ and 13. _____ . 14. _____ which is caused by 15. _____ of protein, is characterized by a 16. _____ look caused by 17. _____ fluids pushing against wasted 18. _____ . 19. _____ , which is caused by lack of protein and 20. _____ is shown by stick 21. _____ , wide eyes, bloated belly, etc. With both kwashiorkor and marasmus come 22. _____ and 23. _____ . But kwashiorkor alone causes loss of 24. _____ while marasmus brings a 25. _____ appetite.

2. _____

6. _____

Ly 3. _____

4. _____

Scientists are working to cope with the food problem but 26. _____ 27. _____ of the world's population live in the 28. _____ countries which have the highest 29. _____ 30. _____ .

Check your answers on page 124.

Possible number right = 30
Number right =
Percent right =

(From *Foundation Reading II, Vol 3* by the Chulalongkorn University Language Institute)

5 Schoolboy Tyranny

Note: Tyranny: *Cruel or unjust use of power*

I still remember–my hands and my finger-tips still remember!–what used to lie in store for us on our return to school from the holidays. The guava trees in the school yard would be in full leaf again, and the old leaves would be lying around in scattered heaps. In places there were even more than just heaps of them: it would be like a muddy sea of leaves.

'Get that all swept up!' the headmaster would tell us. 'I want the whole place cleaned up, at once!'

'At once!' There was enough work there, very hard work, too, to last for a week. Especially since the only tools with which we were provided were our hands, our fingers, our nails.

'Now see that it's done properly, and be quick about it,' the headmaster would say to the older pupils, 'or you'll have to answer for it!'

So at an order from the older boys we would all line up like peasants about to cut and gather in crops, and we would set to work like members of a chain-gang.

If the work was not going as quickly as the headmaster expected, the big boys, instead of giving us a helping hand, used to find it simpler to whip us with branches pulled from the trees.

In order to avoid these blows, we used to bribe our tyrants with the juicy cakes of Indian corn, the couscous made of meat or fish which we used to bring for our midday meal. And if we happened to have any money on us the coins changed hands at once. If we did not do this, if we were afraid of going home with an empty stomach or empty purse, the blows were re-doubled. They hit us so violently and often, and with such devilish enjoyment, that even a deaf and dumb person would have realised that we were being flogged not so much to make us work harder, but rather to beat us into a state of obedience in which we would be only too glad to give up our food and money.

Occasionally, one of us, worn out by such calculated cruelty, would have the courage to complain to the headmaster. He would of course be very angry, but the punishment he inflicted on the older boys was always very small–nothing compared to what they had done to us. And the fact is that however much we complained, our situation did not improve in the slightest. Perhaps we should have let our parents know what was going on, but somehow we never dreamed of doing so; I don't know whether it was loyalty or pride that kept us silent, but I can see now that we were foolish to keep quiet about it, for such beatings were completelty foreign to our nature.

(Adapted from 'The African Child' by Camara Laye.)

1. The writer says, 'My hands and my finger-tips still remember!' because
   A. the work probably made his hands and finger-tips sore.
   B. the work was very hard.
   C. he had to use his hands and finger-tips.
   D. he had to work in a muddy sea of leaves.

2. From the way the headmaster spoke, it seems that
   A. he was ordering only the older boys to do the work.
   B. he fully expected everyone to join in to do the work.
   C. he did not care who did the work, provided it was done quickly and properly.
   D. he wanted the older boys to make the others work, without working themselves.

3. The headmaster's order to have the whole place cleaned up at once was
   A. reasonable, since he was the headmaster.
   B. unreasonable, since he did not provide any tools.
   C. reasonable, since the school grounds must not look untidy.
   D. unreasonable, since he put the older boys in charge of the work.

4. The older boys beat the younger ones so hard
   A. because they knew this would make them offer bribes of food and money.
   B. because they were too lazy to work themselves, and enjoyed being cruel.
   C. because they knew the headmaster would be angry with them if the work was not done quickly.
   D. in order to make them work faster and harder.

5. When the younger boys complained to the headmaster
   A. he became very angry with them.
   B. he gave the older boys a suitable punishment.
   C. it only made matters worse.
   D. it made no difference.

6. 'Perhaps we should have let our parents know what was going on.'
   The reason for their silence was
   A. loyalty.   C. not exactly clear.
   B. pride.   D. foolishness.

7. (*Note:* You would expect a lion to attack a gazelle because it is in its nature to hunt for food of this kind. It would be foreign to a lion's nature to leave a gazelle alone when it is hungry.)
   What does the writer mean when he says that 'such beatings were completely foreign to our nature'? Explain why you either agree or disagree with him.

8. Complete the following sentence, trying not to use more than another 25 words:
   The passage is an example of what can happen in a school if . . . .

(From *Read and Think* by J. Munby (Longman))

6 Pollution

Activity C

△ ○ ●●●●

Read for main points

Below you are given a question, a text on pollution and three incomplete statements.

Look at Question 1. Now read the text quickly to answer the question. Then complete the statements. Re-read the text if necessary. Tick the correct answers.

1.   This text on pollution answers one of these two questions. Which question does it answer?

   (a)   How many kinds of chemicals can be found in the air and in the sea?

   (b)   In what ways does the world become dirty and unsafe for living things?

Pollution

Pollution spoils our environment in many ways. The air we breathe, for instance, is constantly polluted by smoke and by chemicals such as carbon monoxide in the exhaust fumes of cars and other kinds of motor vehicles.

For wild life, however, there are even greater dangers in the pollution of water — of rivers, for example, or lakes and seas. A good illustration of this is the oil released from tankers at sea. It kills all kinds of sea animals, including birds, whose feathers become covered with oil so they cannot fly, as well as fish and other forms of marine life. Other causes of water pollution include power stations, which release warm water into rivers. This kills the fish and plants which live there. These are only a few examples; there are many more.

2.   The two main types of pollution the writer talks about are

   (a)   pollution of the air.

   (b)   pollution of water.

   (c)   pollution by oil.

3.   From the examples in the text you can tell that "pollution" means

   (a)   things that are produced by factories.

   (b)   things which make our world dirty.

   (c)   the deterioration of our environment.

4.   From the examples in the text you can tell that "environment" means

   (a)   the world around us, including living things.

   (b)   water and the air that we breathe.

Activity D

Complete the sentences

Here are seven sentences with blanks.

Use information from the text on pollution to complete the sentences.

Example: Rivers, lakes and seas are all examples of water.

1.   The oil released from tankers at sea is an example of

_____ .

2.   Sea birds are examples of _____ .

3.   Fish are a form of _____ .

4.   Warm water released from power stations is an example of

_____ .

5.   The air in cities is polluted by chemicals such as _____

and by_____ .

6.   Carbon monoxide is found in the exhaust fumes of cars and

other kinds of_____ .

7.   Oil at sea kills all kinds of sea animals, including _____

and _____ .

Activity E

O ●●

Complete the labelling

The three diagrams below have not been completely labelled.

Use information from the text on pollution to complete the labelling.

Examples: Rivers, lakes and seas are all examples of water.

We could express this as a diagram:

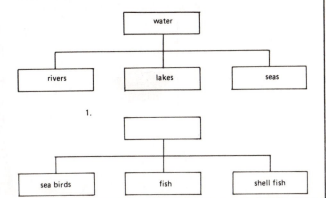

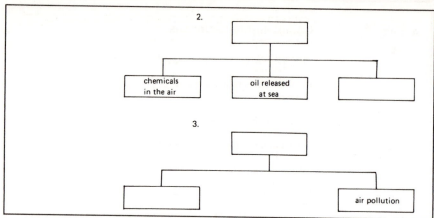

(From *Skills for Learning: Reading for Academic Study by* The Language Centre, University of Malaya (University of Malaya Press/Nelson))

7   The Survival of the Fittest

In this second lesson on evolution you will be able to deepen your understanding of how animals adapt for survival. You will also get an opportunity to practise the skill of prediction and to relate a linear text to tables and a map.

Activity A
△

What are your views on natural selection?

Answer these questions.

1.   Can you think of any creatures which are in danger of dying out?

2.   Can you suggest any reasons why they are in danger?

3.   Can you think of a way in which many creatures are adapted so that they can avoid being seen by their predators?

Activity B
○ ●●●●

Read how creatures adapt to survive (1)

This is a step-by-step activity. At each step in the text you are given a choice of ideas or a question. The text describes the process by which some creatures survive and others die out.

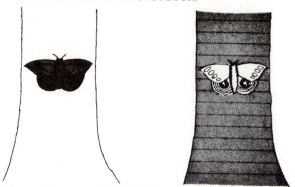

Read each step and say what can logically follow, or answer the question. Tick the correct answers.

Step 1

On each tree there is a moth. They are both quite clearly visible. Any predator would see his prey very clearly. But suppose the light moth was sitting on the light tree and vice versa.

(a)   It would not make any difference.

(b)   The moth might survive.

Step 2

A dark moth on a dark tree would be less visible and have a better chance of survival from the attacks of predators. This is known as camouflage. Some animals, like the chameleon, for instance, are able to change colour according to their background. This kind of change is not evolutionary change (though of course the chameleon has evolved the ability to make this change). However, a change in colour is evolutionary if the new creature is able to reproduce itself so that its young also have the new colour.

The example of the moth is a real one and was investigated in England in the 1950's by a scientist called Dr. Kettlewell. It is a very well-known example of evolutionary change.

The species of moth is the Peppered Moth. It was typically light brown in colour and settled on the trunks of trees which were a similar colour and camouflaged it. Then came a change in the environment. Industry began to grow up in parts of England with the result that smoke and other forms of pollution began to fill the atmosphere. So,

(a)   the moths turned black.

(b)   the trees turned black.

Step 3

The pollution from the factories covered the bark on the tree trunks with soot and grime so the light brown Peppered Moths became very visible to their predators and were eaten. Then, gradually they began to change colour.

(a)   They became lighter.

(b)   They became darker.

Step 4

The darker ones were more likely to survive, so their colour gradually became darker. How did they become darker? This is one of the mysteries of science, but it has been called 'natural selection' since Charles Darwin published his famous book *The Origin of Species* in 1859. Natural selection does not make anything happen. You cannot force a moth to change colour, for instance, nor can a moth decide to change. The point is that every creature has a genetic structure consisting of genes and chromosomes. This structure can change naturally, by accident. Perhaps this change does not matter. Perhaps, on the other hand, it produces a 'deformed' individual which the others reject or even kill because it is different. These things happen all the time. But if the change (or 'mutation') happens to fit the new environment, then the new creature, instead of being rejected or killed by the others will

(a)   die.

(b)   survive.

Step 5

This is natural selection. A mutation (which is always possible) happens to suit a new environment, and the "odd" creature survives because it is better fitted. Then it reproduces and a new type of creature evolves. Meanwhile the others have become unsuited to the changed environment. They must either change their behaviour, or

(a) become extinct.

(b) change the environment.

Step 6

Dr. Kettlewell wanted to discover whether the dark Peppered Moths were in fact a new type of Peppered Moth which had adapted to its environment. In the first experiment, he released light and dark moths into the woods near Birmingham (a large industrial city in England). In the second he released his moths into the woods in a country district called Dorset in the south of England. Finally, he placed examples of each kind of moth on trees of the opposite colour and watched what happened.

Below is a list of hypotheses (things that can be predicted if your theory is right). Which of the hypotheses would support Dr. Kettlewell's theory that a new type of darker moth had evolved in industrial areas? More than one hypothesis may be necessary.

(a) More dark moths would survive in Birmingham than light ones.

(b) More dark moths would be eaten by birds in Dorset than light ones.

(c) The number of dark moths that survived in Dorset would be equal to the number of light moths that survived in Birmingham.

(d) All the dark moths in Birmingham would survive.

(e) The number of light moths surviving in Dorset would be equal to the number of dark moths surviving in Birmingham.

Here are the results from his experiment in Birmingham:

	light	dark
Number of moths released	201	601
Number of moths recaptured	34	205
Percentage of moths recaptured	16%	34.1%

Dr. Kettlewell's technique was to release moths which were specially marked, then recapture as many as possible after a time.

Which of the following statements could Dr. Kettlewell make on the basis of the results? Notice that he released more dark ones than light ones.

(a) Six times as many dark moths seem to have survived.

(b) Just over twice as many dark moths seem to have survived.

(c) I have proved my hypothesis beyond doubt.

(d) The evidence supports my hypothesis.

Activity C

○ ●●

Complete a summary of what you have read

Here is a text with blanks. It summarizes the main points in the texts you have read. A choice of words for each blank is given in the margin.

Complete the text by filling in the blanks with the correct words from the margin.

1.	light dark	Dr. Kettlewell's observations clearly demonstrate that natural selection was responsible for the replacement of (1)_____ forms of the Peppered Moth by dark forms in (2) _____
2.	rural industrial	regions. The theory of natural selection enables us to predict genetic changes in a population from our knowledge of changes in the (3)_____ . If pollution were controlled in industrial areas,
3.	environment individual	and if this allowed forests to revert to their natural unpolluted state, we would predict that the frequency of the light form of the
4.	decrease increase	Peppered Moth would gradually begin to (4)_____ . In fact, smoke control programmes have been introduced in industrial regions in Britain since 1952, and the frequency of the
5.	light dark	(5)_____form of the Peppered Moth has shown a highly significant increase.

Activity D
○ ●●●●

Read how creatures adapt to survive (2)

This is a step-by-step activity. In it you are given a continuation of the report on Dr. Kettlewell's experiments. At each step in the text there is a question and a choice of answers.

Read each step carefully and then tick the correct answer to the question.

Step 8

Later, to find additional support for his hypothesis, Dr. Kettlewell repeated the same experiment in Dorset. The results proved he was right.

Which of these two tables shows the correct results from Dorset?

		light	dark
(a)	Number of moths released	496	473
	Number of moths recaptured	30	62
	Percentage of moths recaptured	6.3%	12.5%
(b)	Number of moths released	496	473
	Number of moths recaptured	62	30
	Percentage of moths recaptured	12.5%	6.3%

Step 9

Finally, he placed an equal number of moths of each colour on trees and watched what happened. He quickly discovered that several species of birds searched the tree trunks for moths and other insects and that these birds more readily found the one that contrasted with its background than the one that blended with the bark.

Which of these tables expresses the results?

		Moths eaten by birds	
		light	dark
(a)	Unpolluted woods	164	26
	Polluted woods	15	43
(b)	Unpolluted woods	26	164
	Polluted woods	43	15

Step 10

Here is a map of the British Isles showing where dark (melanistic) and light (typical) moths were found in the early 1950's.

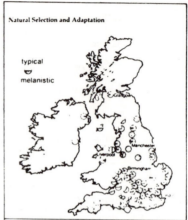

Natural Selection and Adaptation

typical

melanistic

The frequency of melanistic individuals in populations of the Peppered Moth (Biston betularia) in various localities in the British Isles. The map is based on more than 20,000 records from 83 centres collected during 1952–56 (after Kettlewell 1958).

Do the results support Dr. Kettlewell's theory?

(a) Yes

(b) No

(From *Skills for Learning: Reading for Academic Study* by The Language Centre, University of Malaya (University of Malaya Press/Nelson))

8 The House on the Hill

On their way to the theatre, Carl and Rosa went to a bookshop to buy a book each to read at home. Carl bought a book called *The House on the Hill*.

Before reading parts of Carl's book, look at the cover ────────▶

and at the first illustration. ───────

Now answer this question:

What do you think the book will be about?

a crime

b science-fiction

c love

d horror

e war

Now read Chapter One.

THE HOUSE ON THE HILL

PART 1

It was a beautiful summer evening. Paul was happy. No more exams. College was finished. Now he needed a job. He wanted to be a writer and work for a newspaper. But first he needed a rest.

It was hot in the house. There was no wind. 'I'll go for a walk,' said Paul to himself. 'I'll go down to the river.'

Paul lived in a small town and he was soon outside in the country. He walked near the river and watched the water birds.

Suddenly, he saw the girl. She was standing alone, looking into the water. She was young, and very beautiful. She had long, dark hair, and she was wearing a pretty white dress.

Paul went up to her.

'Hello,' he said. 'What's your name?'

'I'm Maria,' she said, and she smiled at him.

Paul and Maria talked for a long time. The sun went down. It was nearly dark.

'I must go home,' said Maria.

'Where do you live?' asked Paul.

'In the big white house on the hill,' said Maria. 'Where do you live?'

'In the little brown house near the market,' said Paul.

They laughed. But Paul was sad. The house on the hill was big and important. Maria was rich, and he was poor. And Paul was in love.

1

1

1 The Characters

The boy

a his name .... *Paul* ....

b wants to be ....

c money: rich / poor? ....

d feelings: happy /sad?
   at the beginning ....
   at the end ....
   about the girl ....

The girl

a her name .... *Maria* ....

b her age ....

c her money ....

d appearance ....

   her hair ....
   her dress ....

(2) Here is another extract from the book. ▶

Before you read this part, you need to know:

Paul lives alone with his mother, a poor, kind woman.

Maria lives alone with her mother, a rich, ugly woman.

In this extract, Paul visits Maria's mother for the first time.

While you are reading the extract, think about:

Maria's mother – her feelings about Paul.

Maria – her feelings about Paul.

Paul – his feelings about Maria and her mother.

Money.

(1) *The House on the Hill* is a love story. Read the first page again, and **while** you are reading, make NOTES. Write one word only, like this:

2 The Place

a Paul walks. Where? .... *river* ....

b Paul lives. Where? ....
   town / city / country ....

c His house: size / colour? ....

d Her house: size / colour?

3 The Time

a Time of year .... *Summer* ....

b Time of day
   at the beginning ....

   at the end ....

c They talk: How long? ....

After you have finished reading, do not look back at the story, but use your notes to write about the boy / the girl / the place / the time.

'So you want to marry my daughter?' The old woman said. Her voice was hard.

Paul looked at her bravely. 'Yes,' he said. 'I love Maria and I want to marry her.'

The old woman laughed.

'You! A poor student! No money, no father, nothing! My daughter will never marry you.'

Paul said nothing. He looked at Maria. She did not look at him.

'I am poor now,' he said. 'But one day I'll be a famous writer.'

The old woman laughed again. 'No,' she said. 'My daughter is not for you. She is going to be married soon. You will never see her again.'

> **After** you have read the extract, try to predict the end of the story.
> Here are five endings. Do you think they are:
>
> **impossible / possible / probable / certain?**
>
> 1 Maria kills her mother.
> 2 Paul kills Maria's mother.
> 3 Maria marries Paul.
> 4 Maria marries someone – but not Paul.
> 5 Paul marries someone – but not Maria.

(From *Reasons for Reading* by Evelyn Davies and Norman Whitney (Heinemann Educational Books))

9 Notices

When she got to Pembroke College, Rosa found a lot of people there. She wondered what to do and where to go. At first, she stood with a lot of other students in front of the college notice-board. Then she decided to ask the young man standing next to her for help.

Rosa Excuse me. Can you help me please? I'm a new student and I want English classes.

Carl So do I.

Rosa Oh! Are you a foreign student, too?

Carl Yes. I'm Swedish. You're Spanish, aren't you?

Rosa No. I speak Spanish, but I come from Colombia.

Carl Well, I think we both go to GENERAL ENQUIRIES ROOM 102.

Rosa But what about ROOM 110 NEW FIRST YEAR STUDENTS? We are both new first year students.

Carl Yes you're right . . . No, wait a minute. Let's look at the whole list first . . .

Rosa What about ROOM 290 ENGLISH LANGUAGE? Do you think that's right?

Carl No, look, further down, near the bottom . . . ENGLISH FOR FOREIGNERS NEW AND OLD STUDENTS.

Rosa That sounds right. What does EFL stand for?

Carl English as a Foreign Language, I think.

Rosa That's it!

Carl O.K. Let's go to Room 310. By the way, my name is Carl, Carl Lindstrom.

Rosa I'm Rosa. Rosa Morello.

Carl I'm glad we met, Rosa.

Rosa So am I, Carl.

Notice Board	
Pembroke College	Enrolment Day
ALL GENERAL ENQUIRIES	Room 102
Hotel Management	103
Business Management	104
Science Courses (DAY)	106
Science Courses (NIGHT)	107
NEW FIRST YEAR STUDENTS	110
Geography	203
History	207
French	237
German	264
Spanish	276
OTHER FOREIGN LANGUAGES	281
English Language	290
English Literature	
Engineering (DAY)	292
Engineering (NIGHT)	293
English For Foreigners	310
(EFL NEW AND OLD STUDENTS)	
Accountancy	296
Drama	294
Art	311
Pottery	357
Yoga	381
ALL OTHER COURSES	390

1

(1) Tick the two correct facts about Carl and Rosa:

They are	old students
	new students
	English Language
	Foreign Languages
	English as a Foreign Language

(2) Complete this sentence about Carl and Rosa. Use the words:

English   language   as   both   They

. . . . . . are . . . . . . students of . . . .
a Foreign . . . . . .

(3) Both Carl and Rosa made a mistake. They both read slowly down the list of subjects and rooms, instead of quickly reading the whole list first.

What was the first word at which Carl stopped reading?

What was the first word at which Rosa stopped reading?

(4) Carl and Rosa are students of English as a Foreign Language. They enrol in Room 310.

Where do these students go?

Meena	a second year accountancy student
David	a third year student of Spanish
Tina	a student doing a second year Science course in the evening
Maria	a third year History student
Paul	a student from another college looking for his sister
Mick	a degree student in his first year at the college
Laura	a housewife interested in yoga
Yoko	a photography student
Barbara	a drama student
Graham	a student of Russian

(5) The room for EFL students to enrol in is on the third floor.

Which floor are these rooms on?

Business Management

General Enquiries

Pottery

Chinese

daytime Science courses

Architecture

Art

German

evening Engineering courses

Hotel Management

(6) Carl wants a **full-time** course in **technical** English.

Rosa wants a **part-time** course in **general** English.

The relevant words for Carl are –
full-time and **technical**.

The relevant words for Rosa are –
part-time and **general**.

In Room 310, they were given this notice:

NOTICE TO STUDENTS EFL	
Please enrol on the correct form	
Course	Form
Part-time course in English conversation	A
Full-time course in general English	B
Part-time course in general English	C
Part-time course in spoken English	D
Full-time course in written English	E
Full-time course in technical English	F
Part-time course in technical English	G

Which form does Carl want?

Which form does Rosa want?

(From *Reasons for Reading* by Evelyn Davies and Norman Whitney (Heinemann Educational Books))

Appendix C

British publishers of graded readers for students of English as a second or foreign language

Those publishers who produce a handbook or teacher's guide to one or more series of graded readers have the letter H after their name. Those who produce recorded versions of some of the readers on cassettes have the letter C. All addresses are in the United Kingdom.

Edward Arnold Ltd 41 Bedford Square London WC1B 3DQ	Leaders, Recollections
Cambridge University Press (C) PO Box 110 Cambridge CB2 3RL	Cambridge Fiction Readers
Cassell Ltd EFL Sales Department 35 Red Lion Square London WC1R 4SG	Spotlight, Structured English Readers
Centre for British Teachers Quality House Quality Court Chancery Lane London WC2A 1HP	Reading Box
Collins ELT (H, C) PO Box 39 Glasgow G4 ONB	Collins English Library
Evans ELT List is now distributed by Bell & Hyman Ltd Denmark House 37–39 Queen Elizabeth Street London SE1 2QB	Graded Reading, Evans English Readers
Heinemann Educational Books (H, C) 22 Bedford Square London WC1B 3HH	Heinemann Guided Readers Heinemann Science and Technical Readers
Hodder & Stoughton Educational PO Box 6 Mill Road Dunton Green Sevenoaks Kent TN13 2XX	Hodder Graded Readers, Modern English Readers, Modern English Library

Longman English Teaching Services (H, C)
Longman House
Burnt Mill
Harlow
Essex CM20 2JE

Structural Readers, Squirrels, Books in Easy English, Simplified English Series, Bridge Series, Technical English Series, Reading Routes (reading laboratory)

Macmillan Press Ltd (H, C)
Little Essex Street
London WC2R 3LF

Rangers, Pattern Readers, Dodd's Supplementary Readers, Stories to Remember, Controlled Readers, Student Series

ELT Department (C)
Thomas Nelson & Sons Ltd
Nelson House,
Mayfield Road
Walton-on-Thames
Surrey KT12 5PL

Nelson's Graded English Readers, Streamline Books, Rapid Readers, Getaway Readers, Tamarind Books

ELT Marketing (H)
Oxford University Press
Walton Street
Oxford OX2 6DD

Active Readers, Active Colour Reading Books, Oxford Graded Readers, New Oxford Supplementary Readers, Oxford Progressive English Readers, Tales Retold for Easy Reading, Stories Told and Retold, English Readers Library, Alpha Books, Delta Readers, Lotus Library, English Picture Readers

Science Research Associates Ltd
Newtown Road
Henley on Thames
Oxfordshire RG9 1EW

Reading laboratories

University of London Press
St Paul's House
Warwick Lane
London EC4P 4AH

Present Day English Readers

Ward Lock Educational
116 Baker Street
London W1M 2BB

Reading Workshops (reading laboratory)

Appendix D: Vocabulary levels of some major series of British EFL readers

*FORMERLY NEW METHOD SUPPLEMENTARY READERS

VOCABULARY LEVELS	UNGRADED	3500	3000	2500	2000	1800	1500	1200	1000	800	700	600	500	300	Publisher
CAMBRIDGE FICTION READERS	CELL Level 6 and 7				CELL Level 5										
CASSELL SPOTLIGHT				Level 6 2100		Level 5 1750	Level 4 1400		Level 3 1050			Level 2		Level 1 350	
COLLINS ENGLISH LIBRARY			Level 6	Level 5			Level 4		Level 3			Level 2	Level 1		
EVANS ENGLISH READERS				Stage 5 2300					Stage 4	Stage 3	Stage 2	Stage 1	Beginner		EVANS
EVANS GRADED READING				Grade 5 2300					Grade 4	Grade 3	Grade 2	Grade 1			EVANS
HEINEMANN GUIDED READERS				Upper 2200		Intermediate 1600		Elementary 1100				Beginner			HEINEMANN
SCIENCE AND TECHNICAL READERS						Science and Technical readers									HEINEMANN
HODDER GRADED READERS						C Intermediate		B Lower Intermediate	A Elementary						
STRUCTURAL READERS						Stage 6	Stage 5	Stage 4 1100	Stage 3 750			Stage 2	Stage 1		LONGMAN
SQUIRRELS*						Stage 6 Stage 5	Stage 4 1400	Stage 3	Stage 2 850		Stage 1				LONGMAN
BOOKS IN EASY ENGLISH							Stage 5 Stage 4		Stage 3		Stage 2 750	Stage 1			LONGMAN
BRIDGE SERIES				BRIDGE SERIES											LONGMAN
LONGMAN SIMPLIFIED ENGLISH SERIES					LONGMAN SIMPLIFIED ENGLISH SERIES										LONGMAN
RANGERS					Range 6 2200	Range 5 1880	Range 4 1530	Range 3 1180			Range 2 830		Range 1 450		MACMILLAN
DODD'S READERS					2000		1500		1000		700	600	500		MACMILLAN
PATTERN READERS			3000		2000		1500		1000			600			MACMILLAN
STORIES TO REMEMBER				STORIES TO REMEMBER											MACMILLAN
STUDENT SERIES			STUDENT SERIES												MACMILLAN
NELSON ENGLISH READERS					Advanced 2075	Intermediate			Elementary						NELSON
RAPID READERS / STREAMLINE BOOKS / GETAWAY READERS / TAMARIND BOOKS		RAPID READERS / Big RR / GETAWAY READERS		TAMARIND BOOKS	STREAMLINE BOOKS	RAPID READERS / Small rr									NELSON
NEW OXFORD SUPPLEMENTARY READERS		6 3500			5 2000		4 1500		3 1000		2 750		1 500		OXFORD
GRADED READERS			3		2 1900		1500		1000		750		500		OXFORD
DELTA READERS			3		2		1 4		3	2 900		1			OXFORD
ALPHA BOOKS							ALPHA BOOKS 1500		ALPHA BOOKS 1000			LOTUS LIBRARY			OXFORD
TALES TOLD AND RETOLD					2							1			OXFORD
UNIVERSITY OF LONDON PRESS PRESENT DAY ENGLISH READERS					E		D 1400		C	B 750			A		OXFORD
VOCABULARY LEVELS	UNGRADED	3500	3000	2500	2000	1800	1500	1200	1000	800	700	600	500	300	

Bibliography

(a) General

Abbot, G. (1976), *What Next?* (London: Longman).
   Listening material to develop the skill of prediction.
Abbot, G. (1979), 'Coherence and the reading text', *Reading 13*, pp. 2–9.
Austin, J. L. (1976, 2nd ed.), *How to do Things with Words* (London: OUP).
   Classic account of speech act theory.
Ball, F. (1977, *The Development of Reading Skills* (Oxford: Basil Blackwell).
   Many activities (mostly for children) and good phonic lists.
Banton-Smith, N. (1966), 'Speed reading: benefits and dangers' in Downing, J.
   (ed.) *The First International Reading Symposium, Oxford 1964* (London: Cas-
   sell), pp. 211–234; reprinted Melnik and Merritt (1972b).
Berman, R. (1975) 'Analytic syntax: a technique for advanced level reading', *TESOL
   Quarterly* vol. 9, no. 3.
   Suggests ways of simplifying/clarifying difficult syntax.
Bright, J. A. and McGregor, G. P. (1970), *Teaching English as a Second Language*
   (London: Longman).
   A classic; Chapter 3 deals with reading.
Brown, G. and Yule, G. (1983), *Discourse Analysis* (Cambridge: CUP).
Brumfit, C. J. (1977), 'The teaching of advanced reading skills in foreign languages,
   with particular reference to English as a foreign language', *Language Teaching
   and Linguistic Abstracts*, pp. 10, pp. 73–84; reprinted Kinsella (1978).
Brumfit, C. J. (1979), *Readers for Foreign Learners of English* (ETIC Information
   Guide 7) (London: The British Council English Teaching Information Centre).
   Lists supplementary readers from British and other publishers, arranged accord-
   ing to approximate level of difficulty.
Candlin, C. N., Kirkwood, J. M. and Moore, H. M. (1978), 'Study skills in English'
   in Mackay and Mountford (1978), pp. 190–219.
   Interesting account of materials development and underlying theories.
Coulthard, M. (1975), 'Discourse analysis in English – a short review of the lit-
   erature', *Language Teaching and Linguistic Abstracts*, no. 8 pp. 73–89; reprinted
   Kinsella (1978).
   Surveys recent work in the field; extensive bibliography.
Coulthard, M. (1977), *An Introduction to Discourse Analysis* (London: Longman).
   A useful book but concerned mainly with spoken interaction.
D'Arcy, P. (1973a), *Reading for Meaning 1: Learning to Read* (London: Hutchin-
   son Educational for the Schools Council).
D'Arcy, P. (1973b), *Reading for Meaning 2: The Reader's Response* (London:
   Hutchinson Educational for the Schools Council).
   This and the preceding book lucidly demonstrate current approaches to L1 read-
   ing in Britain. Section II of 1973b deals with children's reading preferences.
Davies, A. and Widdowson, H. G. (1974), 'Reading and writing', ch. 6 of Allen, J.
   P. B. and Corder, S. Pit (eds), *Techniques in Applied Linguistics* (vol. 3 of *The
   Edinburgh Course in Applied Linguistics*) (London: OUP).
   A cogent account of the principles of reading in a foreign language.
De Leeuw, E. M. (1965), *Read Better, Read Faster* (Harmondsworth: Penguin).
Eskey, D. (1970), 'A new technique for the teaching of reading to advanced
   students', *TESOL Quarterly*, vol. 4, no. 4.
   Suggestions for tackling structural problems, especially nominalization.
Freedle, R. O. and Carroll, J. B. (1972) eds, *Language Comprehension and the
   Acquisition of Knowledge* (John Wiley & Sons).
   Essential reading for anyone who wishes to explore the psycholinguistic ap-
   proach to comprehension.

Fry, E. (1963), *Teaching Faster Reading* (Cambridge: CUP).

Fry, E. (1964), 'Judging readability of books', *Teacher Education*, no. 5, pp. 34–9.

Fry, E. (1977), 'Fry's readability graph', *Journal of Reading*, no. 20, pp. 242–52.

Gilliland, J. (1972), *Readability* (London: University of London Press for the United Kingdom Reading Association).

Goodman, K. S. (1967), 'Reading: a psycholinguistic guessing game', *Journal of the Reading Specialist*, no. 6.
> Classic discussion of reading process, especially the part played by presupposition and prediction.

Grellet, F. (1981), *Developing Reading Skills* (Cambridge: CUP).
> A wealth of useful and imaginative suggestions for exercises to promote reading skills.

Halliday, M. A. K. and Hasan, R. (1976), *Cohesion in English* (London: Longman).

Harrison, C. (1980), *Readability in the Classroom* (Cambridge: Cambridge Educational).
> A very useful account of recent research and thinking; discusses various readability measures.

Heaton, J. B. (1975), *Writing English Language Tests* (London: Longman).
> Chapters 2, 7 are particularly relevant, and include the writing of multiple choice questions.

Hill, J. K. (1981), 'Effective reading in a foreign language', *English Language Teaching Journal*, no. 35, pp. 270–81.
> Describes a successful experimental course in effective reading.

Johnson, T. D. (1973), *Reading: Teaching and Learning* (London: Macmillan).
> Full of clear practical suggestions; good bibliography. Relates to L1 reading in Britain.

Jordan, R. R. (1978), 'The reading interests of lower secondary school children in Africa and Asia', *English Language Teaching Journal*, no. 32.

Kress, G. R. (1976), *Halliday: System and Function in Language* (London: OUP).
> A useful collection of major papers by the linguist whose work has strongly influenced British thinking on language and reading.

Kinsella, V. (1978), ed., *Language Teaching and Linguistics Surveys* (Cambridge: CUP).
> A collection of survey articles from *Language Teaching and Linguistics Abstracts*. Excellent bibliographies.

Lackstrom, J., Selinker, L. and Trimble, L. (1973), 'Technical rhetorical principles and grammatical choice', *TESOL Quarterly*, vol. 7, no. 2.
> Interesting attempt to present a hierarchical model of discourse and to work out the relationship between rhetorical function and grammatical choice.

Lenzberg, A. and Hilferty, A. (1978), 'Discourse analysis in the reading class', *TESOL Quarterly*, vol. 12, no. 1.
> Suggests class activities.

Lunzer, E. and Gardner, K. (1979), *The Effective Use of Reading* (London: Heinemann Educational Books for the Schools Council).
> Illuminating account of a study of reading in British schools, with many useful conclusions and suggestions.

Mackay, D., Thompson, B. and Schaub, P. (1970), *Breakthrough to Literacy: Teacher's Manual* (London: Longman for the Schools Council).
> Describes one version of the language experience approach to the teaching of reading to young children.

Mackay, R. and Mountford, A. (1978), *English for Specific Purposes* (London: Longman).
> Includes some useful articles on materials development with samples of exercise types.

McLaughlin, G. (1969), 'SMOG grading – a new readability formula', *Journal of Reading*, no. 22, pp. 639–46.

Marland, M. (1977), ed., *Language across the Curriculum* (London: Heinemann Educational Books).

A discussion about the place of English in British secondary schools, full of practical and illuminating ideas. Reading is discussed particularly in pages 80–129.

Melnik, A. and Merritt, J. (1972a) eds, *Reading Today and Tomorrow* (London: University of London Press in association with the Open University).

Melink, A. and Merritt, J. (1972b) eds, *The Reading Curriculum* (London: University of London Press in association with the Open University).
    This title and the preceding one are collections of important articles on many aspects of reading.

Moody, K. W. (1976), 'A type of exercise for developing prediction skills in reading', *RELC Journal*, vol. 7, no. 1.

Moorwood, H. (1978), ed., *Selections from the Modern English Teacher* (London: Longman).
    A collection of useful practical articles for teachers.

Morris, R. (1963), *Success and Failure in Learning to Read* (expanded edition 1973) (Harmondsworth: Penguin Education).

Moyle, D. (1970), 'Readability – the use of cloze procedure', in Merritt, J. (ed.), *Reading and the Reading Curriculum* (London: Ward Lock Educational), pp. 159–68, reprinted in Melnik and Merritt (1972b).

Murphy, M. J. (1969), *Designing Multiple Choice Items for Testing English Language* (Nigeria: Ginn/African Universities Press).

Nation, I. S. P. (1979), 'The curse of the comprehension question', *Guidelines for Teaching Reading Skills* (RELC Journal Supplement no. 2) (Singapore: SEAMEO Regional Language Centre).
    This article is discussed in Chapter Seven, p. 109 ff.

Pierce, M. E. (1973), 'Sentence level expectancy as an aid to advanced reading', *TESOL Quarterly*, vol. 7, no. 3.

Pugh, A. K. (1978), *Silent Reading* (London: Heinemann Educational Books).
    Includes useful information about the value of listening to texts for slower readers.

Rees, A. (1980), 'Reading aloud: suggestions for classroom procedure', *English Language Teaching Journal*, vol. 34, no. 2.

Robinson, F. P. (1964), *Effective Study* (new ed.) (New York: Harper & Row).
    Deals with study skills, including SQ 3R.

Saville-Troike, M. (1973), 'Reading and the audio-lingual method', *TESOL Quarterly*, vol. 7, no. 4.
    Includes useful sections on processing complex sentences, inferring meanings of words.

Searle, J. R. (1969), *Speech Acts* (London: CUP).
    Develops the ideas of Austin (1976).

Selinker, L., Trimble, L. and Vroman, R. (1974), 'Presupposition and technical rhetoric', *English Language Teaching Journal*, vol. 29, no. 1.

Selinker, L., Todd, R. M. and Trimble, L. (1976), 'Presuppositional rhetorical information in EST discourse', *TESOL Quarterly*, vol. 10, no.3.
    This article and the preceding one develop the ideas discussed in Lackstrom *et al* (1973).

Smith, F. (1975), *Comprehension and Learning: A Conceptual Framework for Teachers* (New York/London: Holt Rinehart & Winston).

Smith, F. (1978), *Reading* (Cambridge: CUP).
    Frank Smith's books are essential reading; these two are lucid and accessible.

Tadman, J. (1983), ed., *How to make the most of Graded Readers on Cassette* (London: Longman).

Urquhart, A. and Alderson, J. (1983), eds, *Reading in a Second Language* (London: Longman).
    A collection of articles dealing with various issues relevant to reading, especially in a second language.

Vincent, M. (1983), Developing Reading Skills (London: Longman).

Walker, C. (1974), *Reading Development and Extension* (London: Ward Lock Educational).

Full of practical classroom suggestions for the teaching of L1 reading; particularly good on group work.

West, M. (1960), *Teaching English in Difficult Circumstances* (London: Longman). Despite its age, this book still has relevance for teachers in many parts of the world.

White, R. V. (1980), *Teaching Written English* (Practical Language Teaching Series) (London: Allen & Unwin/Heinemann).

Widdowson, H. G. (1978), *Teaching Language as Communication* (Oxford: OUP). A key text for the ideas of this influential thinker.

Wilkins, D. A. (1976), *Notional Syllabuses* (London: OUP). Contains a useful description and listing of concepts and functions.

Williams, E. (1983), *Reading and Reading Comprehension* (London: Macmillan).

(b) Teaching materials

Abbot, G. (1976), *What Next?* (London: Longman). Story telling exercises to promote the skill of prediction.

Allen, J. P. B. and Widdowson, H. G. (1974), *English in Physical Science* (English in Focus) (Oxford: OUP).

Allen, J. P. B. and Widdowson, H. G. (1978), *English in Social Studies* (English in Focus) (Oxford: OUP). Nine books by various authors dealing with the English required for various specific fields of study. Interesting attempts to focus on rhetorical structure, make use of non-verbal material.

Barr, P., Clegg, J. and Wallace, C. (1981), *Advanced Reading Skills* (London: Longman). A wide variety of texts with activities to develop a full range of word- and text-attack skills.

Centre for British Teachers (no date), *The Reading Box* (London: Centre for British Teachers Ltd). 140 reading cards for intermediate learners.

Chulalongkorn University Language Institute (1979), *Foundation Reading Books 1–3* (Bangkok: Chulalongkorn University Press). Aims to develop a range of reading skills required for study purposes.

Clarke, D. (1983), *Inroads* (London: Heinemann Educational Books). Trains students in the strategies needed to analyse relationships of meaning.

Cooper, J. (1979), *Think and Link* (London: Edward Arnold). Trains reading and writing skills by focusing on the organization of text and the transfer of information.

Davies, E. and Whitney, N. (1979–83), *Reading Comprehension Course*, 3 vols. *Reasons for Reading, Strategies for Reading, Study Skills for Reading* (London: Heinemann Educational Books). Ensures student knows why he is reading and is made to apply his knowledge to tasks. Wide range of texts and tasks.

Fry, E. (1967), *Reading Faster: A Drill Book* (Cambridge: CUP). A series of texts of similar level (on tropical diseases) for timed practice.

Geddes, M. and Sturtridge, G. (1982), *Reading Links* (London: Heinemann Educational Books). Specifically designed for group study and oral work, based on the information gap principle.

Johnson, K. (1981), *Communicate in Writing* (London: Longman). A variety of tasks focus attention on how texts are organized, how functions are expressed, leading from reading to written work.

Jolly, D. (1982), *Reading Choices* (Cambridge: CUP). 125 reading cards at various levels.

Laird, E. (1977), *English in Education* (English in Focus) (Oxford: OUP).

Language Centre, University of Malaya (1979–83), *Skills for Learning*, 5 vols: *Foundation, Development, Progression, Application, Reading Projects: Science* (International Edition) (London: Nelson).

Uses current ideas about discourse structure to train students in effective reading for academic study.

Moore, J. D. (*et al.* (1979/80) *Reading and Thinking in English*, 4 vols: *Concepts in Use, Exploring Functions, Discovering Discourse, Discourse in Action* (Oxford: OUP).

A discourse-oriented course training students to understand how writing conveys connected thought.

Morgan, J. and Rinvoluori, M. (1983), *Once Upon a Time* (Cambridge: CUP).

Ideas for using stories in the classroom.

Morrow, K. (1980), *Skills for Reading*, (Oxford: OUP).

Promotes the reader's active involvement with the text by means of a range of intensive activities (sequencing, inference, prediction, etc.).

Mosbach, G. and V. (1976), *Practica Faster Reading* (Cambridge: CUP).

A selection of texts for practice in increasing reading speed, with recommendations for use.

Munby, J. (1968), *Read and Think* (London: Longman).

Texts with carefully conceived multiple choice questions for use as teaching, not testing, devices.

Pearson, I. (1978), *English in Biological Science* (English in Focus) (Oxford: OUP).

Science Research Associates (no date), *SRA Reading Laboratories: Multiread A, Multiread 2* (Henley on Thames: Science Research Associates).

Collections of reading cards with questions.

Sharp, A. (1983), *Storytrails* (Cambridge: CUP).

Stories with alternative developments to practise the skill of prediction.

Walter, C. (1983), *Authentic Reading* (Cambridge: CUP).

Trains students to understand textual structure and develop efficient reading skills.

(c) Journals

One journal (first issue 1983) is devoted solely to this field:

Reading in a Foreign Language

(Published by: Language Studies Unit, University of Aston in Birmingham, Gosta Green, Birmingham B4 7ET.)

Other journals in the fields of both reading and ELT carry useful articles. Apart from those cited in Part (a) of this bibliography may be mentioned:

International Review of Applied Linguistics in Language Teaching
Journal of Applied Linguistics
Language Learning
Modern English Teacher
Practical English Teacher
Reading Research Quarterly
Reading Teacher
System

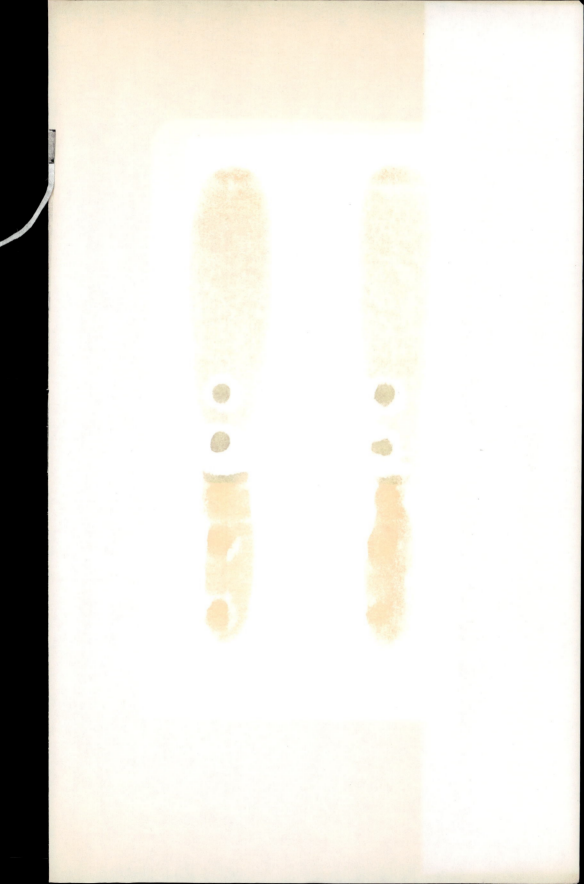

DATE DUE			
APR 19 1997			
MAY 1 99			
DEC 18 01			